Praise for *Politically Incorrect*

"Poignant and painful. Both evocative memoir and sober analysis."

NOAM CHOMSKY

"Easy to read, hard to digest."

DANNY SILBIGER, LAWYER

"Easily the most important thing I have read on Israel in years, perhaps ever. It gets to the structural underpinnings of the tragic 'dead end' of Israeli life."

PROF. TOM HARRINGTON

POLITICALLY INCORRECT

WHY A JEWISH STATE IS A BAD IDEA

A Memoir by
Ofra Yeshua-Lyth

SKYSCRAPER

Originally published in Hebrew
First edition by Nymrod Publishing House,
Tel Aviv, 2004

Second edition by Ma'ariv publishers,
Tel Aviv, 2011

Revised English edition published by
Skyscraper Publications Limited
20 Crab Tree Close, Bloxham
OX15 4SE, United Kingdom
www.skyscraperpublications.com

First U.K. publication 2016

A CIP catalogue record for this book is available
from the British Library.

ISBN-13: 978-1-911072-04-1

Cover design by John Chandler

Typesetting by
Chandler Book Design

Printed in Malta
by Latitude Press

CONTENTS

Part V – Brethren

Part VI – Cousins

Part VII – Hopes (b)

LIST OF ILLUSTRATIONS

For readers unfamiliar with the divisions into which the major groups of Jews in Israel fall, the following are the terms usually used:

ASHKENAZI

Descendants of Jews of Eastern European origin. In ancient Hebrew, Ashkenaz is Germany

SEPHARDI

Literally descendants of Jews from Spain and Portugal, however the term applies to all Jews from Middle Eastern and North African descent who have adopted the Sephardic style religious rituals.

MIZRAHI

Literally Eastern, descendants of Jews from communities in Arab countries of the Middle East and North Africa. With the exception of the Yemenite community, they are also identified as Sephardi. The term “Arab Jews” is unanimously avoided except in small politically conscious circles.

Part I – Hopes (a)

Zionism: the apex of the Jewish national movement which aspired for a normal nation-state but founded Israel instead.

Joseph Agassi, *A Philosopher's Apprentice: In Karl Popper's Workshop* (from the glossary)

1

FALLING STARS

Here by hill slopes,
Before sunset and the aperture of time
By orchards with broken shadows
We do what prisoners and jobless do
We nurture hope

Mahmoud Darwish,
A State of Siege Trans. Mohammad Shaheen

Having set the alarm for one-thirty in the morning, my husband and I loaded our only slightly grumbling, daughter into the family car, and promised her a once-in-a-lifetime adventure. As we set off, we strained our necks towards the night sky, but all we could see were the bright lights of Tel Aviv reflected upwards. Only stopping to join up with a couple of friends and their kids, we passed the city's industrial parks, shopping malls and vast new cemetery, which was already full, then hit the highway leading east.

At the roadblock the soldiers lazily waved us through. Their instructions were to scrutinize incoming traffic only, and we were driving out. Before we knew it, we were cruising along the main street of Biddia. The sprawling Arab city resembled a ghost town at this time of night. The next invasion of Israeli bargain hunters would not start for a few hours. On Saturdays you could barely move your car amid the crush of the bazaar. But now the market stalls were folded away and shuttered. Biddia's merchants were presumably fast asleep, anticipating the next windfall.

East of the town, the hills were still a disappointment. The luminous glow of the metropolitan area brightened the horizon, and powerful orange projectors floodlit the roads leading to the fortified Israeli settlements.

We followed the narrowing road, taking curves at dangerous speed to get away from the artificial illumination. The crest of the Samarian Ridge, though, was reasonably dark.

The deserted spot suited our purpose. Further eastward the road descended into the Judean Desert, and the Jordan Valley lay beneath us, with the Hills of Moab on the other side. The weak street lamps of some distant Arab village seemed unobtrusive enough.

We parked our cars in a lay-by, and spread the blankets we had brought over the hard rocks. Faces turned upward, we were ready to catch the Grand Finale of God's annual fireworks show. The August 1999 meteorite shower was expected to be the best the world had seen since 1956, and the Middle East was positioned for an especially good view.

The trail of a falling star is very delicate. Tiny drops of light burst out of nowhere and disappear at a blink. We soon discovered that you only see the spark if you happen to look in the right direction at the right moment; by the time you spotted one, it was already too late to alert the others. Our shrieks of delight over the celestial objects we managed to spot tore the night air, mixed with bursts of frustrated laughter at the ones we missed. There were long lulls in which nothing happened and then by the time someone called out excitedly, you knew you had just missed a good starburst or even two. When we all noticed a trail at the same time, it was pure joy.

The night was as ordinary and as magnificent as any other summer night in the wilderness. It would have been great to come up here any time and stare at that cosmic beauty, but we were busy urban people with a short attention span, so unlikely to take the time just to gaze at the star-studded dome for no particular reason; we had come to watch some action. Tonight, rocks that had been traveling in space for millions of years were changing shape and spectacularly burning to cinders as they hit the atmosphere, leaving behind just minute trails of light. NASA's website had announced a "Perseids Storm."

Ever since a certain ancient comet crashed somewhere near this spot in space a million or so years ago, earth punctually ploughs through its frozen remains late every summer. This information, gained from the morning's newspaper, was now knowledgeably presented to the younger generation. The presence of the three children was allowing us adults to pretend we had come here to share an educational adventure, but it felt more like an existential one. High up on a bare mountain, gazing at the wonders of creation as man has done for thousands of years, it was easy to think big about being small.

"But what if we are hit by a big meteor?" our friends' practical little son asked with alarm on learning that some of the rocks were pretty large. "We are quite safe," said the adults dismissively. The atmosphere protects us like a great blanket, grinding the rock and gaseous substances to nothing as they violently crash into it. Even supposing that a meteorite should make it all the way to earth in one menacing piece, there is no chance of it hitting us. No reason at all why it should land – of all places – here on the Samarian hills, in the middle of the Palestinian Authority.

"Don't forget to make a wish!" I added, changing the subject.

A moment of silence followed, as we all concentrated on this opportunity. Options were falling out of the sky: time to make a wish and perhaps even see it granted, but where to start? Perhaps we should have drawn up a wish list back home which covered all our worries and hopes, ready to launch at the glittering, falling stars.

Best to focus our wishes on the here and now, I felt: May our life always be as sweet and as simple as it was now in the lovely fresh air! May our loved ones always be so near and so happy. May other people be equally satisfied with their lot and not wish us ill! And, may we, please, live happily ever after?

Over the mountains on the other side of the Syrian African Rift, somewhere above the Hashemite Kingdom of Jordan, the eastern skyline was getting paler. Stars were still falling fast, but with visibility fading the great show was now over. Time to drive home and get some rest before daylight. We folded our blankets and drank up the remaining coffee in the pot.

On the way back, we stopped to stock up on *knafeh* – sweet cheese delicacies – and sticky *baklava* cakes in a famous Biddia bakery. At four-thirty in the morning the road west was already packed with ancient vans and trucks loaded with day labourers and agricultural goods, en route to the checkpoint. The working hands and the products of Palestine were waiting patiently, as they did every morning, to merge into the thriving economy of coastal Israel. Tired soldiers went through the motions of peering at faces, trunks and IDs. In less than twenty minutes, we would be home.

What a luxury it had been to contemplate our position on the planet, pondering the universe at large. The "Who are we" and "What are we doing here" questions had been reduced to earthly perspectives, like the colour of our car number plates and the plastic ID cards we always carry.

* * *

It was a time of unprecedented prosperity. The 1993 Oslo talks, in which Israeli and Palestinian leaders had for the first time sat together and thrashed out a framework for peace, had coincided with the world's biggest technology boom. Israelis, as it happened, were rather good at technology. There was more money to spend than anybody could remember. Our cars were newer and bigger; food portions in restaurants became smaller, beautifully designed, and pricier. We worked harder than we imagined possible, but we had developed some superior leisure patterns. The Israeli middle classes were discovering the charms of Tuscany, Cyprus, and Provence for short, quality vacations. We, however, were fortunate to be introduced by our good friend Eli to the enchanted Mediterranean region that sprawled over the hills all the way to the valley of the Jordan River. It was also known as the Occupied Territories, or Judea and Samaria, or the West Bank. Or Palestine.

Half an hour's drive from where we lived, a new and foreign land, most convenient for short trips and weekend getaways, was being discovered. We could be abroad in no time, without any visa, and use our own currency. Our vehicles took us around cultural milestones and ancient historic or archaeological sites. We could go on nature walks or dine royally for a few gratefully received shekels. As an extra bonus, we could congratulate ourselves on the fact that we were part of a new, blessed era. Every weekend trip seemed to be an act of good will. We were greeted by gentle and smiling people who made great efforts to show the generous hospitality written into their religion. We made an effort to show our appreciation.

Tens of thousands of Israelis enjoyed the welcome Palestinian openness in those days, the last months of the last millennium. With bargain hunters and anybody in need of cheap furniture crowding into Biddia, this bustling market town was the nearest thing to the vision of a binational haven. Every Friday, Ramallah turned into a disco capital for hundreds of young Israelis. In Bethlehem, builders were frantically completing more and more hotel space for the millions of pilgrims expected. Gamblers went all the way down to Jericho, the oldest city known to mankind, and by far the most attractive destination for Israelis in Palestine.

Most visitors disappeared into the Oasis Casino as soon as they arrived. But media reports and word of mouth were all *we* experienced of the classy entertainment that the casino's glamorous halls offered twenty-four hours a day; we were politely refused entrance. Jeans and T-shirts were against the strict dress code, and the premises were out of bounds to children. We knew, however, that every morning a special bus left Tel Aviv packed with housewives to divest themselves of some of the family's budget at the fruit machines. Heavy gamblers checked into the grand hotels designed to evoke the atmosphere of Scheherazade's palace. We once ventured into the Grand Park of Jericho for a drink of cool *tamarhindi* (date juice), watching the gamblers' bored wives sprawled on sofas in the air-conditioned lobby, while their children splashed about outside in the large swimming pools.

We made friends with the manager of the brand-new cable car at the Sultan tourism centre. Rising out of this glitzy commercial enterprise next to the famous archaeological excavations, the cable ride was still in pilot stage, and they did not want our money. "Go up and tell your friends," the manager beamed at us. A PR lady from Ramallah – smart, very slim, and almost too beautiful for this forsaken corner – handed us printed colour leaflets that described, with no exaggeration, "shiny red alpine cars [that] glide over the breathtaking landscape all the way up to the ancient Caranthal monastery, carved deep into the cliffs high above."

Publicity leaflet for Jericho cable car, 1999

"It's going to be a great money spinner very soon", we reassured both of them on the way back, to their delight. Think of the millions of Christian tourists who will pour into this place to touch the very stone that Jesus used as a pillow for forty nights. We saw it with our own eyes. The shrewd, young resident Greek monk was very convincing, relating pious miracle stories in good English, and making it clear that cash donations were accepted in all currencies. After the tour, visitors may enjoy Israeli ice cream in a tastefully built new café terrace, with wrought-iron fittings, overlooking the magnificent panorama of the Jordan delta by the Dead Sea.

In the evening of one of our exciting days in Jericho, we had coffee in the city plaza. It was crowded with Israeli families scouring bric-a-brac shops and patronizing ice cream parlours. All mixed cheerfully with the local people. We knew for a fact that we had a joint future in this warm land that can be made so cosy. The enchanted Levant had always been a meeting point of races, cultures, and religions. It was now our turn to make it the happy habitat it was always meant to be.

Almost all the locals we met could speak our language. We were familiar with quite a few words in theirs. We had a common history, a common recognition of the pain and sorrow that we had inflicted on one another. We also had a vested interest in leaving our bad past behind, and concentrating on a better future, which included gourmet cuisine and superior architecture (theirs) as well as a more robust economy (ours).

A major foreign client of my consultancy had expressed an interest in promoting peace between Jews and Arabs through a technological business project. The initiative was progressing satisfactorily, and I had a rare opportunity to organize a reception in Ramallah's newly finished Grand Park Hotel. Security officials of the Shimon Peres Institute for Peace met their counterparts of the Palestinian Authority for long and tense discussions. There was always the risk that somebody with a grudge would decide to break up the feast to make a violent point. Personally I saw no reason not to be driving in and out of Ramallah unescorted; the security regulations seemed exaggerated. My biggest concern was the need to arrange a piano for the ceremony, but the hotel manager and staff produced one eventually at a reasonable cost.

Our event in October 1998 was a PR success. The Israeli Minister of Regional Cooperation, Shimon Peres, came from Jerusalem. The Palestinian Minister of Finance, Mohammed Nashashibi, came from Gaza. The Managing Director of Siemens AG, Dr. Heinrich von Pierer, travelled all the way from Munich. All three posed to be photographed as they cut the large cake crowned with the logo of the new company. It was truly exciting. Listening carefully, one could clearly hear the rustle of history's wings over the first-ever German-Palestinian-Israeli hi-tech venture. We received excellent media coverage and made the TV evening news, even in Japan.

Signing a German-Palestinian-Israeli commercial agreement, 1998

* * *

In December of 1999, we received a Christmas card from the manager of the cable car in Jericho. The century ended sweetly and the new millennium started, rich with high expectations. Nine months later our fragile peace was shattered into nothing, and all hell broke loose. No one was safe from the horror, and nowhere was sacred. Men, women, and children were being randomly and savagely butchered on a weekly basis, as more and more recruits willingly turned themselves into a bloody mess on buses, in restaurants, shopping malls, and discos. Hundreds of innocent people were maimed for life. Thousands were permanently traumatized.

It did not take too long for the expected revenge to explode. Towns and villages that produced suicide bombers became targets of blind military rage. Many more innocent people were massacred by misdirected bombs and tank shells, crushed under bulldozers that ground their homes to dust. A well-equipped, superbly trained army was activated as a killer puppet by politicians. Incarceration, humiliation, and starvation became the way of life for hundreds of thousands of men and women who have never experienced the citizenship of any country. The frustrated occupiers, determined to satisfy their illusion of omnipotence, only managed to produce more death, more thousands of maimed limbs, more bereaved. An eye for an eye and a baby for a baby.

My land, it suddenly seemed, was making sure that its neighbours would have no other wish than to produce mad human bombs, who in their turn would provide the excuse for continuing the senseless violent grip. The lines of young volunteers seeking dynamite-packed belts for death in the midst of the hated enemy – us – were only getting longer. Families who manage to produce *Shahids* – "martyrs"– were gaining ever more pride and respectability – and better rations.

Oasis Casino and the Grand Park Hotel Ramallah became as devastated as the Israeli economy and Israeli self-confidence. The well-lit, barbed-wired, armed islands that my state had transplanted onto the land of others kept pumping out its resources, blood, and brains as if they were the symptoms of some terminal disease. Every night millions of Israelis and Palestinians went to bed praying that their counterparts would somehow miraculously be wiped off the face of this land. The wish that someday this nightmarish reality would be over, so often exclaimed, did not seem even remotely realistic.

"Do you think that they might reach us too, make it here, to our neighbourhood?" my daughter and her friends would sometimes ask me, as the latest suicide mass murder hit the news. "Could it happen to us?"

"I very much hope not," I answered earnestly, as all mothers should. My voice had none of the authority it had once possessed, when I still could reassure them that that never, under any circumstances, would they ever be hit by a shooting star. Israelis had long ago stopped thinking about questions like "Who are we?" and "What are we doing here."

2

ANYTHING LEFT FOR US TO DO?

"But man's highest purpose in life is to make human society better, is it not?"

"This will never be achieved if all will be making sacrifices and nobody will have a good time."

A conversation (1850) between the socialist Luis Blanc and Russian Intellectual Alexander Herzen. In *My Past and Thoughts: The Memoirs of Alexander Herzen*

Long ago, just before my eighth birthday, my mother took me to visit the hospice where her father, my grandfather, was dying of cancer. We took the bus to Ra'anana, then a big village in the heart of the Sharon Region, surrounded by orange groves. The hospice was a long one-story building with gloomy rooms and large windows overlooking a scrubby garden. The man my mother started talking to did not resemble the Saba Shmuel that I knew. He was half his weight and had acquired a new thin face with a sickly red complexion. As we had never been too close, this was more embarrassing than painful.

It was a perfect sunny winter's afternoon. The ward had the spartan charm of a *kibbutz* children's house, with freshly washed, grey tiled floors and short, colourful, cotton curtains. Saba Shmuel and several other patients were lying in narrow beds arranged along the walls. The grim impression was further enhanced by a dragon-like nurse who kept scolding the patient in the bed next to my grandfather. The poor man had seemingly defied her orders by keeping his hands under the blanket and not on top. I wondered vaguely what Saba Shmuel had to put up with when he did not have visitors.

My mother, then barely thirty years old and heavily pregnant with my brother, was having a very serious conversation, perhaps her last, with her father.

The little I know about my maternal grandfather was learnt long after his death. His divorce from my Grandmother Chaya took place when my mother was a little girl. Savta Chaya always referred to her ex-husband with dramatic exasperation. She accused him of allowing his philosophical ponderings – mostly inspired, she spitefully claimed, by the company of pretty women – to occupy the time he should have devoted to his responsibilities as the family's provider. He had wasted the couple's first and only capital of five pounds, received as a loan from the Jewish Agency when they arrived in Tel Aviv as immigrants in 1925, on a doomed experiment to build a novel kind of chicken incubator. A disgruntled ex-beauty with a frustrated intellect, Savta was openly jealous of grandfather's second wife, a kind, plain woman who had a steady job and some savings. "I am sure that he never really loved her," she sanctimoniously told me, long before I considered myself old enough to be trusted with such intimate confidences.

My grandfather's sister Milka often mentioned with certain pride that they were both children of a rabbi from Odessa. I tried to trace this part of my family during a brief visit to Odessa in 1988, but the Jews I met there mocked the idea that one could find relatives of people who had left town almost seventy years earlier – certainly not when all I had was the family name, which means "an orphan" in Hebrew.

"Yathom? You mean Yuthem," they said, dismissing my Hebrew accent and restoring the correct Yiddish intonation. "More than half the Jews from Odessa are named Yuthem." I thought this was quite interesting. Either all these people were the descendants of one prolific orphan, or this could have been the Odessa Jewish community's nickname for anybody who landed in the city without a family, or had been born without any identified father.

According to the few remaining family photos, Shmuel and Chaya made a handsome young couple. They met at the Odessa University, where he was studying agronomy, and she intended to graduate in child care; both were training for a new life in Eretz Israel. The members of their group of young, well-educated

Zionist Pioneers were all fluent in Hebrew and inspired by the Bolshevik revolution that at least some of them intended to import into Palestine. In Tel Aviv, then a fast-growing Jewish suburb of Jaffa, some members of this group stayed loyal to the PKP (Palestine Communist Party) until they were very old and grey. A few went back to Russia in the thirties and were never heard of again. The rest were swept up by the harsh reality of immigrant life in their new urban habitat. Some obviously had fared better than others. Already as a child I was aware that my grandfather's circumstances were humble.

He had a post office job. A large stamp collection seemed to be his main pride and joy, and I was expected to admire it as we went over the pages during my rare visits to his tarpaulin-covered hut in the Nordia slum, off the fashionable Dizengoff Street, on the very spot where the Mashbir Latzarkan department store stands today. The hut was primitive by anybody's standards. It had a small entrance hall that served as a dining room and a sitting room, and was also the bedroom for my step-aunt Yehudit, who was only six years older than me. Inside was her parents' bedroom, one corner of which served as a kitchen. Water had to be carried in from the taps outside by the communal bathrooms.

Tel Aviv's first glitzy shopping mall, Dizengoff Centre, was to be built on the ruins of the Nordia shacks a few years later by smart entrepreneurs. In a book about this piece of Tel Aviv real estate history, I later discovered (to my mother's complete surprise) that shortly before he died, Saba Shmuel had served as the active chairman of the local residents' association, which had tried to prevent its members' eviction from their homes by the combined power of greedy developers and the city council. In the minutes of the meeting that had elected him to office, Saba is quoted as describing the tenants' struggle against dispossession as doomed, mainly due to internal disagreements among them.

The rightful owners of this precious large plot in the city centre, a rich Arab-Christian family, had been dispossessed a few years earlier when they became refugees during the War of Independence in 1948. Old George Hinawi had built, operated, and rented out the humble wood and tarpaulin homes for poor Jewish immigrants on what used to be a vineyard. He got a good return on his investment, but then paid with his life for cooperating with the Jews. Nationalistic Arabs shot him dead on the corner of King George Street during a rent collection round. Most of his tenants managed to move on to better housing. As the landlord's family could not by then claim their property, the ex-tenants started subletting the shabby huts. As property holders they expected to do even better financially when the neighbourhood was cleared. Saba Shmuel was a subtenant.

As he lay on his narrow deathbed in the Ra'anana hospice, he might have had good reasons to tell his daughter that he was leaving this world with little to show for himself. This is only a guess, as I wasn't really listening to what was being said between them. Grownups always moaned about something or other. But my ears pricked up at my mother's reassuring tone, which came in a memorable little speech.

"Your generation were the pioneers, Abba," my mother was saying encouragingly to her dad. "Israel exists thanks to you people, and look how much your generation has achieved! You all came to this country, and you built it from nothing. Every generation seems to have a mission. My own generation – we would probably be remembered as the Fighters, the Warriors. You gave us a state; we defended it. I wonder, what will they call her generation?" Here she pointed straight at me, capturing my attention. Both were now regarding me with some undefined expectation. "It is too early to say," my mother concluded, "what kind of mark these kids will leave on the state's history, how *they* will be remembered."

With my mother's training as a teacher and her history as a youth movement activist, this form of idealistic Zionist discourse came quite naturally. There was nothing unusual about it where I grew up. The national agenda was on everybody's lips. Our beloved state was part of every serious conversation at home, at school, in the media, and on the streets. Birthday greetings were not complete without "May you grow up to be a good daughter (or son) to your People and to your Country."

Looking back, it seems that my mother could not have chosen more comforting words or a better healing message for her father as he lay dying. Of course I have no idea whether or not she managed to distract his mind from the ultimate failure of his grand scheme to become a farmer-philosopher in the new Jewish homeland, or from his failure to provide adequately for the small, orphaned family he was leaving behind him in the Nordia slum.

My own mind was by now completely focused on the unexpected challenge that had suddenly been thrown at me and "my generation." It was worrying to consider the weight of our combined group responsibility: the day would come – I realized for the first time – when we, too, would have to show that we had contributed something to the State of Israel. This had never occurred to me before, and now it seemed like an enormously difficult question. Was there anything left for us to do?

Like most children I grew up fiercely competitive and determined to prove that my friends and I could beat adults in most games. Now I suddenly faced a new, problematic situation. It was clear – my mother said as much – that our contribution would be measured against the achievements of our predecessors. I could not help feeling that this was grossly unfair.

Solemnly and crossly, I weighed up our options. In order to outperform the previous generations, we would need to come up with something as spectacular as founding the state and making the desert bloom, as Saba and the other pioneers had done; or as heroic as winning a major war for its independence, few against many, beating seven Arab nations single handedly, as Abba and Imma did. The more I thought about it, the more hopeless it seemed.

I knew very well that Israel was unique. The only Jewish state in the world was small but brave, poor but just. Toward the state's tenth anniversary, the children's socialist weekly *Davar L'Yeladim* ran a column with the photos and life stories of ten-year-olds who shared a birthday with the state. I was naturally jealous at the easy glory they had achieved just by choosing such a good time to be born. If only I were two years older! Still, this was my generation. We were the Children of the State.

Our nation, at long last, was enjoying freedom and happiness. At the Tel Aviv A. D. Gordon Educational Home, named after the prophet of Zionist Labor, we had memorized dozens of songs and hymns glorifying the country and its people. We sang before every lesson started and before every meal in the communal dining room. We sang on school trips and outings and during the agriculture practical lessons on the school farm. Once a week we had a singing hour for the whole school. Our music teacher, Meir Noy, a popular composer and a gifted pedagogue, accompanied us on the dining room piano or on the accordion that he used to wear over an apron of blue velvet. The lyrics, specially printed out for us, included solemn vows like "*We shall build our homeland... because this Land belongs to us / this command is in our blood; it is the command of generations! We shalt build... in spite of all our destroyers; we will build the country with our sheer willpower!*"[1]

At home, the two Hebrew radio stations provided a similar musical menu. The airwaves vibrated with the latest patriotic lyrics, serenades to our young beloved country. There were also dances to match:

Our Barns are full of Wheat,
Our Wineries burst with Wine,
Our Homes are packed with Babies –
What Else could you ask of us, Sweet Homeland?[2]

The building of the Homeland was obviously complete.

Even our chance to fight in a decent war now seemed gone. A year earlier, in October 1956, Israel had won yet another great military victory in what it called the Sinai Campaign. True, we in Tel Aviv had to spend a few nights in air-raid shelters (in our case, a mere sandbagged area at the front of our apartment building on Weiss Street). Within a week what was elsewhere known as the Suez war had generated one more uplifting musical hit:

Not a legend, my friends, and not a passing dream.
The Burning Bush is aflame on the Mount of Sinai,
Oh, the Godly Flame in the eyes of the boys
Oh, the Godly Flame with the thunder of engines![3]

---

1 "We Shall Build Our Homeland," words by Avraham Levinson, music by Moshe Beek. All translations by the author.

2 "Our Barns Are Full of Wheat," words by Pinchas F. Elad, music by David Zehavi.

3 "Not a Legend, My Friends," words by Yechiel Mohar, music by Moshe Vilensky.

The Israeli Army had taken over the Gaza Strip and the Sinai Peninsula. To borrow the jargon of a later era, the "terrorist infrastructure" had been eliminated. There had been a considerable human cost also among Israelis, including the pointless deaths of thirty-eight soldiers in an unauthorized military operation: a gifted, over-enthusiastic colonel had independently decided to take the peninsula's Mitla Pass, not an official campaign objective. His exposed troops had been forced to retreat under heavy, unforeseen Egyptian fire. Military historians would quietly argue about the failed operation for years to come, but the renegade who had dreamt up the failed operation would go on to build a career based on self-devised killing sprees that won him the nation's unfaltering admiration. His name was Ariel Sharon.

Our Brave Little Israel was devastated when it became clear that we must immediately pull out of the vast territories that had just been conquered in battle. We had to hand back the fruits of a victory achieved with the military support of our then allies, the British and the French, whose objective had been to recapture the Suez Canal after the Egyptians had dared to nationalize it. Even a seven-year-old understood how unfair both the United States and the Soviet Union were by ganging up on Israel with United Nations backing. They were giving all that support to the Arabs just because they had so much oil!

Davar L'Yeladim, the Labour children's weekly, had on its front cover the poem "Facing Blackmail" by Nathan Altherman, the national poet.[4] It was a simple and powerful fable about a quiet, peace-loving man constantly subjected to violent attempts on his life by a hostile neighbour. One day the Quiet Man had "had gripped the arm that had raised the dagger in midair" and had refused to let go. But then all the other neighbours came running to support the dagger holder and demanded that the victim let go of the aggressor! The poem was illustrated with a drawing of the hand holding the knife. All young readers knew very well that the decent, quiet person stopping the knife-wielding arm in mid-air symbolized our state and the Israel Defence Forces.

[4] *Davar L'yeladim*, February 20, 1957.

We also knew that the Hand Restraining the Knife was forever stretched out for Peace. And Peace was definitely bound to come, one day. By the time we would be old enough to become soldiers, military service would no longer be necessary. This is at least what people wished my expectant mother, on the assumption that she was carrying a boy.

The Hand Restraining the Knife. Cover illustration of the Labour Movement's children's weekly, February 20, 1957

Government advertising calling on children to invest their savings with Israeli Defence Bonds (1967)

So our chances to leave our mark on the nation's history as soldiers did not look all that promising either. I nurtured a modest hope that somehow I might be able to make a remarkable contribution as a ballet dancer. This was, after all, what I really wanted to do.

* * *

In January 1958 my eighth birthday party was cancelled because my grandfather Shmuel had died the previous night. When I started writing this book, I was about as old as he was then. My classmates who survived the many wars that followed are enjoying grandparenthood, and the spirit of my parents' generation of warriors and fighters is dominating our society more than ever before. Younger politicians find it hard to match the legacy of the renegade Mitla Pass officer, who was in a coma between 2006 and his death in 2014 but still enjoyed the reputation of a great statesman and a successful prime minister.

The beloved, orange-scented homeland of my childhood in the meantime turned into a stress-ridden, violent, and uncaring environment. Newspaper editors often use images of doom to describe the life we live in Israel, preferably with a nautical flavour. According to the headlines, we are a "dinghy drifting fast into the Niagara Falls," "The Titanic," "The Ship of Fools," or sometimes merely "A Sad State." "They sit there in the government – a scoundrel, an opportunist and a talk-backer – and we put our lives in their hands," columnist Yossi Klein complained (quoting how the PM, his newly appointed Minister of Defence and the Minister for Education refer to each other) in a piece titled "Israel Is a Powder Keg Waiting for a Match" (Ha'aretz, June 3, 2016).

The economy is doing well for the upper echelons, while crime – petty and organized – is on the rise. Israel is registering embarrassing world records in social gaps, sex slavery, money laundering and military expenditure. It is the most dangerous place in the world for Jews. Its military is currently at risk of being dragged in front of the International Criminal Court in Hague on charges of war crimes.

"You cannot even drink the water in this country," an exasperated neighbour tells me as he and his son lug heavy crates of mineral water and soft drinks up in the lift. He is referring to revelations over yet another scandal, this time involving neglect and pollution of the water resources. "And you know what? The country is even worse than the water," he concludes angrily. He also moans that no foreign European football team would come and play Macabbi Haifa or Hapoel Tel Aviv that summer. I have no doubt that come the next elections, he will once again vote for the leadership that bears most of the responsibility for this sad state of affairs, but who could say that his state of mind wasn't justified?

"Let's face it: what is the alternative?" smarter and grander people are reciting daily.

"Not easy is our way," we all hum listlessly with the radio, together with "Where have we made a mistake; what have we done wrong?"

* * *

I had to drop the fantasy of becoming a ballerina at a relatively early age, having realized that I was not built to dance for my living. It took much longer to realize that the image I had of the wonderful, earnestly hardworking Jewish state I grew up in was also a product of wishful thinking and grand desires, based on a faulty concept (or design).

A major ingredient of the charm of the early days, now talked about with eyes shining with tears of nostalgia, was the belief that dreams of private bliss were inseparable from the great joy of being part of a nation-state.

In the 1950s and 1960s, thoroughly dipped in innocence and devotion, nobody had any reason to worry that by its very definition as the Only Jewish State in the World, the State of Israel was doomed to serve aims that have little or nothing to do with the welfare of most its inhabitants. We had a rich national folklore and a venerable tradition: it was not to be expected that a few anachronisms in this tradition would so soon be leading us to a dead end.

We were raised to a unique, deep sense of Jewish fulfilment. We were educated to be proud of being part of a people that has succeeded, against all odds, in becoming a nation as good as any on the face on the earth – actually somewhat better. The state truly was a great success story – so successful that most of us seriously considered it unnecessary to devote one's life to improving it, or fighting to secure its survival, as we were obviously expected to.

Parents and educators were dismayed and disappointed with this attitude. Newspapers wrote in disgust about the appalling phenomenon of what became known as the "Espresso Generation." Opinion makers found fault with the very idea of young people who unashamedly preferred to consume small cups of expensive coffee made by a noisy Italian machine rather than tea in ordinary Russian-style glasses. Dancing the Twist was denounced as totally immoral. But the boring old dances associated with the Zionist youth movements could not compare with moving one's hips to the sounds of Elvis Presley and Cliff Richard, or doing the romantic "slow" with The Platters and Paul Anka.

"The State of Israel was not created to become a cheap imitation of America," the deputy headmaster of Municipal High

School 5 raged at us from the depths of an offended national-Zionist soul. Time and again we were sent home to change the forbidden blue jeans to the standard blue cotton and synthetic pants and skirts of the school uniform. We knew nothing of the global village back then; its trousers, however, seemed superior.

In an effort to halt the decline toward the degenerate West, the government had seen fit to ban a Beatles concert that was planned in Tel Aviv. I cannot recall any real effort even to explain that totalitarian decision. Somebody high up obviously could not cope with "A Hard Day's Night" that had nothing to do with labouring and fighting for the homeland, or with so unmilitary a "Yellow Submarine." The ever-loyal press was unanimously sympathetic to the banning, the youth too well disciplined to get out into the streets and protest. Only a few of the boys in our class stood their ground and refused, in spite of threats and actual banishing from school, to have their Beatles-styled outrageously long hair cut back. Eventually they were quietly left alone to their wicked ways. It was clear that within less than two years, in time for the draft, the army would effectively sort out their cute heads.

"You guys think of nothing but your own comforts," a relative who fervently believed in socialist-style austerity admonished me angrily one day.

"Well, if humans had not been seeking comforts, we would still all be living in trees," I answered smugly. What better than the joys of good living to celebrate the ultimate Zionist vindication over the two thousand years of Jewish suffering invoked in our national anthem, the Hatiqva.

It was nice to be a "free people in our own land" with a successful local version of rock music, modern theatre of the absurd, sexual liberties and new consumerism. Our '60s started around 1968 and continued deep into the late '70s. We were eager to be in line with the "big world" whose representatives – most of them New York Jews – regularly made pilgrimages to figure us out and almost unanimously found us admirable. "The Israelis" were congratulated (mostly by themselves) as heroes who did not show off, who were straightforward but smart. We even had peace marches, Vietnam style, following the wars that kept erupting occasionally and the inevitable untimely deaths of those young men with proper haircuts, who fell in battle "bequeathing us life with their death," as official Israeli memorials say, while greatly increasing our real estate options.

* * *

The wars did not halt the ongoing celebration of the good life in the booming economy, but not everybody was a member of the Tel Aviv clubbing scene. Half an hour's drive from the city, a curious counter revolution was happening, which most of us considered marginal and weird. A new species of pioneers, wearing skullcaps and growing beards, were settling barren hills in the territories that our wars had occupied, in what seemed like a pathetic imitation of the Zionist settlement movement during Ottoman rule and the British Mandate. Tel Aviv took little notice of these "Dossim", as we sneeringly referred to those sons and daughters of a vanishing world, who had not yet heard that the days of organized religion were over.

They were building segregated residential areas, based on ethnic and religious purity, mostly without any obvious economical infrastructure. We were annoyed but not too bothered about the enormous resources and the massive support that the new pioneers were being given by our state. They often broke government rules, but our glorified Israel Defence Force, whose soldiers and officers were almost all nonreligious, was serving them with a loyalty hard to comprehend. Still, all this would be resolved one day, when peace was at last achieved. Or would it?

Nearly fifty years into the occupation, it is quite clear that the counterrevolution has won. The stunned remnants of the 1970s local elites and their children now find themselves cast to the margins of a hard, grudging, panicking, and aggressive society, which never stops marching into nowhere. Or into the next war.

"One day or another," author David Grossman wrote with bitter irony in the Israeli daily *Ha'aretz* , years before the second Lebanon War turned him into a bereaved father, "we will understand why we have had to spend decades living in a world parallel to the one we were meant to live in. And why we agreed to live our one and only life in a kind of latent death..."

It seems worth reflecting on how it is that Israeli society, once seemingly so modern and creative, almost a human spearhead towards a better future, has been dragged so far backward, into the depressing modes and cul-de-sac traditions that its founders had fled. Why is it that Israeli Jews so willingly accept life in a homemade trap?

Or maybe this situation should force us to accept, at last, the unpleasant truth about the much missed, beloved good old days. Should we not come to terms with the fact that our society had not in fact been as enlightened or progressive as we had been taught to believe, not just fifty-some years ago, "before the occupation"; actually not even sixty or a hundred years ago, when political Zionism was first conceived as a seemingly brilliant idea, inspiring and rich in promises and expectations. Hardly for a brief moment of grace was the future of the Zionist immigration project prioritized over the Jewish past.

* * *

The spirit of my alma mater, the A. D. Gordon Educational Home on Ferdinand LaSalle Street, hovers over the melancholy Israeli left. What a spectacular failure! Socialist Zionism managed to produce a fairly functioning state with considerable achievements, but it lost battle to the ancient Jewish tradition that it had set out to challenge.

The Jewish religion, a serial producer of the tragic "Jewish fate," had defeated the initial Zionist idea that was supposed to have altered the course of this destiny. Its spirit had dragged those who tried to escape it into their present tragic disposition. The founding fathers of Zionism were very conscious of the fact that religion was the major source of trouble for Jews in the sad Diaspora. However, they failed to grasp the harmful potential of "a faith dying of old age," as the Zionist philosopher and publicist Ahad Haam called it.[5] The Old World, with its prejudices and superstitions, is in sound control of the foundations of the Zionist

[5] Ahad Haam (Asher Ginzburg) in a path-setting article, "This Is Not the Road," first published in *Hamelitz*, 1889.

state. My grandfather's contemporaries carried it with them as extra luggage, all the way into the new land they thought would offer them new beginnings. Once here, it was reincarnated, greatly reinforced, to bring down their descendants.

"*The Old World we shall destroy back to nothing*," the Young Guards (*Hashomer Hatzair*) sang daily, to the tune of the socialist "Internationale." The much-loved poet Shaul Tchernichovsky, in a burst of euphoric optimism, announced that the human spirit is bound to "throw off its chains of foolishness." How disappointing that the chains were not only preserved, but are now serving as hanging cords.

The many hardworking immigrants who arrived in the Middle East from Eastern Europe about a hundred years ago had a perfect opportunity to start the dream land they were pining for, if only they had organized themselves into a properly democratic, modern society. Instead they stuck to a Messianic vision intended to redeem only people with a supposedly similar blood group.

The so-called secular society in which I was brought up never really broke with the traditional deeply religious past of its founders. A few years after the Jewish Holocaust, with a deep sense of loss and mourning over the murder of half the Jewish people in Europe, the state founders set to glue the remnants of the community together with the only cohesive substance that they knew.

Religious identity had always been the only common denominator for so-called Jewish self-determination. It was therefore a religious code, lacking any functional relevance to most of the state founders and to the majority of the population at the time that became the single valid ingredient determining "Israeli nationality." No wonder it soon became the dominant element in Israel's political structure. A desire to offer some Jews positive discrimination may have seemed legitimate in the late 1940s, when the country was experiencing waves of grief. But the combination of separatist religious ideology and a vigorously built military ability created a political reality dominated by unacceptable principles. The builders of the supposed "New Society" allowed themselves to be swept far into the gloomy regions of their forefathers' past, chained to the patterns from which Zionism was supposed to have set them free.

The Jewish religion is not merely a monopoly for the business of faith in the State of Israel. It is also the exclusive ingredient in the definition of the national identity and the state entity. To the detriment of the Jewish state, it is an ingredient with a built-in mechanism against the very principle of statehood. Orthodox Judaism is perfectly designed for the mission of preserving a religious minority that lacks a sovereign territory. It is a paradigm totally inadequate for – and until recently, totally uninterested in – running a state apparatus. Quite the opposite is true: Jewish Orthodoxy puts an enormous effort into making sure that nobody will ever be allowed to join its ranks unless they wish wholeheartedly to adopt the faith.

The revolving doors of traditional Jewish society cannot stop its sons and daughters from turning their backs on it, but they effectively block anybody from entering. The Jewish state fully adopted the principles of the Jewish religion. As a result, Israel turned into a political entity devoid of any ability to sustain internal partnerships. It would not accept non-Jews as equals. As a side effect, it alienates Jews who object to blatant discrimination. The state is, therefore, a handicapped entity, acting in a self-destructive manner. The citizens belonging to the caste identified with the state's religion live in constant anxiety of becoming outnumbered. Their attitude to the others who live with them and around them is shaped accordingly.

* * *

There is only one Jewish state in the whole world. It would seem really heartless even to consider challenging its "right to exist." However, it is no accident that Judaism is such a solitary and exclusive human genre.

The seemingly well-meaning attempt to sustain "a Jewish democratic state" has forced Israelis into a peculiar, harmful, and hopeless attempt to preserve – using the might of secular sovereignty – a statutory rule of an outdated system of commandments, dictated by a particularly fanatical version of an ancient religion.

The Jewish majority of Israel is united by no other ingredient than the Jewish religion. Around it is a truly senseless tangle of ideological, theological, and civic principles. Millions of people hold on to this tangle and dare not let go. Israelis dare not even consider proper disengagement from the least useful parts of the Jewish tradition.

Only blindness or extreme exhaustion may explain the fact that nonreligious Israeli Jews have no interest in challenging the harsh and petty methods used by our religion to define our national identity. Both right and left of the political spectrum are united in their earnest zeal to continue fighting over "preserving a Jewish majority" in the State of Israel. The disagreements between the opposite political systems are merely about the means by which to achieve this Jewish majority: should we get all Jews out of regions heavily populated by non-Jews, as the enlightened Left dearly hopes; or should non-Jews simply get their marching orders to quit all lands that Jews desire for themselves, as the nationalistic Right expects?

Israelis and Jews abroad are fiercely defensive of the concept of the Jewish state; they invest enormous energies in squashing any discussion over its sustainability and legitimacy. With all the pressures, the fury and despair of everyday life in this country, its residents and supporters tend to put aside the question of what it is, after all, that characterizes this all-important "Jewish majority" that is critical to the survival of the cherished concept, and what exactly is the "national identity" that they are defending. Universally acceptable characterizations of language, way of life, social and economic parameters, or even local culture are not enough to make somebody acceptable to the mainstream of Israeli society. They mean nothing to a legal system that does not accept non-Jews into the dominant Jewish nationality. Ours is a community in need of total isolation based on its religion.

This is the fundamental Zionist flaw, and there is no way around it. With Jewish Orthodoxy being the sole version of Judaism recognized by the Jewish state, Jews are not even trying – as some other colonial forces have done before them – to become a majority in the land that they occupy, which they could do merely by soliciting local people to join them. They are bound, therefore, to become eventually a minority in the land between the Mediterranean and the Jordan River. Should this land be divided into two states – which, as most honest people will tell you, is not going to happen – Jews might keep their majority in their part for another fortysomething years. Still, as they insist on according a different legal status to non-Jews, they will not be able to stop harassing the growing minorities in our midst. The continued frustration of those who will be cast as second- and third-class citizens will not fail to yield further violence and fury.

Decreeing religion as the national identity had effectively torpedoed, in advance, every chance of creating a genuine new nationhood, the way new immigrant nations have been created and flourished throughout the Old and New Worlds. The cohesive "Israeli society" that was believed to crystallize in the first years of statehood was a particular version of a Jewish-Israeli society. It gradually started to collapse under the pressures produced by the inefficient, anachronistic principles that its members have almost unanimously adopted.

The Jewish citizens of the Israeli state live in a constant logical contradiction between their desire for a good and peaceful life and their complete resignation to a political existence dictated by religion. Right and Left – including even part of what has become known as the "radical Left" – accept the axiomatic superiority of religion above statehood, against the best interests of most citizens. This inner contradiction had reached its bizarre climax with the emergence of a powerful new "secular" political movement that targeted religious privileges. Its charismatic founder and leader, the late Yosef (Tommy) Lapid, followed by his even more charismatic son, TV presenter Yair Lapid (nominated Minister of Finance in 2013 following a fantastic election performance), galvanized a considerable segment of the electorate against the refusal of ultra-Orthodox Jews to serve in the Israeli Army; vowed to fight extra allocations for the ultra-Orthodox extended households and educational institutions; but fully endorsed the national-religious concept of Zionism. Following his late father, Lapid, in opposition as well as in his days as a minister, is a loyal and eager advocate of Israeli policies that are based on the principle of Jewish supremacy.

The occupation of Palestinian areas with the constant abuse and harassment of the population in the West Bank and the Gaza Strip is a natural derivative of the Israeli-Jewish nationality syndrome. The mushrooming of dubious power brokers and the collapsing of legal elements throughout the Jewish state is another aspect of the same malaise. With a norm that places an ideology or a religion above human rights and civil liberties, this should be expected. It is hard to sustain a modern society in the long run without a legal system that works "without prejudice and with no special favours."

Judaism is neither meaner nor more fanatical than other religions. But all religions are flawed in one way or another once they are allowed to hold real political power over a community. Judaism, kind and responsible as it may potentially be, has the capability of inflicting political calamities at least as efficiently as most other faiths.

Our religion is a complex system whose most precious goal is to preserve the uniqueness and exclusivity of a well-selected, scholarly community. It is a community supposedly endowed with a sublime mission of preserving pious justice and morality. In practice, everyday Jewish life revolves around an enormous codex of rules and regulations, designed to prevent or at least to minimize any contact between the Children of the Faith and all gentiles. A special dress code, strict food rules, numerous rituals, unique festivities, and even the re-design of male genitals mark us as a people apart. Together they ensure that we will always be left in a minority, keeping ourselves to ourselves.

* * *

Longing for a homogeneous ethnic-religious texture is not something exclusive to Israelis or to Jews. Most ethnic or national groups tend to reject strangers and foreigners. For many generations Jews have been the wretched victims of such rejection, and they have perfected their own methods of coping with it. From generation to generation, a tradition was passed on that placed the Faith and its commandments at the centre of everybody's life. As ways of life are stronger than most regulations, Jewish communities eventually adopted many of the characteristics, habits, and rituals of the people they lived among. When a new political movement started bringing together Jews of very diverse communities, it soon became clear that the concept of homogeneous ethnicity was a fake. Religious unity did not really supply true communal cohesiveness.

Here lies another problematic aspect of the Israeli-Jewish syndrome. Next to the fervent longing to attain a "Jewish majority," the old Jewish elites of Israel still crave the traditional Eastern European model of the early Israelis. Although rooted in the small towns of Eastern Europe, veteran Israelis – otherwise known as Ashkenazi Jews – are convinced that it is based on the highly prestigious "Western liberal" model. And as the Arabs of the land are stigmatized for their "Islamic, nonliberal culture," Jews of Arab origins have always been considered to be affiliated with this undesirable population. They were courted to join the Zionist project, but at the same time, they were looked upon with an anxiety that perfectly reflects the problematic, basically religious concept of the "Jewish Israeli" brand.

The first Zionists, children of Russia, Romania, Poland, and the Ukraine, carried with them into the old-new Jewish homeland a peculiar ancient language and a rich heritage. Unfortunately, a major element in this heritage was an exclusive club culture.

The indigenous inhabitants of the New Country and their offspring have been expected, from day one of the Zionist settlement, to accept the status of second-class citizens that was accorded to them by the newcomers. This is the attitude that culminated with the declaration of the Jewish state in 1948, when hundreds of thousands eventually lost their homes and became permanent refugees.

As a mirror image of the Nakba – the Palestinian Arabs' disaster – another, seemingly less horrible mass human transfer occurred in the opposite direction. The freshly born institutions of the new state started the complicated operation of transferring masses of citizens of Arab countries, all of them Jewish by religion, into its territory. The idea was to reinforce the fragile Jewish majority within the new expanded borders.

The Arab Jews landed in the new country with a mother tongue and cultural traditions that were embarrassingly similar to those of the native Arabs who had just been kicked out. They were met with a double message that would characterize their life here for the next decades: they were welcomed by the veteran immigrants from Eastern Europe, as members of the specially privileged Jewish nationality, and therefore superior to the local Arabs; at the same time, they were openly despised as culturally inferior, patronizingly defined "The Second Israel," chastised for their blatant Arab manners, and thrust into the deep end of poverty, humility, and ignorance of the new Israeli society.

Well into the seventh decade of Israel's existence, one's head is still dizzy with social gaps, conflicts of interest, and built-in paradoxes in a state that was merely expected to offer a safe haven for one long-suffering national-religious community.

All around us, in the meantime, the world is moving forward toward a reality where racial, religious, and national segregation lines are collapsing, with or without much blood or pain. The unique, unabashed insistence on distinguishing one preferred brand of citizens, and the forcing of this privileged distinction by military force, secures for the State of Israel the status of a pariah in the global village.

* * *

My grandfather Shmuel Yathom was quite careful, in April of 1948, not to criticise openly the decision of his daughter to choose a non-Ashkenazi husband, but he did find a feeble excuse to stay away from the wedding. My parents' marriage was at that time considered a rare "mixed marriage." Had his daughter chosen for herself a "real" Arab, Saba Shmuel, according to a Jewish custom, should have declared her dead.

With time he learned to genuinely love his son-in-law. As we said our goodbyes in the Ra'anana hospice, he asked my mother not to forget to give his best regards to "Moshe." He was never able to come to terms with the fact that everybody else called my dad "Mousa," the Arabic version of the Prophet Moses's name.

The "ethnic demons" that rocked Israel for many years are still there, but with so many Israelis like me who belong to no side of the "ethnic rift" – having parents on both ends – the raging must eventually subside.

Ashkenazi Jews learned to conceal – and many truly got over – their cultural abhorrence of the Arab/Middle Eastern flavours.

Rich idiomatic Arab expressions have become an integral part of Hebrew slang. Tasty Middle Eastern dishes and gradually even the musical quarter-tonality, so vehemently despised in the 1950s and '60s, are now the *bon ton* in elegant social circles. By contrast, a majority of Middle Eastern Jews and their offspring support political forces that keep pushing the rejection of the local Arabs to unacceptable levels of discrimination and dispossession. This cognitive dissonance is yet another bizarre derivative of the religious conception of this state.

Zahara Yathom and Mousa Yeshua, 1947, on a trip to the South

* * *

"We are a villa in the jungle" is a favourite expression coined by ex-Prime Minister, ex-General, often Minister of Defence Ehud Barak, somehow still considered part of the battered Israeli

"Left." It expresses a national consensus and nicely illustrates a twice-erroneous Israeli illusion. In reality Israel is no pretty, elegant "villa," but more of an eclectic urban conglomerate with a disorderly mix of grandeur and refuse. As for the "jungle" element: it is all over the country, inside and out, but has nothing to do with the battered, much-maligned "neighbours."

In fact, with the national energies so powerfully enlisted to keep this land isolated from any non-Jewish element, the Israeli construct has doomed itself to exist as a racially selective *kollel* religious seminary, captive of a user-unfriendly faith and exasperating its environment. Why, I often wonder, do Israelis constantly complain about the "bad neighbourhood" they landed in? Would the Zionist project be more popular if the Jews had decided to plant it in peaceful Scandinavia and tell Finns or Norwegians that they are now an undesirable demographic risk?

Zionism, generally considered part of Western civilization, is actually a religious entity – something at least some of its founders had not anticipated. The thin democratic veneer that is used to disguise the uncompromising nature of this religious state of ours is much cracked already. While the so-called civilized world regularly panics over the belligerence of violent, religious fanatics, it has for years failed to pay attention to the growing religious fanaticism that characterizes this supposed "spearhead of Western Civilization" as Israel's lovers would have it described.

For the last sixty or so years, secular Jewish Israeli jurists, academics, and civil servants have been sparing no verbal acrobatics to try and reconcile the oxymoronic "Jewish and democratic" concept.

Israel is one of two states that were started during the twentieth century with an official intention to create an ethnic-religious homogeneous political entity. The other state is Pakistan, which is also still struggling under this legacy. Nothing but a full separation of church and state might put an end to the present messianic frenzy that carries the "Jewish state" into ever more dangerous abysses. Israeli-Jewish solidarity, often heralded, is in fact contrived and illusionary. It is only effective in making sure that non-Jews, notably Arabs, should forever be counted outside this "national" formation.

Taking religion out of politics would mean the removal of the mechanism that allows the state to rob over a fifth of the citizens – and all the inhabitants of the occupied territories – of their equal, legal civil liberties. It is a move essential for the abolition of the special privileges granted to one favoured religious (though it insists on calling itself "national") group.

At the same time, the only long-term chance for the Jewish community in Israel to survive is to allow the state to live up to its already obvious multinational practical identity. A free-spirited regime, adhering to basic democratic principles, is the only one likely to guarantee this land a balanced, peaceful existence. Continuing the present arrangement guarantees the present collision course (which admittedly is useful for a certain type of politician).

It is only a truly secular, democratic, regime that may contain the amazing variety of ethnic, cultural, and denominational characteristics of Jews and Palestinians – and some others who are neither – and allow them to coexist and further develop. The Israeli obsession with "security," the total compulsive worship of the state's military might, is nothing but an admission of the fact that its present form of government and set of (religious) principles will never be acceptable if not forced by an enormous iron fist.

How sad that the very idea that this land should become "democratic and secular" is being considered by its Jews a code name for a vile conspiracy "to eliminate the Jewish National Home." This, indeed, is Zionism's fundamental flaw. The National Jewish Home has been burning for almost a century on a daily basis because it was constructed as a fire trap.

* * *

There is good reason to believe that human nature is stronger than even the most rigid political structure. During the last decades of the twentieth century, bigger empires than ours have collapsed like packs of cards as new generations refused to take any more tyranny, violence, and deprivations in the name of grand ideas that captured the imaginations of their grandparents. We live in a life-loving place. The human variety populating the areas under the control of the Israeli state is still capable of shaking off the unfair rules of the game imposed on it by a confused and inefficient legal code, riddled with inner contradictions.

One must only open a window to observe that the global village has reached us after all, in full blossom.

I can remember times when, in the height of the heavy Israeli summer, the only sprays of colour in our public parks belonged to the local deadly poisonous oleander bush. Parsimonious with its water consumption, well adapted to the meagre sandy base, it dominated the gardens with its plain flowers in white and faded pink.

Now the roadsides are alive with the rich, Hawaiian-class colour schemes of the dainty bougainvillea, made possible by economical watering systems, an Israeli contribution. Around our multi-storeyed residential homes, the Far East glory is alive with jacaranda and callistemon, poinciana, hibiscus, purple bohenia, and azedarach China-berry tree, all blending nicely with elegant desert palms. In the spring we shall have yellow exuberant acacias and the pink-purple flames of the cercis. Its Hebrew name is *Kllil Hachoresh* ("Perfections of the Woods"), but the English viciously nicknamed it Judah's Blood.

The human landscape mix of our Tel Aviv neighbourhoods is equally astounding. Cleaners from Ghana and Nigeria work for landladies whose parents were born in Hungary or Morocco, next to housemaids from Columbia and Guatemala. Gentle Filipino men and women lovingly care for frail geriatrics and for the children of parents who are too busy to stick around. The grass is cut by Thai dayworkers who have escaped hard labour in the southern villages of Israel, where they have replaced Palestinians, now unwanted and feared. But in the elegant northern housing estates, all the pharmacists and most cashiers, as well as half the medical staff in all hospitals, are educated Palestinians, already part of the new middle classes whose aspirations are so similar in Tel Aviv and in Ramallah.

In the small playground next to our flat, Russian Orthodox grandmothers discipline their blond grandchildren, and Israeli girls of unspecified ethnic beauty demonstrate supple, agile bodies on the swings. Chinese and Romanian bricklayers walk silently to the bus stop having completed a hard day's work in a nearby building site. Some Ethiopian students are on their way back from Tel Aviv University. A newspaper article reported harsh discrimination among Ethiopian Jews; apparently some of them are considered blacker than others. Maybe in another twenty years this, too, will be but a bitter memory.

Social gaps keep mounting mercilessly, there is no public housing, public health and education are constantly deteriorating as the military keeps inflating and the rich get richer. Still, for the majority of people all over the world, Tel Aviv offers an option far superior to what they have in their homes. Refugees and labour immigrants arrive here rife with expectations, ready for any hard labour, just like my own Grandfather Shmuel and Grandfather David, who landed in Jaffa many years ago as penniless immigrants. The new guest workers' children wear red scarves to cheer the Hapoel Tel Aviv soccer team, or go for the yellow of rival Maccabee; they should be considered just as Israeli as I am, with no Immigration Police to hunt them as undesirables. Immigrant societies have characterized Palestine for centuries, which is why Jaffa was nicknamed "*Um el Gharib*" – the mother of foreigners. Rather than spend all our energies pushing new people out, it is time we start to consider how to accommodate them, as well as the many who had to leave this land many decades ago and are still pining for their ancestral homes.

The new communities that are gradually emerging all over this land would otherwise have to start fighting for civil rights in a manner similar to that chosen by furious Palestinians, now trapped and locked behind fences and barbed wire. Confused Israeli soldiers – Jews, Druze, Bedouins, and some Russian Christians – make sure that only those officially recognized as Jews should be allowed to drive freely on specially allocated asphalt roads that were built over what used to be old olive groves.

Zionism was started – or so I was educated to believe – as an idea to create a solidly stable, productive community based on sound economic and social principles, as opposed to the way of life forced on Jewish communities elsewhere. For many years it grieved me to realize that "my generation" has been digging itself and the country ever deeper into the failed traditions that Zionism was meant to eradicate. It took even longer to realize that in fact the will to break up with an unsound past was not there even in the times of my pioneering, avant-garde-style, Russian Ukrainian grandparents.

The following chapters are an attempt to comprehend why and how millions of people who are not impressed by divine teaching have allowed the illogical rules of an unreformed religion to bring their national existence to the brink of moral and practical bankruptcy. Are we dealing here with the most efficient brainwashing in the whole world, or does the indoctrination start elsewhere, in other body parts?

3

THEODORE'S BUSINESS PLAN

A Jewish colony might become "a ghetto within a ghetto with all the prejudices of a ghetto... It would be small and petty, orthodox and illiberal, and keep out non-Jews..."

Nathaniel Lord Rothschild
writing to Theodore Herzl, August 18, 1902[1]

In Herzliya, a sprawling modern town just north of Tel Aviv, real estate sharks are busy covering the last plots of rich agricultural land with concrete, creating ever more residential buildings. The city is perfectly positioned on the Tel Aviv-Haifa highway, smack in the middle of the crowded Dan conurbation, the heart of the Land of Israel. But a whiff of the old farming scent, a fragrant reminder of the days long ago when Herzliya was known as a "colony,"[2] may still be noticed around the city centre, next to the old central bus station and the small avenue nearby. One block away from the station, my mother's aunt Milka (Milla) and Uncle David Lutzki used to live.

I used to be sent there during the summer holidays, to ensure that my lungs would take in some clean country air and that my parents might enjoy a few days of peace and quiet. I loved the cookies Aunt Milla baked specially for me on these occasions and the creaking, lazy sound of the wire door that protected her

---

1 Theodore Herzl, *Die Judensache*, Diaries 1885-1904, v.3, edited by Michael Heymann and Josef Wenkert, Byalik Institute.

2 Colony is the generic Israeli term for a village of private farmers, without communal property or organized production.

kitchen from flying insects. By the time I had finished reading the books I brought with me, I moved on to the old bound copies of *BaMa'ale,* the weekly magazine of the Labor youth movement, lovingly preserved from the thirties and the early forties, when my mother's cousins were devout members of *HaNoar HaOved.* Next to heroic tales and well-adapted political commentaries, the publication carried a satisfactory collection of modestly romantic tales with a social and patriotic message.

A shack under the lemon tree by the little brown house was called "the goat's shed," a reminder that once upon a time, a real goat actually resided in it. Behind the house was the Lutzki's private orchard: two rows of orange trees that seemed so long, I never ventured to check where they ended. In the early sixties, my great aunt and uncle allowed the orchard to dry up, and for several years, the oranges picked from its trees were particularly sweet and well shrunk, up to the day when the trees were uprooted altogether and the land sold to a developer. Uncle David and Aunt Milla lived for a while in a flat in the long residential building that replaced their plot, and then it was time for them to move into a nursing home. In the yards surrounding the typically long apartment blocks that replaced Herzliya's orchards, lemon trees still grow, next to the ancient cypresses.

To the west of the highway is the more fashionable side of the town. Affluent families live in the large private estates of Herzliya Pituach. The prettiest villas, housing millionaires and foreign diplomats, are perched on the cliffs overlooking the seashore. This area becomes crowded every Fourth of July as a few thousand men and women, the most prominent members of Israeli society, make the annual pilgrimage to the American ambassador's barbecue and garden party. While they rub shoulders around the sunken swimming pool at the bottom of the garden, handsome uniformed marines at the gates protect the elegant residence, with its beautiful private park spilling up and down a gentle slope to the Mediterranean. The wet rocks surrounding it in the water are well covered with rusty barbed wire to defend this strategic point against any terrorists who might choose to enter the grounds from the sea.

North of the residential area, the remains of a shabby neighbourhood, left over from the time of mass emigration in the fifties, are still to be seen. Overlooked by the large Sidna Ali mosque, a sacred site for Muslims, they are a remnant to the Arab village that used to be here until 1948, high above one of the most beautiful beaches in the country. The southern part of Herzliya Pituach is the most prestigious Israeli business zone. This is the place to be if you run a high-tech enterprise, a venture capital fund, or a trendy restaurant. A fast-growing maze of green-glassed, white and grey marble-tiled towering office blocks and expensive shopping malls sprawls over an area that was sand dunes until the early 1990s.

To get from the highway into this "Little Manhattan," one turns off at the busy HaSira (Boat) Junction. A real boat, about the size of a fishing smack, has been installed high on a dune in the middle of the asphalt and concrete traffic-congested junction. It commemorates the illegal immigration to Palestine of Jewish refugees from Europe in the late 1940s. Such small smacks, loaded with sad but hopeful human cargo, steered for these dunes, as members of the Haganah and Palmach Jewish militia waited under cover of darkness to pick them up as they hit the wild beach. My father was a member of Palmach in those days. My mother and her friends in a Socialist-Zionist youth movement used to stage diversionary riots to distract the British police away from the illegal landings.

The illegal immigration was commemorated in Nathan Altherman's famous poetic verse "A toast to the boats making their way." At the boats' actual landing point by the cliffs of Herzliya, a huge yacht marina was built in the 1990s. Breaking almost every environmental and planning regulation, an influential construction consortium poured thousands of tons of concrete over ancient coarse sand rocks to create the docking area. The mile-long walk along the breakwater is most enjoyable on sunny winter days. The marina restaurants are packed on weekends and almost every evening; patrons are not deterred by the high prices of the well-presented dishes. Only the bulky, ungainly sight of the most expensive apartment buildings in the country, all built on a scam and registered misleadingly as holiday homes, spoils the harmony of the sea view.

Overlooking HaSira Junction is another piece of public art. Mounted on a disused water tower, the city fathers placed a large metal black-and-white wire picture of Theodore Herzl, the founder of modern Zionism, after whom the town was named. "Herzliya: A Fairy Tale of a City," the Hebrew inscription under the picture reads. It is a paraphrase of the closing lines to Theodore Herzl's famous book *The Jewish State* that nicely fits the purposes of municipal branding. Photographer Alex Levac captured the large portrait during renovations, adorned with a huge sign that reads, "Works by Mahamid Muhamad, Stone and Marble Works." This ironic photo makes the cover of Levac's inspired photo album *Our Country*.[3]

Theodore Herzl would have approved of Herzliya. Smart and prosperous, the town comes closer than any other in the Jewish state to Herzl's own futuristic description of a modern ideal Jewish political entity. It's too bad that only a few Israelis would be familiar today with Herzl's manifested vision that is considered to have laid the ideological foundations for our lives here.

* * *

Herzl's short manifesto, published 1896 in Vienna, managed to stir up the Jewish world and create the political Zionist movement well over a century ago. The movement, possibly one of the most successful theories put into practice in the twentieth century, has been fast to abandon major principles of the founder's professed intellectual legacy; indeed, its present leaders go to great pains to deny this legacy.

Herzl's image disappeared from Israeli bank notes in the 1980s. By that time, his books had long since been removed from the curricula of Israeli schools. My own copy, which combines *The Jewish State* and *Altneuland* (1904), is part of a special Hebrew edition that was republished in 1960 to commemorate the 100th anniversary of Herzl's birth. It was offered that year as a gift to all elementary school graduates in Tel Aviv, still in the archaic translation made sixty years earlier. I got it from a second-hand book dealer and discovered that the book's previous owner was a Tel Aviv high school library. The empty library card

---

[3] MOD Publishing House, Jerusalem, 2000.

glued to the inside cover and the good condition of the volume silently testified that it had not been borrowed even once.[4]

Reading Herzl reveals that the man we call "The Visionary" of Zionism – a name that evokes a particularly dreamy, spiritual, and unearthly character – actually was the most realistic and hard-nosed entrepreneur. *The Jewish State* is a perfectly modern business plan. *Altneuland* is a futuristic technological novella, packed with practical inventions, which conveys a belief surprisingly trendy today: that the world might become a better place if only the right mixture of sensible economical leadership and social responsibility would be applied. Dr. Herzl worked out, down to the minute details, all the inputs and mechanisms needed to establish a settlement capable of providing Jews with adequate living conditions. He also displayed amazing ability in organizing grand international conferences full of excitement and pomp to support his project and managed to produce a media buzz that would have made today's PR gurus green with envy.

Herzl's business scheme quantified the initial investment needed to get started (one billion pounds sterling) and suggested simple and practical methods for raising the necessary funds. Attention was given to every detail. Clearly and unambiguously Herzl dealt with all the possible aspects of the Zionist project: rules, legislations, and the democratic mechanism to monitor and control their applicability; land and agrarian policy; real estate and property management; and communications and public awareness campaigns. He outlined organizational charts and offered solutions and instructions for problems of human resources, equipment, and means of transport. He anticipated modes to allocate resources and methods of remuneration. Special emphasis was put on technology and the project's robust profitability to investors. Within a few years, Herzl had actually established a bank that has since managed to survive and prosper better than any of the founder's other ideas.[5]

---

[4] In 1997 Babel Publishing House issued a new and modern translation, but it sold poorly and is unavailable in most outlets.

[5] Bank Anglo-Palestine has since become Bank Leumi, presently one of Israel's largest banks.

In *Altneuland* ("Old-New-Land") Herzl went one step further and set his creative imagination loose. *Altneuland* is recognized as a didactic novel, which carries moral insights as political futurism. But an unbiased reader might easily define it as science fiction. The prophet of Zionism is revealed as an enthusiastic fan of modern technologies, some not yet invented. His Jewish state thrives on the power of electric energy activating ploughs, ships, locomotives, and large trucks. Automated industrial machines, large water works, and other engineering marvels are the things that turn the Zionist vision into reality. It is modern technology that makes the settlement of hundreds of thousands of jobless Jews, lacking any formal education and professional training, in the most neglected and deserted regions of the Middle East, into a guaranteed success. One must not forget that during Herzl's time, the European model of successful colonialism had already been put into practice in Ottoman Palestine. It had started with the German Templars' colonies and was followed by the first Jewish settlements, already practicing modern agricultural methods by the end of the 1890s.

Struggling dot-coms in Herzliya and elsewhere would be surprised to learn that over a century ago, Herzl already predicted the communications revolution, fully realizing its social and economic significance. He had, for example, identified the potential of the telephone, at that time just becoming familiar to the Europeans. Using the telephone to create a network for broadcasting live news was one of the ideas that sprung into his mind. He could not predict, at that stage, that radio could also be wireless, but in his futuristic Jewish state, the visitor was introduced to an amazingly insightful description of what can be done by "oral (or telephonic) newspaper" and how one can make money from its captive listeners:

Its advertisements command the highest rates. The reader of a printed newspaper is not obliged to look at the advertising columns. But he is defenceless against advertisements that come through the receiver.[6]

---

[6] Altneuland references are from the *Altneuland Book* on the Jewish Virtual Library.

The entrepreneurial conception of this communication system is strikingly similar to today's license fee arrangements for telecommunications:

Under our streets, tunnels have been provided for the reception of all kinds of pipes and cables (present and future) for gas, water, sewage, and so on... You may, if you like, regard this as symbolic of our whole system... we knew just what utilities a modern city required, and therefore laid tunnels under our streets to accommodate them... Since this telephonic newspaper also runs its wires through the street tunnel, it must pay a rental in proportion to its income. This rental accrues to the public treasury.

It should be noted that Altneuland's administrators are constantly listening in to wired communication "so that there will be no mishaps and that this device will not be used to promote lies, exaggerated news or profane language" (!). A professional journalist himself, the writer accepted benevolent censorship as part of the game. How remarkable that even this idea, considered reprehensible for years, is being seriously considered today.

Get a desolate, thinly inhabited piece of land, put on it some sophisticated, hardworking European engineers, back them up with a modern bureaucracy and enough capital to purchase the latest industrial know-how, and the hungry Jewish masses would follow and do their best to succeed. Their own prosperity, as well as a fair return on capital for the investors, seemed guaranteed. The Jewish state was no prophetic whim. It was a fully realizable business plan.

Herzl did not need to invent his business model. He not only copied it but also gave credit to the original. In the 1890s, such entrepreneurial ventures were realities in several parts of the world. Available wasteland was being upgraded into profitable means of production. In the North American Midwest; in California; in large parts of Australia, Argentina, and South Africa, the model of mass emigration was already proven as a well-paying concept. In the frontier zones, pioneers, supported by heavy mechanical machinery, had been growing agricultural commodities using novel agrarian methods. Urban industrial centres flourished nearby. Engineering projects involving electricity, telegraph and telephones, railways, and irrigation systems had already made deserts and prairies bloom and made a lot of money for daring entrepreneurs who were fast enough to spot real estate and other opportunities on time. All Herzl had to do was to repackage this pioneering model and adapt it to the needs of penniless Jews. For this, he requested, "Let the sovereignty be granted us over a portion of the globe large enough to satisfy the rightful requirements of a nation; the rest we shall manage for ourselves."[7]

Herzl shocked many of his supporters by his readiness to accept any piece of land that would prove viable for his plan. Seemingly prepared to abandon the traditionally yearned-for homecoming of the Jews to the Land of Israel, he called for the acceptance of the "Uganda solution" put forward by the British. He even considered other locations for the "Promised Land" in places like Brazil and Argentina. Readers of *The Jewish State* had no reason to be surprised. Eventually, Herzl came round to the view that Palestine was not only the best but also the only viable option for a modern Jewish state. The historical roots and the emotional attachment were too fundamental to give up. In *Altneuland* he had fully come to terms with this aspect of the national concept.

This was inevitable for that particular period. To have a normal, modern life in the Europe of 1900, you had to have a national identity of some sort. The very "Jewish National Problem" that Herzl set out to solve and to ultimately end was the anomaly the Jews were experiencing in those days: a religious group, identified with the middle classes everywhere, finding it more and more difficult to fit in with the European environment that put an increasing emphasis on its own national self-determination. Zionism was, after all, a derivative of current mainstream Western political thought. By the end of the nineteenth century, nationalism was a rising political creed. The radical solution for the "Jewish Problem" was therefore well adapted to the times: to create from scratch a Jewish national identity, based on self-sovereignty.

Reading Herzl, however, one discovers that he himself was one step ahead of nationalism. He could see through it into an

---

[7] *The Jewish State* (New York: Dover Publications, 1988 [translation]), p. 92.

era that today we call global and multicultural. While expressing loyalty and fondness for Jewish traditions, his ideal society was universalistic, based on a pan-European model. Universalism was a favourite theme with intellectuals in Herzl's days, people who found the growing nationalistic passions of their times exasperating.

It was not a coincidence that Jewish thinkers were in the forefront of this line of thinking, which became attractive to both Marxists and to multinational capitalists. It was also not a coincidence that some years later, Nazi Germany's raving nationalism targeted Jewish "cosmopolitans" who presented an alternative to a *Weltanschauung* focused on ethnic purity.

The Zionist "entity" for Herzl was part of a global vision. *Altneuland* is packed with references to social experiments and reforms in other parts of the world. The leaders of the "New Lands" see themselves as members of a benevolent worldwide movement that aims to maximize the welfare of all human beings. The novel features a well-publicized cruise of an international group of intellectual celebrities. Having enjoyed themselves as guests on board the good ship *Futuro*, these wise men and women publish their favourable impressions of the Jewish New Homeland in a collection of their discussions that immediately becomes a best seller all over the world.

In emphasizing the cosmopolitan nature of his Zionist ideology, Herzl was merely following a respected tradition of emancipated Jews in Europe. The French revolutionary ideas of "liberty, fraternity, and equality" were a gift to European Jews. Members of their communities were for the first time able to turn their backs on the Jewish ghetto and acquire general education and professional status, while still practicing Judaism. The enlightenment movement turned Jewish communities in some European countries into open societies that bred outstanding individuals like Freud, Marx, Einstein, and Herzl himself.

How far ahead of his time Herzl was in matters of human rights is demonstrated by his suggestion that, having liberated themselves from enslavements to other people who dislike them so much, Jews should lead the world in emancipating other peoples. He specifically pointed out the need to help black people achieve equal rights. This, by the way, did not stop him from including handsome, elegantly clad, black servants as appropriate Zeitgeist status symbols in the households of the good and the great in his imagined Old New Land.

* * *

True to his vision of the Jewish state as part of a general vision for a better human condition, Herzl naturally included in it the original inhabitants of Palestine. He could see no reason why they should not be well integrated into his predicted technological settlement enterprise.

Herzl's idyllic vision of the harmonious relations between Jews and Palestine's Arab inhabitants has often been criticized and even mocked as naïve and unrealistic. In *Altneuland* the Arabs are represented by the Ottoman Muslim Rashid Bey. Contemporary readers find the fictitious Rashid unconvincing. A chemist by profession and landowner by birth, Rashid is a proud intellectual who keeps his womenfolk at home while he joins his Jewish friends on their sightseeing expeditions. He seems happy to be a part of the new state's elite, enjoying the prosperity brought to his land by the Jewish newcomers, displaying no signs of a wounded national ego.

Rashid Bey may have been the product of Herzl's wishful thinking, but then so are the too-good-to-be-true Jewish personalities he conjured up in the novel: an amazing collection of self-sacrificing bureaucrats, businessmen, and politicians. Even Rashid's position on women's issues is not at all far behind that of his Jewish friends, as Herzl's liberalism stopped short of social change for the ladies. ("Girls don't go on such tours... We believe that the place of a growing girl is beside her mother," beeps his young Jewish heroine, Miriam.)

In Israel today one would not find a single affluent, well-educated Arab who had integrated well into the local Jewish elite. The reasons for this have nothing to do with Herzl's colonialist vision and everything to do with the serious deviations from its original layout.

Reading *Altneuland* today, one is struck by the adequacy of its economic and technological predictions, compared to the seeming irrelevance of its social and political vision. History tells us that Arabs have resisted Zionism as long as it has existed, and that Jews have retaliated with increasing military ferocity. Herzl failed to predict this simple fact.

Or perhaps he only failed to convince his successors of the vital necessity to annul a hopelessly distorted set of priorities. Herzl was no naïve ignoramus (the Jewish version[8]), and he was hardly a conspirator of an imperialistic plot (as the common anti-Zionist viewpoint goes). He was an entrepreneur with a sound enough reason to believe that Jews and Arabs could live side by side, on a daily basis, in the Holy Land. The option of coexistence was rejected – not, as we have been asked to believe, by extremist Arabs who managed to coerce the majority of their communities into supporting their position, but first and foremost by a crushing majority of the Jewish population and its leading elites.

Herzl spoke out unequivocally against any religious meddling in the affairs of the state, and he warned against tampering with his design. He clearly foresaw the risk that certain Zionist leaders might be attracted to a national-religious ideology that he was not prepared to tolerate. But he could not guess that this, eventually, would become the winning ideology in the Jewish state.

In fact, while setting out to create Jewish Nationalism out of almost nothing, Herzl actually chose to apologize for the very idea:

It might be more reasonably objected that I am giving a handle to Anti-Semitism when I say we are a people – one people; that I am hindering the assimilation of Jews where it is about to be consummated, and endangering it where it is an accomplished fact.

So unflattering was the contemporary image of his own people to Herzl that he sounds as if he is almost rationalizing antisemitism:

Anti-Semitism increases day by day and hour by hour among the nations; indeed, it is bound to increase, because the causes of its growth continue to exist and cannot be removed. Its remote cause is our loss of the power of assimilation during the Middle Ages; its immediate cause is our excessive production of mediocre intellects, who cannot find an outlet downwards or upwards – that

---

[8] Adopted, for example, by liberal Professors Amnon Rubinstein and Alexander Yakobson in *Israel and the Family of Nations* (Tel Aviv: Schoken Publishing House, 2003).

is to say, no wholesome outlet in either direction. When we sink, we become a revolutionary proletariat, the subordinate officers of all revolutionary parties; and at the same time, when we rise, there rises also our terrible power of the purse.

But in accepting the fact that "when civilized nations awoke to the inhumanity of discriminatory legislation and enfranchised us, our enfranchisement came too late," and that it was "no longer possible to remove our disabilities in our old homes. For we had, curiously enough, developed while in the ghetto into a bourgeois people," Herzl had no intention of letting the rules of the ghetto be involved in the actual running of affairs in his future Jewish state. His position on this was uncompromising:

We shall keep our priests within the confines of their temples in the same way as we shall keep our professional army within the confines of its barracks. Army and priesthood shall receive honours as high as their valuable functions deserve. But they must not interfere in the administration of the State which confers distinction upon them, else they will conjure up difficulties without and within. And if it should occur that men of other creeds and different nationalities come to live amongst us, we should accord them honourable protection and equality before the law.

No priests interfering in the administration of the state? No professional soldiers allowed out of barracks? No wonder the father of political Zionism is such an irrelevant figure in the Israel of the twenty-first century. No wonder that "men of other creeds and different nationalities" are unable to be accorded "honourable protection and equality before the law." Religion and the military are the predominant forces of Israeli politics and society. Together they devour the lion's share of the country's resources.

Jewish religious bigotry must have been all too familiar to Herzl. *Altneuland* includes a particularly unflattering description of the rabbi Dr. Geyer – a religious leader who "fights and swears" against the building of the Jewish state, then joins it and tries to take over its politics. In a vivid anticlerical speech uttered by Chief Engineer Steineck, the secular, patriotic administrator, Herzl's views are made crystal clear:

These rabbis who sought the immediate advantage made our lives a burden to us. Geyer is doing the same thing now. In those early, difficult days, he did not so much as want to hear the name of Palestine mentioned. Now he is more Palestinian than any of us. Now he is the patriot, the nationalist Jew. And we – we are the friends of the alien. If we listened to him, he would make us out to be bad Jews or even strangers in his Palestine. Yes, that's it. He wants to turn the public against us, to sow suspicion between you and me. This pious man rolls his eyes to heaven and all the time seeks his immediate advantage. In the old Ghetto days, when the rich men had all the influence, he talked to suit their notions [...] He and his ilk invented the myth of the Jewish mission. The function of the Jewish people was asserted to be to instruct the other peoples. Therefore, they alleged, we must live in the dispersion [...] The fact was, of course, that we not only did not teach the other nations, but that they taught us – day by day and year by year – bloody, painful lessons. Finally, we roused ourselves and sought our way out of Egypt [sic]. And we found it. Then, to be sure, Dr. Geyer also came here, and brought with him all his old arrogance and hypocrisy.

Nowadays, thank God, the Jews conduct their public affairs differently. It is not the rich alone who make the decisions, but the whole community. Communal leadership is no longer a reward for success in business. Leaders are chosen not for their wealth, but for their talent and their ability to command respect in the eyes of the public. Therefore, the instincts of the masses must be flattered. A theory for the immediate advantage of the masses must be found, or at least for what the masses imagine to be to their immediate advantage. Therefore, an anti-alien slogan is proclaimed. A non-Jew must not be accepted by the New Society. [...] If you adopt that stupid, narrow-minded policy, the land will go to wrack and ruin. We stand and fall by the principle that whoever has given two years' service to the New Society as prescribed by our rules, and has conducted himself properly, are eligible to membership no matter what his race or creed.[9]

Altneuland's fictional bigot fails after nearly succeeding in hijacking the new democratic entity. Jewish religion's prestige is redeemed in the novel by the honourable Rabbi Shmuel, who

[9] *Altneuland,* the Jewish Virtual Library.

condemns Rabbi Geyer while admitting that the community had given birth to "quite a few of his sort."

Herzl was not hostile to religious authority. Quite the contrary, his utopian manifesto *The Jewish State* outlined the important role of "Our Rabbis" in a specific chapter dedicated to these vulnerable figures:

Every group will have its Rabbi traveling with his congregation. Local groups will afterwards form voluntarily about their Rabbi, and each locality will have its spiritual leader. Our Rabbis, on whom we specially call, will devote their energies to the service of our idea, and will inspire their congregations by preaching it from the pulpit... The Rabbis will receive communications regularly from both society and company, and will announce and explain these to their congregations. Israel will pray for us and for itself.[10]

It would have been inconceivable to Herzl that rabbis should have a sovereign status in the bureaucracy of the state, and that an enormous religious-political establishment should openly and successfully oppose the very idea that non-Jews might become citizens with equal rights.

* * *

Densely populated Israel continues to show a surprisingly resilient economic potential, which proves that the founder's business sense was sound enough. But a clear majority of Jews in this country seem to accept the concept of this state as an institution to preserve the hegemony of a Jewish majority, rather than an organization whose prime aim is to facilitate its inhabitants' personal welfare and a good, secure life.

This erroneous concept is often attributed to the calamity brought on Europe's Jews by European nationalism during World War II. The Holocaust that destroyed six million Jews no doubt scarred the survivors forever. It is easy to identify with the passionate urge that drove the Zionists to the immediate creation of an ethnic national state for Jews, as an antithesis to the pathological ethnic hatred of Jews that they experienced from the Nazis. One can

---

[10] *The Jewish State*, p. 125.

even sympathize with the principle of affirmative action for Jews, which underlined the UN partition resolution and the decision of the new state's legislative system to decree a Law of Return[11] for the benefit of the Holocaust's survivors. But it is still hard not to be amazed by the carelessness by which the state's secular founders accepted the problematic Jewish *Halacha* religious code as the final decree above the civil legislation in matters of civil and residency privileges. It is a status that from the outset mocks any Zionist pretence for enlightenment and democracy.

With blatant defiance of even the most basic element of Herzl's plan, the State of Israel failed to adopt any commitment to human rights. The Jewish Halacha, with its oddities and clear major faults, is binding on all the citizens of Israel, overruling basic civil liberty considerations.

Religious politics is a central driving force on the Israeli political scene. Civil servants, legislators, and even professional soldiers have no problem in declaring publicly that their loyalty to the Jewish religion overrules all other loyalties they might have, including the need to obey the civil law and to comply with international conventions.

* * *

History sometimes plays funny tricks. It is common knowledge that Herzl's interest in finding a solution to the "Jewish Problem" stemmed from his witnessing the trial in France in which the Jewish army officer Alfred Dreyfus was wrongly accused and convicted of treason. In French politics, the Dreyfus Affair was a milestone. Prompted by the ugly manifestations of nationalism and prejudice that it evoked, French intellectuals, led by the writer Émile Zola, eventually succeeded in bringing about the separation of church and state in France.[12]

Herzl covered the Dreyfus Affair as a correspondent for the Austrian newspaper *Neue Freie Presse*. He then returned to Vienna

---

[11] This very basic Israeli law bestows automatic Israeli citizenship on every Jew who lands in this country and wishes to become a citizen.

[12] By the act of parliament in 1905.

and conceived *The Jewish State*. The Jewish state eventually became a reality, but with an unexpected twist: the travesty of church-state entanglement that Herzl had warned against so passionately became a cornerstone of the modern State of Israel.

The majority of Israeli Jews used to be secular, but their proportion is constantly dropping. Still, 49 percent of Israeli Jews described themselves as non-religious in a 2014 survey. Many of them would tell you, if asked, that they support the separation of church and state in Israel "as soon as possible." But an overwhelming majority would stop short of accepting a proper disengagement, one that includes a detachment of the Jewish majority from its special privileges over state-controlled public resources.

In fact, in the present Israeli political scene political activity toward decreasing religious involvement in state affairs is identified as political suicide. One would immediately be accused of jeopardizing the fragile Jewish solidarity – so vital to a "people in a constant state of war." Never mind that the state of war is a direct result of the insistence to preserve national-religious supremacy.

It is no use to claim – as secular-liberal Israelis would tell you – that we cannot deal with the problems inflicted by our religion "because we have a much bigger problem to deal with, namely our regional conflict." The truth is, religion and state *is* the "big problem" Israel imported to this region. Our so-called national solidarity really is merely a religious solidarity. Just watch the smug, expensive campaigns calling for "brotherhood and unity" that appear on billboards every few months. They are obvious efforts to mobilize Jewish fraternity against anybody who is not Jewish.

For the last hundred years, the bloody conflict in this country has been described as a battle over territories and sovereignty. But in fact, the fight has always been over religious control and supremacy.

* * *

Zionism is not meant to be racism. There are Jews of all colours and races, and members of any race may be accepted to Judaism. But Zionism does practice serious discrimination based on religion. The actual practice is often no different from the practice of racism.

The Jewish population of Israel sees nothing but animosity and growing nationalism when it looks at Palestinian Arabs. The more isolated the Jews feel, the more frightened and anxious they become. But this isolation is homemade. It is a fact that many Jews feel threatened by very mundane contacts with the other inhabitants of the land.

Israel continues to congratulate itself on being "the only democracy in the Middle East." But when the principles of democracy clash with Jewish edicts, as interpreted by the Orthodox school of Judaism, democracy inevitably gives way. "National unity" and "security necessities" are the usual excuses. Above it all hovers the spectre of the "Demographic Problem" that paralyzes the good judgment of secular Israeli liberals. The persistent "Peace Now" demonstrators have been marching for years demanding an end to the occupation of the West Bank and the Gaza Strip. From day one of this movement, I considered "Peace Now" a political and ideological home. It took too long to realize that in this home, we were united by the belief that Jews and Arabs must live their separate national lives on opposite sides of the historical "Green Line." In other words, we accepted Zionism's Jewish model of life apart.

In 2003, following the Palestinian second *Intifada*, the hottest argument between Right and Left in Israel concerned the building of the Separation Wall, a monstrous undertaking in every aspect and dimension, designed to keep Palestinians ultimately out of Israel as the only way to stop suicide bombers from infiltrating densely populated Jewish areas. The Left campaigned for a less destructive fence and objected to its usurping vast areas belonging to the Arab population.

But it was – and still is – united around the basic concept; namely, *They* (namely, all Arab Palestinians) should be left over *There* (namely, in the occupied territories), and *We* (namely, Israeli Jews) should be left alone, to live our peaceful life *Here* (in Israel's pre-1967 borders).

This leaves a basic question unanswered: Who, actually, are *We*? In the Israeli state, Jews are a mixture of immigrants from dozens of lands and their descendants, very different in their original cultural and linguistic heritage. About twenty percent of the population is non-Jewish, mostly Arab-Palestinian, the indigenous population that includes a variety of religious and ethnic groups. Arab Druze and Bedouins, for example, have made enormous efforts to become "Israelis": serving in the Israeli armed forces and fighting no less zealously than most Jews. The non-Jews also include some hundreds of thousands of Russian Orthodox and several thousand Christian Ethiopians who arrived in Israel under the auspices of the Law of Return. Unlike the Arab non-Jews, they are to be considered part of the collective "we". The peculiarities of the identity politics are best illustrated in the case of a large group of South Lebanon Army soldiers and their families. This Christian militia had to escape Lebanon when the Israeli army pulled back from this country after 17 years of occupying its southern areas. Initially the families tried in vain to integrate into Israeli society, which seemed natural after having spilled their blood for years serving the Zionist entity. Most have eventually left for Europe or returned to Lebanon. Even more unfortunate are the thousands of Palestinians who agreed to cooperate and to collaborate with the occupying nation against the best interests of their neighbours and families, in return for a chance to feed their children. But as non-Jews they are considered just as "demographically dangerous" as the Palestinians of "East Jerusalem" who found themselves residents (but not citizens) of Israel following the official annexation of their city. Estranged, and frustrated, hundreds of thousands are kept in the purgatory of residency without citizenship, never knowing when the next separation wall, giant motorway, bureaucrat, or would-be settler should appear to shake up their lives.

* * *

Herzl's bourgeois vision of society used to be accepted even by the conservative "General Zionistic" party that in 1973 became part of the right-wing Likud. In fact, the "General Zionists" even objected to the partition plan in 1947. Present supporters of a "state for all its citizens" in Israel are considered "raving lefties" (if they are Jews) or suspected for high treason (if they are Arabs of any denomination).

On the other side, the Palestinians in the occupied territories may easily be presented as a torn-apart, confused society, still searching for a unanimously accepted sense of nationality, other than the deep resentment of the long and humiliating occupation.

Not even the best-supported international agreements, packed with good will and padded with money, would conceivably pull off the Independent Palestinian State trick, so fashionably and officially flashed and waved by sleek, hypocritical politicians and their media chorus.

There is no way to preserve so fictional a religiously-based ethnic purity in a local, isolated bubble, as Israel has been trying to do for the last seven decades – not in a global era of unprecedented openness characterized by a powerful flow of humanity among the five continents. Monolithic cultural conceptions could survive in the ages that knew no mass transport or cellular communications. Presently they are swept away in favour of more appropriate structures. Technological progress, having materialized way beyond Theodore Herzl's wildest dreams, and a healthy lust for life might still give this country a fair chance to pull itself together and fit in with the new, rapidly changing world.

The confused communities that live in Israel in a state of constant conflict must get over the bad habit of reincarnating obsolete instructions of ancient religions as orders of the day for all kinds of military organizations. Cultivating cultures and religions is one thing, but enforcing the special whims of these cultures and religions on others with the heavy hand and the armed forces of statehood – or a militia – is something else altogether.

As soon as religion is, once and for all, banned from the realms of the economy and the legal system of the State of Israel; once religious considerations no longer dictate building regulations, food regulations, taxation, budgeting, leisure patterns, and funeral arrangements, it will be possible to turn the Holy Land into the flourishing haven it was meant to be. It is possible that even a truly high-level international football team could be started, at long last. Palestinians returning from refugee camps surely have a lot of talent to offer.

A hundred and twenty years ago, Theodore Herzl's plan seemed just as unlikely, but this did not deter him. The bottom line of his book is the golden rule of every successful entrepreneur: "If you really want it, it is no fairy tale."[13]

[13] In English, it is often translated to, "If you will it, then it is no dream."

Part II – Duties

...that religion is a form of government, its precepts a code of laws; that priests are gatherers of divine taxes, officers of divine police.

Winwood Reade, *The Martyrdom of Man*[1]

---

1 Watts & Co., London, first published in 1872.

4

MONSEY, NEW YORK STATE

The source of all problems is the absolute contradiction between the basic concepts – one that upholds a state based on the principles of law and order, democracy, human rights and civil liberties, on the one hand, and one that aspires to a state with one and only basic principle: the Halacha above all, the people upholding the Halacha above all others.

Levi Yitzhak Hayerushalmi,
The Power of a Yarmulke[2]

The only thing my late grandfather Shmuel and the late Rabbi Abraham Weinfeld of Monsey, New York State, had in common was that they were both Ashkenazi Jews who prematurely died of cancer. By the time I met Rabbi Weinfeld, in the autumn of 1987, he already knew that his days were numbered. At fifty-seven, the Rabbi was a well-respected rabbinical authority in the New York non-Hassidic ultra-Orthodox community. A long list of published works containing his interpretations of various scriptures had won him acclaim and recognition in the relevant circles. Like most of the world's ultra-Orthodox rabbis, he disapproved of the Zionist experiment, but genuinely cared about the future of the Jewish nation in the State of Israel. He watched with growing concern as his fellow spiritual leaders gradually increased their involvement in Israeli politics. Their considerable success in squeezing perks and compromises from

[2] Hakibbutz Hameuchad Publishers, 1997. Yerushalmi (1927- 2007) was a senior Israeli journalist, chairman of the Israeli Journalist Association, a top publicist for Maariv, and a dear friend. He was born and raised in Jerusalem, to a family of 7 generation Jerusalem Ashkenazi rabbis, but chose secular socialism over the family tradition.

both the legislative and the executive sectors did not please him at all. On the contrary, he thought they were making a grave mistake – so much so that he had found it necessary to express his views in the traditional form of a rabbinical pamphlet, titled *Wake Up, the Sleepers!* It was written with the clear intention of stirring things up and starting a fierce argument within ultra-Orthodox communities in Israel and abroad.

Truly devout Jews, the rabbi propounded, have a responsibility to protect the good name of their faith. It was intolerable and shameful that nonreligious Israelis had become accustomed to viewing Orthodox Jews as "parasites" and "blackmailers." They were accepting money from the Zionist entity, which made it seem that they were recognizing its authority together with the unacceptable concept of a Jewish state. The constant demands made on the secular Israeli state inhabitants by religious politicians were completely out of order and harmful to the integrity of the believers.

Any true and observant Jew knows for a fact, Rabbi Weinfeld stated categorically, that most secular Jews are almost beyond redemption for the Jewish religion. The righteous need to concentrate their efforts on preserving their own achievement, and to find independent ways to cultivate their own communities, as Jews have been doing for hundreds of years. There is no point in coming, hat in hand, to their renegade brethren of the Israeli state. On the contrary, this behaviour gives way to the painful – but sadly convincing – accusation that the Orthodox are hypocrites and only really interested in power and in money.

Having put these controversial opinions in writing and making sure his booklet was distributed to the target population, Rabbi Weinfeld braced himself for the expected ensuing outrage and was ready to take the consequences. Rabbinical disagreements on a much smaller scale had always been a sure trigger for an outpouring of colourful condemnations and name-calling. To his surprise and considerable disappointment, the intended earthquake didn't happen. The blatant publication failed to create the slightest tremor among Orthodox society. There was no reaction at all, as the "sleepers" wisely had no intention of waking up.

Rabbi Weinfeld's terminal illness was progressing, and he knew he was about to depart from this world at a time when true Judaism was facing a real crisis. He cared too much for the integrity and prestige of the faith to keep quiet. On learning that his days were numbered, he decided to pass his message to the believers via the secular Israelis and their media. He knew the Hebrew press would be sympathetic to his concerns. At the same time, he had every reason to expect that the very idea of supplying moral ammunition to the secular enemy's camp against his fellow Orthodox rabbis would be conceived as scandalous. A potential clash with the powerful ultra-Orthodox communities of Jerusalem and Bnei Brak did not scare him. On the contrary, he was hoping for one last good fight before he died.

Ma'ariv, Israel's second-largest Hebrew-language newspaper, was considered more acceptable to religious readers than the rest of the secular press at the time. The editors were contacted by one of the rabbi's admirers to suggest an interview. They didn't need to be asked twice. Nobody had ever previously heard a respected rabbinical authority come out against enforcing religion on secular Israelis. Since at that time I was the newspaper's US correspondent, I was immediately dispatched from Washington, DC, to Monsey to get the story.

My then-husband came along to take the rabbi's pictures. We travelled by a night train to New York and took the direct bus to Monsey from the bus station on 42nd Street early in the morning. Rebbitzen Elisheva, the rabbi's young, very good-looking second wife, picked us up at the bus station in Monsey, as had been agreed. Her tightly tied headscarf nicely matched vivid blue eyes. We set off in the back of her all-American station wagon, with her newest baby girl napping in its carry cot in the front seat. When we entered the house, a yarmulke was placed – probably for the first time – on my non-Jewish husband's head. Discreetly but firmly the Rebbetzin passed me a large scarf with which to cover my own hair during my meeting with her husband. Only unmarried women leave their hair uncovered in the presence of men. The Halachic (Jewish religious) ruling is that for a woman to expose her hair is tantamount to exposing her private parts.

Rabbi Weinfeld received us with great hospitality. He treated us to fruit and insisted that we eat so that I could say grace (he explained this is one rare ritual that women, too, are privileged to exercise). He spoke good Hebrew, interspersed with Yiddish and English expressions. My insistence that his picture be taken distressed him; he was a proud man and could not bear the thought of being photographed, so thin and emaciated with cancer. The loss of most of his beard, presumably from chemotherapy, was particularly upsetting for him. But he was a vivid and articulate interviewee. He did not spare his fellow rabbis and particularly denounced the Israeli National Religious Party. The NRP's position that "Jewish national unity counts more than religious teaching" he considered a serious deviation from the faith. Passionate and even entertaining, he made no secret of the fact that as far as he was concerned, there was little affinity between people like myself – a secular Jewish woman – and his own flock.

"The Torah lived in our people long before the state was established," he said. "We do not need you [the nonbelievers] to take care of it. Do us no more favours. We wish to have no more crumbs from under your table. We do not want any compromises and humiliation. The time has come to break up this unnatural partnership between Orthodox Jewry and the institutions of the Zionist state."[3]

He scornfully rejected the common pious warning, often used by those of the National Religious Party, that the country risks a "rift" in the Jewish people in Israel, if civic procedures for marriages and divorces ever should be allowed in the Jewish state. Truly religious Jews, he announced, have no business worrying about how the secular ones wed. As a matter of fact, he was all in favour of civil weddings for those Israelis who do not wish to stand under a *Chuppa*. After all, anybody who does not adhere to the Torah was considered unacceptable to the Orthodox community in any case.

"Our people would not marry your people under any circumstances," he revealed. "For us the fact that someone's mother was Jewish means nothing. We will not have them if we do not know for certain that this mother kept all the regulations of the purity of the family."

---

[3] Quotes from author's own article, *Ma'ariv Weekend Magazine*, October 17, 1986.

This was not entirely new to me. Ultra-Orthodox Jews are among the most particular communities on earth when it comes to the issue of mating. The *yichus* – the origins of one's family – is the most precious asset in the complicated negotiations surrounding matchmaking. To have an important rabbi as an ancestor raises the value of a young man or a young woman on the marriage market. Equally, a "black sheep" in a family – for example, a single member who had become a non-Orthodox – spoils the *yichus* for his or her relatives. Such a dropout would forever be burdened with the knowledge that he or she had deprived a dozen siblings of their chance to make a decent match.

At the very bottom of the yichus pecking order, one finds the handicapped and their offspring, as well as relatives of petty criminals in the community and the "born-again" Orthodox Jews. The latter might be devout and well behaved but still forever undesired, as children of parents who did not refrain from touching each other during the mother's menstruation period. They are encouraged to intermarry, and should be pleased that their own children and grandchildren will be considered worthy of starting to climb the social ladder when their time comes.

The rabbi had a heart-breaking story about a born-again Jew in his community, "a real genius" from a New York Jewish family. He had all the potential for becoming a renowned student of the Torah, the rabbi told me with a sigh. But when the time came to find him a suitable match, a terrible truth came to light. Apparently the boy's mother, before marrying his father, had divorced her first husband by civil procedure only. This turned her son into a "bastard according to the Halacha" – the fruit of the fornication of an adulterous, still-married mother. Such a blemish disqualifies one from marrying a Jew, not for one generation but for ten generations to come. Rabbi Weinfeld had to break the terrible news to his protégé, who went nearly mad with grief and shame.

From the heights of his purist ultra-Orthodox position, Rabbi Weinfeld observed, with loathing and dismay, efforts by the sidekicks of some ultra-Orthodox Israeli rabbis to introduce ever more religious legislation in the Knesset. At the time of my interview with the rabbi, the new laws on the agenda were the "Pig Law", aimed at forbidding the sale or consumption of pork in any Jewish-populated area; as well as the "Law of the *Chametz*" (fermented dough), which demanded the prohibition of the baking of provisions containing yeast during the Passover holiday. Attempts by liberal parties to legislate a constitutional decree guaranteeing "human dignity and liberty" were being bitterly opposed by religious politicians, as a law securing liberties would legitimize the consumption of non-kosher foods. Rabbi Weinfeld understood perfectly why people like me and most readers of the newspaper I was writing for were angry at the very idea that the law should have a position on what we are allowed to eat, and when. He considered it a complete waste of time. Eating pork or not did not make the slightest difference to the fact that we were already outside what he considered the proper Jewish community.

"It is not that I do not believe in enforcement," the Rabbi said, explaining his logic. "The Torah positively supports enforcement. The Torah is not democratic. Because it is the 'true word,' it has the right to enforce its rules on renegades against the Halacha. We religious people see you, the secular Jews, as sinful children who are not aware of your actions and on whom it is permissible to exercise enforcement. Parents, too, educate their children without asking them whether they like it or not. But this can only work as long as the children are with their parents and accept their authority. The reality is that you are no longer children, and we have no authority over you. We cannot enforce things upon you. One cannot use state law to interfere in the private affairs of people, other than in extreme cases of violence and crime. We cannot send a policeman to arrest every person who lights a cigarette on the Sabbath."

He had no time for the crucial and recurrent dilemma that has been shaking Israel ever since its early days: the legal definition of *who is a Jew*. The Israeli definition for a "proper" Jew is vital to immigrants, as the Israeli "Law of Return" grants automatic citizenship and a package of perks to anyone who can prove their

Jewish identity. The criteria are purely religious.[4] Rabbi Weinfeld knew very well that by that time, two Israeli governments had been brought down by these thorny questions, but as far as he was concerned, the entire issue was irrelevant, and pretty ridiculous.

It was just another pointless burden on people. In the kindest possible way, Rabbi Weinfeld made it clear that he considered me, together with my potential offspring, as too contaminated to mix with his own family and community, at any rate for several generations to come. I did not hold this against him. He was welcome to his beliefs and to his way of life and eating habits as long as I did not have to share them.

I was really quite taken with the rabbi. He was a highly intelligent, educated, and dedicated man, proud of the legacy he would leave to his own numerous descendants. The dazzling Rebbetzin Elisheva, I learned later, had been a childless young widow who was honoured to be offered a match with the rabbi after the death of his first wife, the mother of eight children. Together they had three young kids.

Rabbi Weinfeld obviously enjoyed our interest in the prosperous community around him. He took us on a guided tour to the synagogue and *beit midrash* (study hall) that was lodged in the basement of his spacious house.

I boldly asked about the economics of his comfortable situation, and he was pleased to enlighten me. His community had twenty-five families of *Balebotim*[5] – successful business people who commuted every day on the bus to New York City and came back in the evening to pray and learn. These families provided for the rabbi as had their fathers and grandfathers before them in Eastern Europe. Their children spoke Yiddish and had their own *Cheder* education. It was a self-sufficient bubble in the middle of New York State, peacefully coexisting with its gentile neighbours and other

---

[4] The legal status in 2010 Israel: A Jew is anybody who was born to a Jewish mother or who had been converted according to the Halacha. The Halacha is decreed by Orthodox rabbis only. Conversions by Reform and Conservative rabbis, who represent the majority of the practicing members of the American Jewish Communities, are not valid in Israel.

[5] Yiddish for "homeowners" – an indication of affluence.

Orthodox Jewish communities in the area. Rabbi Weinfeld's small intellectual community kept its independence next to that of the Satmar, a large Hasidic court that is more familiar to contemporary Israelis. In the 1960s, the Israeli Satmar Hasidim created an uproar when they sent an official delegation to King Hussein of Jordan asking him to become their sovereign, as they could no longer tolerate the sacrilegious rule of the Zionist secular state.

The rabbi had, he charmingly admitted, warm feelings toward us, the Zionist Jews living in the Promised Land. He even sent his sons to spend several years at yeshivas (religious schools) in Jerusalem.

Later in the afternoon, as we went back to New York City by bus, together with one of the rabbi's older sons, a fine young man of eighteen, I had a chance to inquire about his experiences of the holy city. The boy's English was all American, but he was fluent in Hebrew and Yiddish as well. While endorsing his father's view that a Jewish state was undesirable before the coming of the Messiah, he freely admitted that he loved living in Israel. It just felt great to be in Jerusalem among friends who dressed and lived as he did.

"One feels at home; we go out late at night, after a long day of learning, and have great fun together," he told me. "It is our place."

From his description, life in a Jerusalem yeshiva sounded very attractive. The long hours of hard work at the spiritual rock face of Judaism had its rewards in warm camaraderie and boys' nights out on the town.

Rival yeshiva students, recognizable to each other by minute variations of their traditional black dress, were constantly challenging, competing, gossiping, and even rebelling against authority by smoking or missing lessons. A good time was had by all, it seemed.

Somewhat sourly, I agreed. These guys had so little to worry about compared to most other youngsters in Israel. Military duty, compulsory in Israel for everyone of this age group, does not apply to yeshiva students. There are no financial worries, as state-sponsored grants, free tuition, and subsidized accommodation easily provide for the sparse needs of these eternal students. In due time a suitable, well-trained, hardworking wife will be provided, and she will produce children, run the household, and usually have a job to support the family, while the husband may pursue the life of learning and socializing, fully paid for by the state. In the *Schules,* the religious seminaries of Jerusalem and Bnei Brak, it is the rabbis who are taking care of their students' material needs – quite the opposite of the Monsey Schule model.

New York's Central Bus Station at 42nd Street was not a nice place to be in the mid-1980s. Young men wearing the Jewish traditional dark clothes could often expect to be crudely cursed, and occasionally even punched. But our cheerful companion said he was used to these incidents and seemed unfazed, certainly not scared or bitter as we were about to disembark. At peace with his own mission and vocation, he thought downtown New York City was as good a place as any other to prove one's manly determination and good breeding. In his own way, I concluded admiringly, the young Weinfeld was an American hero, going peacefully about his business against any evil provocation as any good cowboy would do.

* * *

I thought that I had a very good story. Naturally I hoped that the readers of *Ma'ariv* would be as excited and intrigued by the American rabbinical bombshell as I was. I anticipated cheers from the Left as well as angry jeers from the national religious and ultra-Orthodox Right.

This is not to say that the two last communities constitute one single monolithic block. The national religious adherents follow the teachings of different rabbis and their religious practices vary from group to group. They also differ on the relationship pious Jews should have with the Israeli state, supporting different political parties or none.

Jews within the national-religious block are committed to extensive involvement in Israeli life, including army service for their sons (but not daughters). They run separate religious schools which teach Israel's mainstream curriculum, but with expanded religious instruction and a strong emphasis on the sanctity of the land. They have been at the ideological forefront of the settlement drive.

Ultra-orthodox *Haredi* Jews, on the other hand, see themselves, above all, as guardians of the traditional Jewish customs and faith. They have their own neighbourhoods and employment schemes and run schools which largely disregard the secular world. Rejecting military service, their young men commit to a life-time study of religious texts. While national-religious Jews and *Haredi*s sometimes lock horns on theological issues, they share a deep attachment to the biblical sites, many of which are in the occupied territories.

However, putting Judaism at the heart of the Jewish state and life has always been their central objective. As a result, conflicts and even violent tensions over religious issues have always been a key feature of Israel's public debates. As the Orthodox communities were growing rapidly in numbers, thanks to an extremely high birth rate and a grant system that became a negative incentive to secularization, more and more quarters of Jerusalem absorbed neighbours who were educated not to tolerate irreligious behaviour in public. This included people driving of cars on the Sabbath, wearing immodest dress, and the serving of non-Kosher food in shops and restaurants. So-called "Sabbath Wars" broke out, fuelled by the ever-growing orthodox demands to seal off whole streets, including main arteries, to traffic during Saturdays and religious holidays. When the authorities refused to do so officially, thousands of young men and children, with rabbinical approval, would improvise barricades and even throw stones on passing traffic.

If any concessions were made to secular needs, the Orthodox leaders complained bitterly about the infringement on the "status quo." When, for the first time in Israel's history, cinemas started opening on Friday nights, thousands of Orthodox men took to the streets for months to stage massive, angry demonstrations. Given Rabbi Weinfeld venerable position, his appeal to true believers to lay off the infidels should have ignited a heated discussion. Or so I believed.

Ma'ariv's weekly supplement published my story, but the provocation just did not succeed. Rabbi Weinfeld called to thank me for what I wrote, but he was as surprised and disappointed as I was with the indifference that had greeted his message.

The professional ultra-Orthodox politicians and their rabbis wisely chose to ignore the harsh criticism of their fellow rabbi. Being called manipulators and parasites was by then a normal state of affairs for religious politicians, and the fact that this time the utterances were from within made no difference.

In spite of the disappointment, the rabbi graciously invited me to the forthcoming wedding of one of his daughters. It was going to be an impressive event in Monsey, and I thought it would be a good opportunity to follow up on the story, maybe with a new angle. This time, I suggested to the rabbi, Israeli television should also be invited. A TV item featuring American ultra-Orthodox Jews, proudly self-supporting and calling on the separation of church and state in Israel, would, I figured, be difficult to ignore.

Rabbi Weinfeld was ready to accept even this challenge, and I had already started discussing the idea with my colleague Nissim Mishal, who was then the Israeli TV correspondent in Washington, but sadly it was not to be. A few weeks before the wedding, Rebbetzin Elisheva called to tell me that her beloved husband was now *niftar* – he had passed away.

I offered my deepest sympathy for her great loss. We had a long talk over the telephone as the Rebbetzin seemed keen to talk about the man she so adored. She spoke about his greatness in the Torah and about his kindness; she felt lucky and honoured to have been the mother of his children. As young as she was, she was determined to dedicate the rest of her life to keeping the extended family on the path that he would have approved.

I thought she was a great lady. Widowed twice when she was hardly thirty years old, with stepchildren almost her own age, ready to take on any task, armed with faith alone. Two thousand years of Jewish survival were made feasible by women like the Rebbetzin Elisheva Weinfeld. I believe she is still out there, running a super-kosher home and living the way of life she was born into. I would be surprised, however, if at least some of the rabbi's offspring had not by now become a little less religiously observant than their deceased venerable dad.

5

A MAN FROM ANOTHER PLANET

In the mind history of every land there is a time when slavish imitation is inoculated as a duty, and novelty regarded as a crime... Theology turned her into stone. Conventionality was admired, then enforced. The development of the mind was arrested: it was forbidden to do any new thing.

Winwood Reade,
The Martyrdom of Man

Coming directly towards me from the bus stop in the Hadar Yosef neighbourhood of Tel Aviv was a man dressed in the traditional black outfit of the ultra-Orthodox who seemed keen to address me. I locked the car, and my standard brush-off remark was ready before he even started speaking.

It is a common experience for Israeli women to be approached on the street by well-meaning *haredi* (ultra-Orthodox) men. Their aim is often to solicit charitable contribution, mostly to support their own needy family of many children. Alternatively, Hassidic disciples, usually in teams of two or three men, are on a mission to persuade women to perform one of the rare rituals (*mitzvot*) reserved for females in the Jewish tradition. On Fridays they would offer two plastic-wrapped candles for the Sabbath and a copy of the blessing to be said when lighting them. During the *Sukkot* (Tabernacles) holiday, the ladies are presented with a citron-like fruit and various tree cuttings assembled for this particular holiday, so that they may say the prayer of the "Four Species" designated for this occasion.

I opened my mouth to let out a sarcastic "Thank you, but shouldn't you find a proper job?" and immediately had to bite my lip in shame. This *haredi* gentleman, in a typical cheap black suit, white shirt without a tie, and large black hat was merely asking whether I knew a local computer shop. He was pointing at an advertisement in a newspaper that he held in his hand.

I remembered that such a shop had indeed recently opened on the other side of the little piazza and pointed it out in my friendliest manner, to cover my guilty conscience over being so suspicious. The man, in his mid-forties, continued to walk with me and then asked, with a worried expression, "Is it a good business? Are they reliable?"

I paused. I had no idea about this particular shop, and as far as I know, no computer is ever reliable, even when sold by the most respectable folk. So I said I was sorry, I did not know.

But he was not letting me go. "Do you work with computers?" he suddenly asked.

"I do," I replied, "but this does not mean I know much about them."

"Where would you buy one?" he shot his next question. He looked as though he really needed to know.

I was more than willing to help. Ultra-Orthodox people emerging from their Talmud ghetto to acquire expertise with modern technology is good news for all taxpayers. I tried to understand what kind of purchase he had in mind. Did he need a desktop computer for a business? Was he buying a computer for his children? What programs did he want to use?

Israeli media often fêted the alleged success of ex-yeshiva students in computer programming. It is an occupation that seems to suit those who decide to start earning their own living. This is probably because their minds have been trained over the years to perform repetitive, discipline-demanding tasks for many hours each day. I assumed this man was another clever religious nerd, looking for an upgrade of his old equipment.

He unfolded the section of the newspaper that carried the advertisement. It was from a *Ma'ariv* special supplement dedicated to the world of computers, Internet, and new gadgets. Pointing out a news item about an innovative thin plasma screen, he said casually that he thought this might be a good thing to buy. What did I think?

It would be expensive, I said, eyeing the state of his shoes. Besides, there was nothing in the story to suggest that this particular gadget is even available in Israel, and I did not think the local shop in Hadar Yossef would be the first in town to carry such an item. Then it gradually occurred to me that this shopper did not really understand that the monitor was not a computer, and would be quite useless on its own. Indeed, my new acquaintance knew nothing whatsoever about PCs. But he seemed desperate to get started and eager to talk about it.

"I buy this newspaper every Sunday," he explained, pointing at the supplement. "I read all the articles. I would like to do computer graphics. I think I would be very good at it." This was still a secret, he confessed. In his yeshiva, or at home, they would not look kindly on this new passion.

He then asked about the computer I used for my work and tried to figure out what I did for a living. I told him I was a partner in a public relations agency and that, as it happened, I knew something about people in his predicament. For a couple of years, we had been granting pro-bono services to a charity known as Hillel, the Right to Choose. It is an association that supports young *haredi* people who bravely break away from their communities to "go over" and start to live a productive secular life in modern society. The serious gaps in these people's education are a major theme that Hillel deals with on a daily basis.

To my surprise, the man in black knew a lot about Hillel. He also correctly assumed that this association would not be able to help him if he was contemplating a breakaway move. He was too old, already the father of five children and married to an unsympathetic wife who would never consider altering their lifestyle. Although devoted to his family, he could not stop daydreaming about connecting to the big world via the Internet.

I noticed that he was using American expressions in a way that was not typical for an Israeli. I soon discovered the reason. Aaron Cohen (the name he gave me is equivalent to John Smith, and might have been invented for the occasion) was born in Israel to Polish-born parents. When he was five, his family immigrated to the United States. Their ship docked in New York on the very day John F. Kennedy was elected president. I was thus able to determine that he was forty-four years old.

It seems that his parents were promised a better chance of making a good living if they joined the Satmar *haredi* community, which is known for its strict rules and uncompromising stand against Zionism. As a kid, Aaron was bright in mathematics, but his future had to be made in Talmud studies. Sometime in the 1970s he returned to Israel to study at a local yeshiva, got married, and settled in Bnei Brak, registering as a state-supported Orthodox student.

He never stopped talking, inundating me with details of his life past and present, which I found fascinating. Luckily I had forty-five minutes to kill. I was on my way to a local bakery intending to have a cup of tea while waiting for a meeting, so I invited him to join me.

He was apprehensive about having anything in the bakery. The "kosher" certificate on the wall was not up to his standards, so he refused to have a cake and insisted on being served his tea in a Styrofoam cup to avoid the shop's china, which he also suspected of falling short. I ordered *nana* (spearmint) herbal tea, which came with the customary abundance of mint leaves in a glass. Aaron was fascinated. Could he have the same? By the time his plastic beaker was presented to him, he happily inhaled the scent, and then asked knowingly, "This is very addictive, is it not?"

I took a minute to realize what he had in mind, and then I understood: he was convinced that the modest coffee shop was offering patrons intoxicating substances, boiled in water. About as addictive as parsley, I said mischievously. His disappointment was obvious, and I immediately felt sorry for the cruel shattering of his fantasy. The situation seemed to have worked heavily on his hyperactive imagination, deprived by decades of life in the monolithic Orthodox environment. Having plunged into the hedonistic world of middle-aged women who wear trousers, drive cars and buy cups of tea for strangers, he expected no less than the public consumption of drugs. Everybody in Bnei Brak knows that the nonbelievers are up to their ears in debauchery and sin. It was hilarious, but then I started to worry that in his fantasy Aaron might also interpret my interest in him as romantic, and made very sure he realized that I was at least six years older than him.

"So what do you do?" I asked.

"I learn in a yeshiva," he shrugged unhappily.

"So you are bored to death," I concluded easily. He confirmed this with a helpless smile.

He had spent many days considering his desperate situation, he confessed. His wife would not hear of moving out of the community, or allow him any liberties, even in secret, as some people do. She was a daughter of a respected and important family, and this *yichus* obviously meant a lot in their world. There was also the matter of feeding five children. The family was fully secured as long as he was acting as one is expected to within the community, showing up for learning and prayers around the clock. Any rumours about possible deviation would spread like wildfire and undermine his position in the *beit midrash*, which would mean an immediate disaster – financially, socially, and in the family. However, he was now completely resolved to purchase a computer and teach himself how to use it. He was convinced that it could not be that difficult. Fortunately he was fluent in English – a great advantage over his Israeli peers who spoke and read only Yiddish and Hebrew.

Now Aaron's bluish eyes lit up. He reached into his pocket and pulled out a tiny box. His first purchase, he revealed proudly. The box contained minute earphones, the kind you get with any Walkman or as a giveaway on some airlines.

"What do you think?" he was now inquiring. "They told me these are the best quality."

"Seem very good," I lied to please, from the heights of my suddenly presumed technological superiority.

Aaron explained: Good earphones were critical for him. Once he possessed the intended computer, these earphones would give him the freedom to listen to anything he wants. He was particularly interested in listening to modern music – jazz, rock, that kind of thing. Of course he had no stereo system at home – his wife would not even have a radio. That would be unacceptable in the community and would give the family a bad name. But a computer is different. With the computer nobody would know. He would be listening with these first-class earphones. No fear of being found out by the dreaded "Modesty Patrol" that severely sanctioned any deviation from the strict ban on undesirable elements in the Orthodox communities. His first step into the free world was already taken.

I stared at his gentle, excited face, framed by a thin, fair, curly beard, thinking what a heart-melting spectacle it made. So much fantasy and hope was hanging on this one dollar's worth that lay in Aaron's palm. For him, it was the key to all the entertaining sounds and information that the rest of us take for granted throughout life. I could not make myself tell him how far he still was from access to the web and the free-for-all music. All I could think of was: what a wasted, miserable life.

* * *

Some research shows that at least 40 percent of the members of ultra-Orthodox (*Haredi*) communities in Israel maintain the strict discipline of the Jewish Halacha not out of a deep religious conviction, but more to comply with social and family pressure. [1] It is widely known that in the world of the yeshivas and study halls, much undercover secular activity is taking place. Behind closed doors people watch banned videos and TV. There is plenty of social drinking, smoking on Saturdays, and even spending time with 'easy women.' Mostly, this is a men's-only world; home and family are kept strictly in line. Most *haredi*m make their living out of being *haredi*. The jobs of kosher controllers, yeshiva teachers, instructors or house masters, *mikve* (ritual bath) operators, undertakers, and many others are reserved for the large army of clerks and officials belonging to the steadily growing religious state bureaucracy. Any deviation from the strict display of purity and self-deprivation might have serious economic implications for a family of many children.

I have heard from young people who have joined Hillel that some changes did occur. Small groups of young couples meet away from

---

[1] Mainly by Professor Menachem Friedman, Bar Ilan University. For example, "Life and Book Tradition in Ultraorthodox Judaism" in Harvey Goldberg, ed., *Judaism Viewed from Within and from Without: Anthropological Studies* (Albany, NY: State University of NY Press, 1987), 235-255.

home and the searching eyes of the community, and spend time in hotels or on the beach "just like normal people." For a short period, they desert the uniform, sometimes get into fashionable swimming costumes, and forget about kosher and sabbath restrictions. But these youngsters dare not exercise the liberties in public. As they lack the qualifications to become integrated into productive society, they are condemned to eternal social and economic dependency within their respective *haredi* communities.

The power to enforce ignorance over the children of the flock is the most valuable asset of the Israeli *haredi* communities. It is with this power that these communities preserve their abilities to continue growing, in spite of the many temptations of society around them. It allows them to increase the influence they exercise over nonreligious Israeli society from one generation to the next. It is the Israeli secular establishment that bestowed this enormous power on the *haredi* establishment, against the best interests of at least some of the captive flock. For the veteran secular establishment, this was no idle carelessness but the result of a clear and conscious long-term strategy.

The study halls of Jerusalem and Bnei Brak are thus fundamentally different from the private *beit midrash* of Rabbi Weinfeld of Monsey, which in turn is the direct and legal heir of the self-imposed Jewish lifestyle model in nineteenth-century Europe. While the Monsey rabbi depended on his *Baal Botim* students for his own livelihood as well as for the maintenance of his small community needs, the ultra-Orthodox in the Holy Land depend totally on designated rabbis and apparatchiks, the people who hold the power to confirm or withdraw the student's right to state allowances.

The ultra-Orthodox educational system would be considered an aberration in any other modern country. Ironically enough, the term "Babies in Captivity" was often used patronizingly by prominent Jewish religious personalities to describe secular Jews. According to this assertion, secular Jews are not responsible for their sins. This is because they simply do not know any better. But it is the offspring of the large *haredi* families who are born into a system that in our own cultural terms could be defined as a seriously deprived childhood, often bordering on child abuse.

When, in the 1970s, Yasser Arafat bragged that "the womb of Palestinian women" will be proved the most successful "secret Arab weapon" against Israel, Israelis reacted with a mixture of alarm and disdain. But twenty-first century Israel has been cultivating the *haredi* child-making machine as a means to maintain the Jewish demographic advantage over the Arabs.[2]

This must be the main reason why Israeli governments of all times have actively upheld the *haredi* indoctrinatory mechanism, which is officially known by the Orwellian name "Independent Education." It is a mechanism singularly adapted to the creation of fully dependent human beings. The non*haredi* Israelis generously finance this enormous system of emotional and intellectual oppression from cradle to maturity, which makes us all accomplices to the consequences.

Thousands of minors grow up in our country into a system – fully supported by Zionist Israel – that is openly geared to do everything to prevent them from having any future in a modern, open society. These young people are innocent of any acquaintance with the most basic themes of general education; cocooned in inadequate outfits for toddlers as well as for adolescents; restricted in games and physical activity; forbidden to freely exercise their natural curiosity and their natural imagination; force-fed with endless, ignorant superstitions; and tamed to aspire to one single form of personal fulfilment: marriage at the earliest age permitted by law, shortly after puberty, and starting new, large, *haredi* families, modelled on the same sad pattern from which most of them originated.

* * *

Only the brave and the different actually make it to Hillel, the charity that supports young *haredi* people who want to break away. As soon as they change into "civilian" clothes and have a shave and a haircut, they look and sound like any other young person. But they readily explain that they forever feel like visitors

---

[2] Ariel Sharon (1928-2014) said in May 1977, "I do not know if our offspring will be Jewish; the *haredim* will keep the fire burning." Quoted in *Yedioth Aharonoth,* January 6, 2006, as Sharon lay in a coma.

from another planet. Hillel's volunteers have prepared a special booklet for families ready to adopt young *haredi* men and women who have left the ultra-Orthodox lifestyle. The booklet aims to help the families cope with the difficulties facing the products of the *haredi* human grinding mill.

Most of the booklet's content is confidential. The sensitive young people who come to the organization would be embarrassed by a public discussion of the gaps in their social and behavioural experience. "The young ex-*haredi* arrives in the secular world equipped with first-class learning qualifications," Dr. Nechama Yelin-Lipshitz and Anat Nevo, who prepared the booklet, state in the chapter dedicated to schooling, which focuses on young males:

He displays significant intellectual abilities to absorb new information, excellent learning skills, and a strong will to study in order to excel and make his mark.

The gaps in knowledge are evident with respect to many general subjects related to modern life, including some very basic concepts. Some examples:

Foreign languages – with an emphasis on English.

Natural history and the sciences (mathematics, physics, chemistry, biology, agriculture, geography, geology, anthropology, medicine, etc).

Social sciences (sociology, psychology, economics, the law, international cultural concepts, international relations, foreign nations, etc).

Non-Jewish music.

The humanities (general literature, philosophy, archaeology, history, etc).

The universe (the solar system, space, theories about the origins of the cosmos, human achievements in space, etc).

These gaps stand out and become a nuisance on a daily basis, with the emphasis changing from one community to another. The feeling of inadequacy is acute and may impair the normal ability to cope. Ego and pride are hurt as it becomes clear that others, including much younger people, are in command of better understanding of the world around them. This greatly increases the lack of self-confidence. Examples:

Orientation – reading maps or an atlas.

Understanding and operating mechanical or electrical equipment, even the most common gadgets.

Understanding and recognizing works of art and cultural milestones, as in the cinema, literary works, poetry, the theatre, music, etc.

Using public libraries, resources on the Internet.

Understanding human anatomy and functionality directly connected to ideas about health and sports.

Sex and relations between men and women.

Interpreting natural phenomena like day and night, summer and winter, eclipses of the sun and the moon, climate changes, earthquakes, volcano, etc.

The proper names of animals, flowers, birds, etc.

The proper names of important sites in Israel and abroad, including famous high mountains, rivers, seas and lakes.

The history of the State of Israel and of the Jewish people, general history of other nations, basic concept of democracy.

And the list is still long, too long.

* * *

Haredi children do not have pets. Raising cats, dogs, or even aquarium fish is considered an unwanted gentile habit. Eventually the young people "Coming Out" need to find out about *Little Red Riding Hood*, *Goldilocks and the Three Bears*, as well as *Snow White*. It can be very awkward when, during a casual conversation, one does not understand the meaning of expressions like "Dumbo" or "Sleeping Beauty." I have met a young divorced ex-*haredi* who was deprived by the rabbinical court of the right to host his five young children for visits at his own home or even meet them unchaperoned. The court accepted the complaint of his ultra-Orthodox ex-wife, that in his home the children were exposed to animated Disney films on video. This was ruled as subversive influence. In family affairs in Israel, the rabbinical court has exclusivity, for secular and religious people alike.

Artistically inclined children may tend to suffer an especially cruel fate in the *haredi* community. In March 2002 the Yellow

Submarine club in Jerusalem displayed a particularly poignant photographic exhibition by artist Rotem Weiss. Weiss – formerly Shmuel Kovalkin – produced the works during a long term of hospitalization in Eitanim psychiatric hospital. To a radio reporter who came to interview him, he explained that people with his level of sensitivity find it hard to keep their sanity under the constant social pressure of *haredi* society.[3] In a private talk, he also speculated that his own father – a fanatic and violent *Hassid* who used to beat his many children savagely – was himself mentally broken, but never treated. Rotem could not get over his own self-destructive impulses. It was with great sadness that we heard, a few months after the exhibition, that he took his own life.

It is customary in Hillel to celebrate a "Second Seder" following the Passover holiday every year. The festive meal focuses on singing and reading texts from a specially prepared *Hagada,* based on the book of Exodus but written by ex-*haredi* contributors. The traditional Passover texts, the great tale of the liberation of the Children of Israel from slavery in Egypt have been altered to describe the move of their modern descendants from life in the ultra-Orthodox community into modern secular society. It is by no means a poetic exaggeration. For the participants, the Hillel *Hagada* is a fair description of the reality that they are still going through.

* * *

Nonreligious Israelis as well as the modern religious often express anger and even disgust with the seemingly strange *haredi* lifestyle. Frequent belligerent attacks by ultra-Orthodox leaders and newspapers on the so-called secular state make them unpopular. They seem to be constantly demanding more funds, more tiresome religious legislation, more "consideration" and exemption from duties, creating antagonism that sometimes turns into true secular panic. But an objective observation reveals enormous misery in dense ghettos bursting at the seams with uncontrolled population growth. The Torah students are not exactly "getting killed in its

---

[3] Interview by Anat Davidov in *Reshet Bet, Kol Yisrael,* March 25, 2002.

hut," as their pious rabbis often declare[4]; but many certainly get crushed on a daily basis under their harsh vocational burden.

I remember passing through a large crowd that gathered following community leaders' calls to demonstrate against the Israeli Supreme Court of Justice. Numerous signs complained against the wrongs done by the supposedly "anti-Jewish" court: mainly a ruling that women should be allowed to participate in the regional religious councils and a ban on discrimination against babies adopted from abroad who were converted to Judaism by non-Orthodox rabbis. The items on the agenda did not impress me as tragic enough to induce tens of thousands of adults into loud sobbing in public. But they were crying all right. The newspaper headlines on the following day reported "An Ocean of Tears" at this demonstration. Solid grounds for tear shedding were easy to spot. One only had to see the shabby, inadequate clothing for an Israeli summer day, and the tired, listless faces in order to fathom the impact of slums, poor food, insufficient provisions, and impossible social pressure. Inside the incredible uniform of black coats, black hats, wigs, headscarves, thick stockings, and long sleeves lives and suffers a large, dispossessed, underprivileged community. In July 2009 TV's Channel 1 aired a rare aspect of this extreme misery: poor young *haredi* families living in storage spaces in the underground parking areas of apartment's blocks, with no ventilation or proper sanitation.

We usually shrug at their difficulties. They should get a job and make a living. They should join the army and become soldiers like everybody else.

It is convenient to forget that two or three generations ago, we were all where these people are today. Had it not been for our forefathers rebelling against this obsolete lifestyle, would we not all be standing there (God forbid) as *haredi*m, miserably lacking in material as well as nonmaterial assets?

* * *

---

[4] "Being killed in the Torah's hut" is a favourite Orthodox metaphor describing the presumed social service of a yeshiva student that justifies his exemption from military service.

I gave Aaron Cohen my business card and encouraged him to call my office if there was anything he thought I could help him with. I thought I should give him the name of a PC equipment supplier who might find him a free second-hand computer to start with, or at least an inexpensive one. He could, I told him, apply for an introductory computer course sponsored by the Ministry of Labor and Welfare. If he needed the right address, I was ready to find it for him.

As a parting gift, I offered him the paperback that I intended to read during my break. I thought the book – a collection of amusing short stories in English written by young women – would be a refreshing introduction to the world that so intrigued him. His first schooling, after all, was in New York, and he could read and speak English well. Aaron leafed through the book and sadly handed it back to me. There was no way, he explained, that he could risk having such subversive literature in his possession.

To my amazement and that of our office staff, he turned up on our doorstep the very next day. It was just as well I had started the morning by telling my colleagues about the bizarre encounter of the previous evening, or they would have been completely mystified at the sight of Aaron's figure marching in to engage me in yet another long conversation.

He had brought me a present, he explained, in return for my unaccepted gift of a book. I appreciated the opportunity to decorate the shelves in the office with a free copy of the Zohar, one of the most celebrated texts of Jewish wisdom.

Aaron insisted on reading me the annotated lesson of the day. I listened, first with mild interest, then with disgust. The lesson went into details about bodily functions, mainly to do with male libido, related bodily fluids, and the proper techniques to control them according to the *halacha*.

If Aaron's intention was to show me how liberated and free-spirited his learning was, then I was missing the point. The subject matter was not just unsuitable but also excruciatingly boring. I suggested we put the holy book away and move to the more earthly subject of finding Aaron a cheap PC or a state-sponsored computer course.

He was, however, more interested in talking about himself, relating past ventures into several forbidden fields. Proudly he revealed that he had once studied Reiki – he claimed that he had actually received a degree as a healer in this "pagan art," as he had described it. His instructor had become his mistress for a while. The "pagan symbols" fascinated him, but he fully accepted the strict ban of his superiors, and sadly abandoned a half-baked plan to offer his healing services as a Reiki expert to members of his own community.

With all his childish rebellious gestures and intelligent penetrating remarks, Aaron displayed astounding ignorance and blatant preposterous racism. Blacks and Arabs "appalled" him. In America, he informed me, "even the most miserable Jew could at least look into the mirror and bless the creator who had not made him a Negro." Chinese wisdom, he acknowledged, could certainly be appreciated, but then, "It was mainly copied from the Jews."

This verbal avalanche exposed a distressed, unhappy soul. Life was passing him by, he freely admitted in his misery. Most men experience some kind of a midlife crisis at forty, but Aaron felt that he had not lived at all. While most of us suspect the grass is greener next door, Aaron did not have any green on his side. He spoke eloquently about stifling boredom and degenerating poverty, a life totally divorced from the offerings of the developed world at the opening of the third millennium.

He was a clever, probably bright guy – a curious, passionate, and independently thinking individual. He made no secret of his attraction to the secular, open environment. And yet he ruled out from the outset the very idea that he might simply throw himself into this environment by moving a few blocks from where he lived, getting a haircut and a shave, and buying some new clothes.

All in all, he would have been a fool to trade his warm and reassuring habitat for a life as an insecure alien elsewhere. With all his frustrations and present disenchantments, once outside this community, he would have missed much more than the meagre income paid by an insignificant job and the yeshiva allocations. Yeshiva life also meant camaraderie, neighbourliness, and the festive holidays and Sabbath spirit. There was also a wife and five children to consider. Aaron was devoted to his children. Two of them, he told me, suffered from learning difficulties, and he expected the community to come up with the necessary special tuition. His position as a *mashgiach* (supervisor) at the *beit midrash* was the single anchor for his life.

Did Aaron ever try to make any change in his lifestyle? Had he made any use of the telephone numbers, addresses, names and opening hours' data that I had collected for him that morning, or was he merely after another hour or two of idle talk, showing off his experiences with hedonistic secularism and asking weird questions? I would never know. At a certain stage, realizing that my subtle hints were passing unnoticed, I had to tell my guest that the visit had to come to an end. On his way out, he made a point of manifestly shaking my hand. We both knew that he was committing another delinquent act, breaking the rule against any physical contact of that kind between people of the opposite sex who are not first-degree relatives.

I encouraged him to report to me about any further progress, but I never heard from him again.

* * *

On the day Aaron came to see me in my office, he explained that I had earned the pleasure of the visit because he had a day off. This was due to a special funeral that was taking place in Jerusalem. The body of an extremely important rabbi from the United States had just been flown to Israel in order to be laid to rest on the Mount of Olives. Many thousands of ultra-Orthodox men, including all the yeshiva students in Bnei Brak who belonged to this particular stream of Judaism, travelled to Jerusalem by buses to fulfil the *mitzva* (commandment) of having paid their last respects.

Aaron was exempt from this particular commandment because his last name was Cohen, which means a priest, and indicates that he is an offspring of the Biblical Aaron, brother of the great Moses. People who are a "Cohen" should never enter a graveyard, as this is a profane environment, and priests should always keep perfectly pure in case they will have to serve in the temple, should it be resurrected after the ever-imminent coming of the Messiah, which might happen any minute. The fear of profanity to Cohens is so intense that in 2001 an attempt was made to instruct El Al, the Israeli airline company, not to fly over the Holon cemetery grounds so that the menacing contamination might not hit Jewish men named Cohen, or Kagan, or Catz, or Kaplan, or Kahane who might happen to be on the plane. As this was refused, the pious sometimes hid under thick black nylon garbage bags during the supposedly profane passage in the sky.

Back in 1968, a special bypass road for people with the Cohen extended family surnames was built, at great expense, around the Mount of Olives, just taken over by Israel as part of the 1967 occupation. The old Jordanian road had cut through the hill, which is the most coveted resting place in the world for all Jews, wherever they are. When the Messiah comes, this will become the site for the great resurrection of the dry bones as prophesized by the prophet Ezekiel. Jews of the Diaspora, whose bones will be far away on the Day of Judgment, will have to go through the extremely painful "dragging through the tunnels."[5] To avoid the torture of having one's skeleton and skull pushed and shoved through underground holes all over the globe to the Mount of Olives, it is wise to invest a small fortune for the purchase of a resting place on site.

It is well known that the Jewish Messiah is expected to reach the Mount of Olives for the Last Judgment riding on a white donkey. According to the interpretation of modern Jewish mysticism, the blessed animal is already with us. The creature is incarnated in the image of the Zionist secular state and its infidel inhabitants of Jewish descent. Israeli secularism, the national religious piously claim, should be tolerated, as it is paving the road for the coming of the Godly Jewish Kingdom. Indeed, the Israeli state is devoted to the role of the heavenly beast. It often seems to be efficiently carrying us all the way to Armageddon.

The Mount of Olives is a favourite first stop for experienced Jerusalem tour guides. Buses and limousines are always parked next to the Observation Point by the Intercontinental Hotel of East Jerusalem. It is a great place to bombard fascinated tourists with anecdotes of the Holy City's religious-political mayhem.

---

[5] *Gilgul Mechilot* as in Ezekiel 37, 12: "I will open your graves and cause you to come out of your graves, and bring you into the land of Israel."

The terrestrial meeting place of the three ancient monotheistic religions is beautifully laid out in the crisp Jerusalem air, spoiled only by the burping and excreting of a few decorated camels, there for authenticated photo opportunities. Against the backdrop of Jerusalem's best panoramic view, one may be photographed for posterity aloft these haughty "ships of the desert," looking upon a unique, powerful mélange of spirituality and bigotry.

Due west are the silver and gold domes of the Al Aqsa Mosque on the Temple Mount, built over the ruins of the great Jewish temple of Jerusalem. Nationalistic Jews never stop plotting to take over control or at least to increase visiting rights in this sacred site. Any attempt in this direction generates a literally explosive Muslim reaction, and with a billion Muslims all over the world, this should be taken into consideration. Fanatic Jews make no secret of their desire to blow the hated mosques to smithereens, while fanatic Muslims are constantly working on the removal and destruction of any remains of past Jewish glory. Only a small part of the temple's marvel of architecture may be visited underground. The builder, incidentally, was none other than the non-Jew King Herod, in a vain attempt to be accepted by the Jewish priesthood and aristocracy. Any archaeological attempt to explore the temple further is bound to result in tremendous bloodshed.

In Muslim tradition the Temple Mount is the site from where the Prophet Mohammed set off to heaven, mounted on his stallion Al Burak. Before the leap the horse patiently awaited his master while tethered to the Western Wall of the destroyed Jewish Temple, a spot also known today as the Wailing Wall. It was reclaimed as a site for Jewish worshippers in 1967. The area in front of the wall has been turned into a large open-air synagogue with male and female worshippers duly segregated.[6]

Down the western slope of the Mount of Olives, the golden onion cupolas of the Church of Gethsemane glitter to indicate the very location of Christ's last prayer with his disciples the night before his crucifixion. The Russian Orthodox Church is the exclusive keeper of this sacred place. Further west into the Old City, the large silver domes of the Holy Sepulchre sombrely

---

[6] For attempts by women to pray at the wall, see chapter 11.

rule the Christian Quarter of the Old City of Jerusalem. This, tour guides point out, is a famous site of incredible animosity between some of the relatively esoteric Christian Churches who share the proprietary rights over Christ's burial place. Turf fights between the Ethiopian and the Coptic-Egyptian Christian monks who reside in the complex have deteriorated more than once into violent incidents between the men of God, who often had to drag in Israeli police officers and foreign diplomats of their respective governments. Most of the grounds of the Holy Sepulchre are held by Catholics, Armenians and Greek Orthodox Christians who take turns in performing their separate daily prayers and rituals. The Anglican Church's fathers – late arrivals – discovered there was no way to purchase a foothold anywhere near the sacred grave, and displayed admirable Protestant resourcefulness. In the late nineteenth century, they announced that Jesus could not actually have been laid to rest in such proximity to the city, and identified the Garden Tomb, outside the original city walls, as the final resting place. This has since become the central venue for English-speaking Protestant pilgrims.

Israelis who often get frustrated with the illogical and annoying aspects of our own faith may be somewhat comforted by the ample evidence Jerusalem supplies of the bigotry, stupidity, vicious belligerence and general craziness that is also characteristic of other major religions. They conveniently ignore, however, that of all the lunatics in Jerusalem, the Jews are the only ones who made religious decrees into laws of the state.

6

THE RABBIS' GREAT-GRANDCHILDREN

The hundreds of years of preservation of the Jews as an ethnic-religious group were enabled by their development of extreme self-segregation.

Professor Uzzi Ornan,[1]
Ma'ariv, January 30, 1974

I remember being quite surprised to hear from my Great-Aunt Milla that her father – my Great-Grandfather Yathom – was a rabbi. Today I would be surprised to discover any contemporary Jews who do not possess a rabbi somewhere up their family tree a few decades earlier.

Saba Shmuel had passed away long before I was able to converse with him, so I shall never know what really made him turn his back on the rabbinical court – I assume it must have been a fairly minor one – that was run by his father. I did get to hear a lot about how his father-in-law, Nachum, Savta Chaya's father, became a secular Jew just before the turn of the nineteenth century. Great-Grandfather Nachum grew up in a Jewish family in a Ukrainian village. He had somehow developed a great passion for music and managed to procure for himself a small violin. To practice, he used to escape from the *cheder* (schoolroom) to the fields. There he played his tunes clandestinely, hidden deep in the high corn.

---

[1] In 1999 Professor Uzzi Ornan published *The Claws of The Devil – 8 Chapters in Secularism* (Einam Publishers [Hebrew]). Ornan, a highly respected linguist, born 1927, is still leading major human rights struggles in 2016 Israel.

When his devout father found this out, he did his pious duty and exercised the necessary violence on his child. "He told us he had been beaten almost to death, time and again, but he always came back to the violin," Savta Chaya used to tell me encouragingly when I was a kid. The story was meant to inspire me to be more passionate about my own work on the violin, which became a family obsession. Pushing children to follow a traditional path did not disappear with religion, and I had to put up with practicing the demanding instrument for several years before I gathered enough confidence to stand up for myself and drop it when I was thirteen. Great-Grandfather Nachum, at this age, had had his precious violin smashed into small pieces by his father. He then promptly ran away from his home in the village, never to come back.

The escape took him to Odessa, the regional metropolis. There he lived on the streets, finding odd jobs as young rebellious boys did in those days, having dropped out of depressingly deprived traditional communities. The swinging city of Odessa was a haven for modern Jews at the turn of the century. The thriving Jewish business community belonged at least partly to the powerful Jewish underworld of the town. When I visited Odessa in 1988, I was surprised to discover how fondly the Communist authorities preserved the memories of the local Jewish crime circles. The Municipal Museum has a whole section dedicated to the Isaac Babel stories memorializing Jewish petty – as well as big-time – delinquents. They all came from deeply religious families and nurtured a sentimental loyalty to Jewish traditions, which in later years was demonstratively displayed by some of New York's big Jewish mafia bosses.

Seemingly, Great-Grandpa Nachum had been a law-abiding citizen. I have no idea at what stage of his life he adopted – or received – the Russian last name Chestno, which Savta Chaya (Chestnaya) kept all her life. The meaning of this name is "honest" or "straightforward." He soon realized it was too late for him to become a professional musician. Having married a like-minded young Jewish woman, he had to settle for a small family business, where he and his wife made a living by manufacturing sweets. Their main merchandize was Turkish Delight (*Rachat Lokom*).

The sight of Turkish Delight always reduced my Grandmother Chaya to tears. She closely identified the sticky treat with the image of her loving mum and dad slaving over the sickly sweet smells at the back of the house, labouring to give their children a chance in life. The candy business kept the family just above the poverty line. During the hard times Odessa went through in the First World War and the Bolshevik Revolution that followed, a certain supply of rationed sugar, poppy seeds, and peanuts always landed at the shop to be made into sweets, and this had saved the family from the famine that raged in the city.

The five children received classic Russian-Hebrew tuition in Odessa's excellent Jewish educational system. Chaya-Gittel, born in the year Theodore Herzl died, was proud that people always commented that her father seemed a replica of the great Jewish political visionary. Like Herzl, Nachum Chestno was a handsome man with a powerful black beard and burning eyes under thick eyebrows.

Great-Grandfather Nachum Chestno, Odessa 1912

It was a mutual admiration. Chaya-Gittel – in the gymnasium she was known as Clara – was the apple of her father's eye. She was the youngest of his brood, and the only one who learned to play the violin. Her musical talent was evident, and Nachum was the happiest of fathers when she made her successful debut as a soloist in an amateur concert.

Both her parents sobbed bitterly as they said their last goodbye to her in 1925. She boarded the ship in Odessa on the way to Jaffa, Palestine, and they never saw her again. She wrote very little, mainly perhaps as there was little good news to relate. Shortly after arriving in Eretz Israel, Chaya-Gittel, who at home never so much as learned how to prepare an omelette, became a single mother who earned a meagre living as a home help. In this market, Odessa university graduates like her competed mainly against Arab and Yemenite women. One of those was my other grandmother, Miriam.

* * *

My father, born in 1924, had exercised his first rebellion against the Jewish religion when he was eight years old, about forty years after his father-in-law's musical mutiny in the Ukraine. The penalty, however, was identical, as should have been expected: a savage beating.

He was his parents' third child. The family had lived in modest accommodations rented from an Arab landlord in Tel Aviv's Kerem HaTeimanim (Yemenites' Vineyard) suburb. When he was three, he was sent, as was the custom, to study with a *morrey* (Yemenite teacher) in a *cheder*. The *morrey* had only one book for his pupils, and the children, who sat round in a circle, learned to recognize the letters upside down if their position happened to be opposite the teacher.

Graduates of the *cheder*, which in those days functioned as a kindergarten, moved on to the Yemenite religious school on Kalisher Street, next to what is today Tel Aviv's Carmel Market. In his second year, the schoolmaster announced to David and Miriam, proud parents of young Moshe, that their gifted child was marked for a considerable promotion. He had been invited to become a member of one of the city's best religious educational establishments, the Ashkenazi Talmud Torah on Rothschild Avenue.

My guess is that some well-meaning bureaucrat had decided on some kind of an integration experiment in the early 1930s' educational system, in favour of bright Yemenite youngsters. My father used to insist that he had no recollection of what triggered his rage against this Talmud Torah but he was obviously pushed to the wall there at some stage. Savta Miriam told me this chapter of the family saga more than once, with great relish. The child Moshe stormed home from school one day, sobbing furiously; he refused to answer any of his worried mother's questions, and before she knew what was happening, he had snatched her sewing scissors. Within a few seconds, and before anybody could do a thing to stop him, he had chopped off both of his long sidelocks that had decorated his face in the typically pious Jewish style.

"I beat him until I was too exhausted to continue," Savta confessed to me many years later, amused and retrospectively proud of her strong-headed boy. "When his father returned from work and heard what happened, he spanked him even more, as did his older brother Israel. But he just stubbornly said he would never set foot in that school again and never agreed to explain why. He just wept and said 'all of those a*dukim* (religious lot) are thieves!'"

The boy Moshe returned to Kalisher, and towards the end of the eighth grade was predicted to have a promising rabbinical future. He chose, however, to start his working career at the age of fourteen and fitted easily into the secular company of other working boys, most of them, like himself, children of poor immigrants from different countries. As the group spent most of their leisure hours on the beach, they soon started calling themselves the Society for Ameliorating the Sea (*Shippur Hayam*). When the Palmach, the Haganah's crack troops, were started up, the group was drafted en bloc to the Tel Aviv Company that went out on a long training haul in the Ben Shemen forest. My father, then sixteen, was among the youngest of this group. Friends of *Shippur Hayam* marked with us the celebration of his eightieth birthday in January 2004; the remaining few joined us on the *Shivaa* following his death in 2009, weeks before his eighty-sixth birthday.

Most of my father's siblings had found their way away from religion with less drama. The youngest, my uncle Yitzhak, remembers that his brother Abraham simply snatched his yarmulke from his head one day as he passed him on his bicycle. It was enough to make the necessary change. Yitzhak was active in the Working Youth socialist movement, and in the early fifties, when it was time for him to be drafted to the new Israeli Army, he joined a kibbutz, together with his friends in the movement. It was a period in his life that he remembers very fondly to this day.

Contemporary activists of religious ethnic parties cultivate a holy rage over the memory of Yemenite, Moroccan, and other immigrant children who were sent to be educated in kibbutzim when they arrived as new immigrants to Israel in the early fifties. They were made to cut off their sidelocks and get rid of their skullcaps and were fed non-kosher food for the first time in their lives. The criticism is probably justified; there was no need to force the change so abruptly. Left to their own resources in the new country, those children would have probably been quick enough to discover for themselves that one is better off riding a bike and playing soccer on the Sabbath than spending the holy day in the synagogue. I would certainly challenge anyone to find a single Yemenite girl who was not happy to be given the chance to learn reading and writing, in defiance of hundreds of years of the deplorable Yemenite Arab-style tradition of keeping the womenfolk illiterate.

* * *

Almost every secular Jew living in Israel or abroad, regardless of what his or her family origins might have been, should be able to tell you where and when, in the family history, the strictly religious lifestyle was deserted. We all originated in ultra-religious Jewish homes, and by a natural process, some of our ancestors decided that the religious environment was no longer suitable for their contemporary needs. The major task of religious education is to halt this natural process. Thwarting the rebellion is often successful, but next to the success stories, tragedies also still occur.

Le'an ("Where to?") by Mordechai Ze'ev Fierberg is a passionate autobiographical story by a talented young man, recording the suffocating archaic tediousness of life in a 1870s Jewish *schule* somewhere in a small town in Eastern Europe. The emotional but unsentimental story relates everything an Israeli Jewish youngster should know about the yeshiva world that his or her family escaped in their time.

Le'an vividly describes the dead end that youngsters ended up in, having followed the traditional Hasidic education. More than anything else, the young protagonist, Nachman, is enraged by the stifling intellectual diet offered by the ancient scriptures that he is force-fed. He craves real knowledge of the world around him and longs to live a healthy life, in harmony with nature. "I do not desire to be appointed the guardian of old graves. I long to live, to live like any other man! I do not wish to be buried alive!" goes his fervent internal monologue.

But trapped by the love of his father, the old rabbi, and the urge to be loyal to the old Jewish tradition, the young man is unable to openly reject the Jewish vocation. His inner conflict yields nothing but madness, then premature death.

The author, Mordechai Fierberg, died in 1899, aged twenty-four, shortly before his masterpiece was published by Ahad Haam. Throughout the 1950s and 1960s, Israeli kids were not encouraged to be sentimental about the traditional Jewish world that people like my great-grandfather had escaped. Secular Zionist education set out originally to make sure that the younger generations understood Zionism as the only true alternative to rabbinical Judaism. Our own syllabus was studded with pearls of the early Hebrew classics that were dominated by the leitmotif of "Rejection of the Diaspora" (*Shlilat HaGalut*). While we were studying *Le'an* in the sixth grade, it was presented to us as the story of a bygone world, part of our people's tragic history. We would never have guessed that forty and fifty years later, scores of thousands of young people in the new Jewish homeland would be subjected to the ordeal suffered by Nachman, Fierberg's condemned hero, this time with the sovereign state's sponsorship. We could certainly not have imagined how fast both Nachman and Fierberg would evaporate from the secular state's school program. along with the works of other Jewish writers who criticised the narrow-mindedness of life in Eastern Europe's small Jewish towns at the end of the nineteenth century. This was hardly surprising: since the 1960s, most Israeli government coalition agreements have given the Education Ministry to the National Religious politicians. No time was wasted before their appointed bureaucrats uprooted any manifested reservation concerning the stagnancy of religious thinking. The supposedly secular educators did not complain. Who would want to be called anti-Jewish?

Having seriously studied *Le'an* as a young person, one could never end up with "hatred for the ultra-Orthodox Jews." The story of the wretched Nachman carried an unambiguous message for the young Israelis in junior high school: those Jewish ways of life were no longer an option by the end of the nineteenth century. The energies that pushed frustrated young generations out of the dying communities and their depressing yeshivas erupted as the powerful forces of the secular Zionism. At age sixteen we could all easily relate to the stormy narrative that was so fitting to the then-desired Zionist indoctrination.

That the yeshiva energies would eventually take over the whole Zionist political entity, and that we, the great-grandchildren of the not-so-fictional rebellious young Nachman would stoically sponsor the takeover could not have entered the heads of any of us at the time.

* * *

For contemporaries of Herzl, Chaim Nachman Bialik, and Berl Katzenelson, a Jewish homeland in Zion was needed to escape the tragedy of a people trapped by the traditional Jewish fate. Nazism and the Holocaust irrevocably supported the forces that already worked against this perspective. Jews who arrived in Palestine in the 1930s and onward as refugees mostly endorsed the Zionist project without ever going through the process of "rejecting the Jewish Diaspora" state of mind. Sadly, and peculiarly, the Holocaust thus provided an important leverage to the reactionary national Jewish religious interpretation of Zionism.

Almost all Israelis will tell you that it is the lack of a militarized national Jewish entity that made possible the Holocaust, turning this into the ultimate justification for our raving national militarism. The rich literature analysing this travesty of logic has so far made little impression on the collective psyche; with such effective brainwashing, the *Shoa* (Holocaust) is often celebrated as a bizarre pinnacle of Jewish self-righteousness rather than a made-in-Germany monstrosity.

Millions of the Holocaust victims were religious Jews. It seemed natural that three years after the Holocaust, the new Jewish government, secular as it was, should grant special privileges to the tiny ultra-Orthodox community that was already in the country or en route from the displaced persons camps in Europe. The state – also under pressure from Jewish American organizations – condoned an independent *Haredi* educational system, using public resources but immune to public scrutiny and regulation; and it agreed to exempt all ultra-Orthodox students of the Halacha from military service. To avoid misuse of this particular privilege, it was decreed that once the pious scholarship is over, the young man will be conscripted. He would be banned from any professional occupation before paying this important obligation to the newly formed militaristic entity. At the time, these seemed minimal humane gestures towards the remnants of a world that was dwindling and disappearing anyway.

Orthodoxy accepted the challenge. Its survival mechanisms, perfected in hundreds of years of solitude, enabled it to become, within one generation, the centre point of the Israeli experience. The secular state and its secular politicians acquiesced with this development, eyes wide open. As it happened, so-called secular Israeli society failed to present any secular alternative to the definition of Jewish national identity. It never gave itself a chance.

Generously sponsored, and fully financed by the state's apparatus, Orthodoxy has ensured its own unrestricted natural propagation by the traditional method. In his book *The Ruling Yarmulke*,[2] veteran journalist Levi Yitzhak HaYerushalmi describes a 1995 meeting with three friends he had grown up

---

[2] Hakibutz Hameuchad publishers, 1997.

with as a young *haredi* child in Jerusalem some sixty years earlier. As soon as the elderly men started discussing their offspring, it transpired that Levi, the only one in the group who had deserted Orthodoxy, accounted for "only" four grandchildren. Every one of the other three boasted around a hundred grandchildren and great-grandchildren.

Less than 3 percent of Israeli children attended the *haredi* independent educational system in the 1960s. In the year 2016, this system took exclusive care of 25 percent of Israeli children. In Jerusalem, 66 percent of all Jewish kindergarten children were *haredi*.[3] These are the institutions that produce adults like Aaron Cohen, confused youths like the "Hill Gangs" of violent orthodox youths in the settlements in the occupied territories, and the yeshiva dropouts known as the *Shabab* delinquents of Jerusalem. Many of these youngsters eventually alienate themselves from the ultra-Orthodox system of rigid religious discipline. Their chances of fitting in with the more productive sectors of Israeli society are limited, as they cannot easily compete with the graduates of the secular or the national-religious state educational system.

The phony national superiority complex bestowed by religious education lingers on. Graduates of Orthodoxy, as well as most graduates of the national-religious state system, have not been trained to have an interest in a democracy or in human rights and civil liberties. This is fertile ground for nationalistic manipulators of the worst possible kind. It enabled the racist and self-proclaimed "Rabbi" Meir Kahane to attract hundreds of supporters who still regularly carry out random violent attacks on Palestinians. In 1994, one of Kahane's supporters, medical doctor Baruch Goldstein, opened fire on Palestinian worshippers during Ramadan prayers in Hebron's Ibrahimi Mosque, killing thirty of them. Goldstein was subsequently proclaimed a "Jewish martyr" by the religious right and a cult has grown up around his grave. Horror attacks on innocent Palestinians, like the the kidnapping and murder of Mohammed Abu Khdeir in July 2014, and the firebombing of a Palestinian family home in the village of Duma, which cost the lives of a baby and his

---

[3] Figures from the *Haredi* news publication *Hidubrut*, May 2016

parents, were committed by young Jewish terrorists with ultra-religious background.

Violent religious rightists can draw on theological support. In 2011 Israeli liberals were shocked and outraged by a book called *Torat Hamelech* (The Teaching of the King) by Rabbi Yitzhak Shapira and Rabbi Yosef Elitzur, published by the reputable Institute for Torah at Yeshivat Od Yosef Chai, 2009. Its teachings were so objectionable that even Israel's police made a feeble attempt to "investigate" its authors and supporters, but the public prosecutor decided to drop the case. The publishers pointed out that the book was merely a collection of the Jewish rules and legitimate reflections which permitted the killing of unarmed gentiles – namely Arab Palestinians. Jewish teaching – greatly adapted to the needs of the settlers' movement in the post-1967 occupied Palestinian lands – has been, after all, the driving ideological force in Israeli politics for many years.

It seems that most souls born into the harsh discipline of the *haredi* ghettos eventually find their way into the less demanding environments of nationalistic-secular or the national-religious sectors of the population. Like the parents and the grandparents of most Israeli liberals, they gradually do away with most of Judaism's enormous list of demands and commands. They continue, however, to be imbued with the most meaningful heritage of their earlier habitats: the deep abhorrence of living together with non-Jews. It is an attitude they share – alas – with most of the officially secular Israelis, much further removed from their rabbinical ancestors.

7

DIVINELY ALONE

The People shall dwell alone, and shall
not be reckoned among the nations.

Numbers 23: 9

Self-development and independence are too often
accompanied by isolation; and nations, like individuals,
become torpid when they retire from the world.

Winwood Reade,
The Martyrdom of Man

In Cairo's airport, of all places, I received eye-opening information about the importance of keeping a kosher diet.

"Do not eat their food; it will make you stupid," a nice-looking Jewish man warned me during security check before flying home, upon hearing that I was on my way to the airport cafeteria to have some breakfast.

My fellow traveller's outfit clearly indicated his political and religious affiliation – the uniform of a dark suit, middle-size beard, and a dark brimmed hat. I actually saw him fishing the hat out of his luggage upon arriving in the terminal, to replace the less conspicuous cap that he had been using during a visit to Alexandria, the purpose of which I failed to extract from him in two hours of small talk. I was intrigued because at the time, the second Intifada was at its peak, and Israeli-Egyptian relations were at an all-time low. Most Israelis did not consider Egypt a good place to visit in those days. Meir Cohen – so he introduced himself – was a Jerusalemite from the Rav Nof fashionable Orthodox neighbourhood. Fending off my curiosity about the purpose of his trip to Egypt, he very kindly urged me to share his large pack of nuts to keep me clear of the presumed perils of buying food from the terminal's buffet. I was unable to shake his conviction that what seemed like a totally innocent display of bakery products actually had a devastating effect on human brain cells. Non-kosher eaters were all stupid, he told me as a matter of fact.

"What about Albert Einstein?" I protested, displaying my own silliness by finding nothing smarter to say. "Was he also stupid?"

"Yes," Mr. Cohen said unflinching. I was not surprised to discover that he made his living as a kosher controller. He very eloquently made the case for his specialty and was altogether a remarkably charismatic man, obviously experienced in the art of rhetoric, so I did not ask him how damaged my own brains should be due to my non-kosher food habits for the previous fifty-two years. The answer threatened to be too depressing. But not giving in altogether, I boldly ventured a challenge: "And what about Arik Sharon?"

As expected, a raw nerve was touched. Rabbi Cohen was not prepared to condemn the elderly national hero turned prime minister, who was known for his unrestricted passion for all kinds of foods, including some real abominations, strictly forbidden by the Halacha. But his answer was swift and powerful: "Sins may be forgiven; the Lord takes care how he punishes and rewards. Sharon is a great Jewish hero; anybody as great as that – a Jew who single-handedly saved the People of Israel so many times – would be pardoned in the Last Judgment."

At that moment the announcement was made that the flight was delayed. As the only two Hebrew speakers expecting the Air Sinai jet, we had ample time to kill and nobody else to talk to, so the chat continued quite pleasantly. We disagreed about almost everything under the sun, but we were both argumentative Jews, and each of us seemed to believe that the other might eventually come around to admit his or her erroneous ways. The trouble was, Cohen was quite touchy with my teasing heresies. He would hit the roof with holy rage each time I seemed to be pushing the freedom of speech too far. "Touch Not My Messiah!" he shrieked angrily when I critically quoted some idiotic utterances of a very major rabbi whom the press was full of several weeks earlier.

Cohen's preaching was in a genre I was familiar with. Tapes and recently CDs, full of rabbinical pearls of wisdom landed regularly in everybody's post box in my neighbourhood. They usually carried calls to nonbelievers to repentance, using a rich repertoire of stories about incredible miracles. Rabbi Cohen's own collection of fantastic tales about divine interventions in favour of the believers filled me with an irresistible urge to reward him with products of my own imagination. I should be ashamed to admit that at this stage in our conversation, I pulled out the Egyptian souvenirs that I had purchased a day before in Cairo's famous museum – small forms of cats, mummies and beetles – and informed him with a straight face that I was advised by people whose opinions I value that these copies of ancient Egyptian gods and spirits are very effective good luck charms.

He was shocked and appalled, as expected, but what clearly shook him was that I actually took a tour to the Pyramids. I happened to mention that my limbs still ached due to the difficult crawl inside the narrow cavity leading to the tomb of Pharaoh Cheops.

"How could you? This is most dangerous!" He reproached. "The profanity in these sites is enormous!" He was now eyeing me with new disgust. If I were to turn into stone or dirt any moment, he should not have been surprised.

"But every graveyard is profane to Jews," I reminded him. "Some rabbis claimed recently that one may be hit by profanity even by merely flying over a cemetery. When you think about it, actually, the pharaohs' belief that they would come back from the dead is quite similar to the Jewish creed in the Resurrection of the Dead and rolling through earth to the Last Judgment. Moses, after all, had learned much of ancient Egypt's wisdom and brought it into Judaism."

This last impudence earned me yet another furious lecture. The Torah of Israel was handed to Moses directly from the Almighty, and the very idea that the Jewish prophet had been at all influenced by his unholy teachers, the Wise Men of Egypt, was a terrible blasphemy. The People of Israel is the Chosen Nation, Rabbi Cohen kept repeating with total conviction and the all-too-well-recognized self-congratulation.

It was now my turn to lose my temper. "Chosen for what purpose?" I asked desperately, because I already suspected the answer.

"Thou hast chosen us from all the nations" is a major Jewish concept, forever floating on the cusp between the sublime and the ridiculous. At its best, this concept encases the moral heights of Jewish philosophy. But it is often abused for vicious manipulations. Its teachings endow the faithful with a phony sense of superiority, legitimizing the demand for subdued acceptance of the endless suffering entailed by the Divine Choice.

The boarding announcement fortunately released Meir Cohen and me from the urge to jump at each other's throats. The plane was almost empty. Two backpackers, an American who looked like a diplomat and a handful of Thai labourers on their way to Tel Aviv, would have been somewhat baffled to hear two Israelis passionately arguing over Thou Hast Us Chosen. The two of us carefully chose seats as far from each other as possible, in order not to stretch our mutual intolerance any further.

* * *

William Winwood Reade was a gentleman explorer and adventurer. Having toured Africa, the young Reade had spent much time considering the role of religion in the human culture. In his view, the inner need to believe in a creator and to worship a superior entity is a very basic human and social force, which had been energizing the cultural development of all civilizations. Reade had also identified the religious engine's tendency to become stale eventually and to degenerate as priests increase their political clout, taking over control and dragging great societies into corruption and oblivion.

Reade's *The Martyrdom of Man* was published 1872, to become a bestseller only many years after the author's premature death, and then sink back into oblivion. It beautifully surveyed the rise and demise of the West's major religions. In the chapter dedicated to Judaism, Reade expressed admiration of Diaspora Jews following the destruction of the Second Temple. He considered them a uniquely important intellectual elite who had contributed greatly to the cultural progress in the Middle East as well as in Europe. He compared them sneeringly to the provincial fanatics of Judea who did not go into exile:

Those Jews of Judaea, those Hebrews of the Hebrews, regarded all the Gentiles as enemies of God: they considered it a sin to live abroad, or to speak a foreign language, or to rub their limbs with foreign oil. Of all the trees, the Lord had chosen but one vine; and of all the flowers, but one lily; and of all the birds, but one dove, and of all the cattle, but one lamb; and of all builded cities, only Sion; and among all the multitude of people, he had elected the Jews as a peculiar treasure, and had made them a nation of priests and holy men. For their sake God had made the world. On their account alone empires rose and fell. Babylon had triumphed because God was angry with his people; Babylon had fallen because he had forgiven them. It may be imagined that it was not easy to govern such a race. They acknowledged no king but Jehovah, no laws but the precepts of their holy books... It is only in severity that the Jews can be admired.[1]

Expressions like "the Chosen People" or "Thou hast us Chosen" were used sneeringly when I was young, merely to express some dismay about the less appealing aspects of contemporary society. This is no longer funny. Too many Israeli Jews sincerely believe that boons and privileges have been designated for them personally by the good Lord, who had marked us as his special favourites.

Zionist educators must have been aware – long ago – that nonreligious idealistic youth, trained for socialism and the human brotherhood, would not possibly look kindly on the concept of "Chosen People," so fundamental to Judaism. Perhaps in order to pre-empt this – and still keep us happy with our Jewish tradition – the first term of our sixth grade was dedicated to a serious study of *The Khazarian*, a religious-philosophical tract written by Rabbi Yehuda Halevi in the twelfth century.

The Khazarian offers a worthy explanation for Judaism's values in the form of a theologian legend and discourse. The story

---

1 Reade, *The Martyrdom of Man*, p. 167.

is about the King of the Khazarians,[2] who invites representatives of the three major monotheistic religions in order to choose the best discipline for his kingdom, on quitting Paganism. He listens carefully to the wise men of Islam and Christianity but it is the Jewish *Chaver* who impresses him most.

God – explains the *Chaver* – had indeed chosen the Children of Israel, but not in order to let them have a good time in this world. On the contrary, they have been elected to carry the burdens of all other men upon their own shoulders. It is the sacred duty of the Jewish people to assist the good Lord in the eternal struggle between Good and Evil, to support the Sons of Light as they stand up bravely against the constant attacks of the Sons of Darkness.

This explanation threw a new light on the difficult tasks every Jew needs to fulfil every moment of his waking hours: the endless *mitzvot*, the many taboos and self-denials, all presumably serve the purpose of sustaining an extremely special brand of people, totally committed to divine spirituality in the service of humanity, morality, and God's grace.

It was a brand one could be proud of, even from without. I could sympathize with the choice of the *Khazarian* King. For many years I stayed convinced that Judaism was based on an altruistic, sublime vision of universal humanism. Many years before Karl Marx's ideas had challenged the legitimacy of eternal private possessions, the Wise Men of our religion had already found the middle ground between socialists and capitalists; they had recognized the individual's right to use one's talent and hard work in order to get richer and accumulate assets. But at the same time, they had decreed that once every seven years, the entire harvest of the land should be contributed to the community. They also set a rule of full land reform once every fifty years, on the year of the Jubilee.

I could not, at that time, realize that ideas in *The Khazarian* or Judaism's universal altruism would end up so far away from the political and religious reality of the Jewish state. The dominant versions of present-day Jewish Orthodoxy have very little in

---

[2] Based, as commonly assumed, on a real nation somewhere near the Black Sea.

common with the Spanish Golden Age poets and philosophers, who considered their Jewish faith a spearhead of progress and morality for all mankind. Mediaeval Judaism might have been "a civilization of mind and emotions" that was at least two generations ahead of Christian theology and Christian philosophy, as German historian Friedrich Heer had claimed. But this same Judaism was already starting to show "signs of ossification remarkably similar to the ones observed in Christian thinking." As Heer put it, "the Jews have dug themselves into... a narrow, self-encircled piousness. They did not wish to recognize any open windows to the world outside it."

Progressive elements in Judaism that tried to take it out of this mental "ossification" normally had to pay a price. In 1233, staunch supporters of the Orthodoxy were so enraged with the popularity of the great Maimonides's new teaching, that they blew the whistle on the great rabbi's followers to the Holy Inquisition in Montpellier. "Persecutions made the Jewish Orthodoxy ever more sinister" – this is how Heer explained the victory of Jewish conservatism in the fourteenth and fifteenth centuries. His commentary sounds relevant enough to the twenty-first century.

Almost all Jewish immigrants to Palestine in the nineteenth and early twentieth centuries had emerged from deeply religious Orthodox communities. The highly educated Jews and members of Reform communities had mostly opposed Zionism, which they considered yet another method to deepen traditional Jewish self-isolation. Only a few of the scholarly trained had emigrated to the Holy Land, bringing with them their rich and enlightening personal interpretation of European Modernism. (One shining example is Judah Leon Magnes (1877–1948), a reform rabbi and one of the founders of the Hebrew University in Jerusalem. Magnes, a renowned pacifist, strongly disapproved of nationalistic aspects within Judaism and together with other members of the Brith Shalom movement also opposed the Partition Plan of Palestine into a Jewish State and an Arab State.)

All this might explain quite a lot about the making of the New Israeli type of person: one who had switched to his or her presumed secularism directly from the strictest Orthodoxy.

* * *

Apparently, you cannot have a Chosen People if anybody is allowed to join in. For hundreds of years, Judaism had groomed itself as an exclusive club for children of Jewish mothers, with an extremely strict entrance committee for special cases. Only a deep religious commitment coupled with intensive long learning, followed by meticulous and often humiliating examination, can turn a non-Jew into a Jew. The system is geared toward making conversions as inaccessible as possible.

The nonproselytizing nature of Judaism had always been considered evidence of our high moral standards. Unlike the Christians with their pushy missionaries and their Inquisition, unlike the Muslims with the holy Jihad, Jews would never ask strangers to convert into our religion, let alone force them to do so – God forbid.

This self-image of tolerance and virtue has of course a darker side. Judaism is wary of any too intimate a relationship with members of other religions. Rejection might take a gentle, self-isolating style, mainly when the Others are members of those sectors in the population that hold the power and the control. But when the Jews are the ones running the show, this rejection might be conceived as hostile, painful, and insensitive.

In fact, Judaism's energies and resources are very much focused on stopping its sons and its daughters from assimilating into other peoples and religions. This is done with the help of some very effective isolation mechanisms, geared toward making sure that the faithful would not find themselves in any close contact with outsiders. Contemporary nonreligious Jews in Israel are affected by these taboos mainly through the legal codex of the state.

The Halacha's rituals keep religious Jews busy most of their waking hours. To outsiders, the multitude of rules and regulations in Judaism seems tiresome and bizarre. But a simple analysis indicates that almost every one of the commands of our religion is cleverly conceived to achieve two chief strategic goals: the preservation of the community in isolation from its non-Jewish environment, and the preservation of community control in the hands of the elders.

The male control span goes from the community's chief rabbi through the heads of the *schules* all the way to the head of the family. Social life runs around the synagogue school, and family life is geared toward the needs of the family's father. The mother's role in this system is crucial, as she is the one almost exclusively responsible for the kosher food.

The complicated kosher diet is the major axis of Jewish life. Ensuring the kitchen is kosher at all times guarantees that women will also be fully employed by their home duties. It also rewards them with the prestige and the satisfaction of those in charge of keeping the family pure and safe. Fasting and taboos – like the taboo on eating any yeast produced in a bakery during Passover – keep the Jewish Israeli nation busy throughout the seasons and the holidays. A kosher observer is forever on alert counting the hours since his or her last meal, to make sure to not accidentally break the ban on mixing milk and meat products. The panic of unnoticed bakery crumbs that might have been left to contaminate a corner of the home in spite of all the laborious cleaning and purifying efforts pushes whole families to move into hotels for the seven days of Passover. Modern young observers have discovered the marvels of disposable plastic utensils, which take away the fear of unseen bread and cake contamination. They start using those over a week before Passover even starts, in the days of scrubbing and sterilizing.

Judaism has an obsessive fixation on foods. Unauthorized (non-kosher) foods are considered an abomination, and an observing Jew would rather starve if there are no provisions for adequately kosher nourishment. Many Jews who are no longer observant preserve the acquired instinctive disgust to eating "creeps" (crabs and shellfish, for example) or pork. It is hard to beat the elated feeling of satisfaction and togetherness of a festive kosher family meal, so complicated to produce, so nourishing and fulfilling. Years after having severed their ties with the religious community, people would speak longingly about these happy weekend and holiday occasions, with the singing of the Sabbath prayers inspiring an intimacy with "our Father and King, Creator of this World" that nothing else can resurrect.

Contemporary marketing experts should admire the concept of a totally captive market that makes the kosher diet idea such a long-term winner. An observing Jew is unable to dine in the company of non-Jews and must always stay close to authorized religious suppliers. Granting the kosher certificate easily translates to mighty economic as well as political power, held by the various rabbinical courts. These courts, state sponsored or self-appointed, may decide to declare a food supplier or a rival court *treif* (non-kosher) for their own flock, which could mean financial ruin. Thousands of jobs are available as kosher supervisors in restaurants, food producers, and retailers. From time to time, even the secular Israeli media report new turf fights between different rabbinical disciplines. Powerful rabbis display their hold on their respective communities by setting new, tougher requirements for food provisions or banning whole supermarket chains and suppliers – often to the benefit of suppliers with good contacts to someone in the rabbi's entourage. In 2003 the venerable Ashkenazi Rabbi Yosef Shalom Elyashiv announced that it is no longer kosher to eat fruits and vegetables grown by Jews in the Seventh Year (*Shmita*). Chief Sephardi Rabbi Mordechai Eliyahu had to cave in, after he had earlier solemnized the Israeli food products by the usual practice of symbolically "selling" the whole production to a cooperating non-Jew. Food importers stood to make a fortune from overseas kosher vegetables at the expense of local growers, if Rabbi Elyashiv's decree had been accepted by the State Rabbinate.

More than two hundred years ago, such a fierce struggle was going on in Amsterdam. It happened at the turn of the eighteenth century. New decrees set by Napoleon granted civil rights to Jews for the first time in Christian Europe. Jews with modern ideas decided to start a new community, the *Naye Kille*. They met a fierce opposition from the Orthodox rabbinical establishment that was bitterly opposed to any modernization of Jewish community life. Rather than start an assault on the very idea of enlightenment, the Orthodox *Parnosim* (elders) of the *Alte Kille* (the old community) set out to attack the kosher standards in the *Naye Kille*.

In the power struggle that erupted, both sides displayed remarkable mass media skills. Using the new technique of printing cheap pamphlets, so useful and popular with the French revolutionaries, they started putting up street *Pashquills* (news sheets) packed with bitter criticism and slander against their opponents. They were written in the form of smart dialogues between fictitious speakers, who spoke ancient Dutch Yiddish printed in Hebrew letters. Most fortunately, a whole set of these publications survived, and experts in Jewish history managed to decipher them for research that became a delightful book.[3]

Reading today accusations by members of *Naye Kille* that *Parnosim* of the *Alte Kille* are motivated by greed in exercising their power over the kosher slaughter franchise (and thus causing members of the community to pay dearly for low-quality meat); learning how the *Parnosim* of the *Alte Kille* were quick and ruthless to declare that all meat from the *Naye* slaughter house is a non-kosher abomination, a deadly risk for any Jew who might consume it – one could easily make the mistake of assuming that these *Pashquills* had been freshly printed and published in either Bnei Brak, an ultra-Orthodox town near Tel Aviv or in the exotic Mea Shearim *haredi* neighbourhood of Jerusalem. The streets there are often decorated with furious printed admonitions.

About half the population of Israel (in the past it used to be about three quarters) has no real interest in the kosher regulations, but meekly accepts the need to subsidize the state's large bureaucracy responsible for monitoring food production and food distribution all over the country, and for issuing the kosher certificates. Israelis must be the most submissive-by-nature population, Zeev Hefetz commented more than twenty years ago in an article discussing the ban on quality meat imports. A Finance Ministry report, kept secret until exposed by the financial daily *Calcalist* in April 2016, revealed that the kosher food supervision overheads amount to NIS 2.8 billion a year, 3 percent of the overall national expenditure on food products, and a major cause of the relatively high prices in the Israeli food market. Imported foods – which normally help bring prices down, due to competition – become 5 to 27 percent more expensive in the Israeli market due to the kosher certificate regulations. Nobody would put up with so much trouble had it

---

[3] Joseph Michman and Marion Aptroot, *Storm in the Community: Yiddish Polemical Pamphlets of Amsterdam Jewry 1797-1798* (Cincinnati: Hebrew Union College Press, 2002).

not been for a prize that comes with it. The prize in this case is the preservation of the country's presumed Jewish identity. The Halacha, this grim and sterilizing legal religious code, had been the formaldehyde liquid responsible for the preservation of Jewish religious communities all over the world for generations, keeping Jewish rituals and Jewish priorities identical, wherever Jews lived. The Israeli state's legal code is saturated with this preserving substance, activating mechanisms that forcefully estrange all Israeli Jews – religious and secular alike – from anybody who is not Jewish according to the Halacha.

In order to ensure the isolation of God's flock, religious rituals are imposed at crucial junctions of every Israeli Jew's life, in a way that often seems offensive to nonbelievers. Trying to circumvent these religious invasions is tricky, and one might end up in some bizarre situations. Like many other people, I have personal experience with such absurd scenes. Once I even played a leading role.

IDF Purchasing Kosher Dog Food for Passover

It is not even Chanuka yet, but in the IDF preparations are in full swing towards Passover. The Army Food Center will soon purchase Kosher-for-Passover dog food.

All dogs serving in the security forces as guards and on other active assignments will this year be able to munch their Bonzo without worrying that they are eating food that contains bread and yeast. The IDF has now decided to take care of this problem.

A military source explained yesterday that the army would not merely see to it that the dog food will not contain yeast, but also that it should no longer resemble foods that are forbidden for Jews over Passover. "We make sure that what is not to be found is also not to be seen, so the dog food would not look like food for humans which is not kosher for the holiday; for example, it will not look like croutons, which are rich in yeast."

Ma'ariv, *November 22, 2002*

Part III – Commandments

All we may expect from our future is our past.

Doron Rosenblum, *Israeli Blues*

A woman may use tainted powder for her face on Saturday, as this is perishable, but one need to be strict about lipstick, which is not allowed on Saturday, and blush is also to be strict about. But there is no ban on a woman to eat berries and red beetroot and other colour giving fruit, even though by her consuming she is colouring her lips.

Rabbi Ovadia Yosef in a public weekly lecture, according to *Ma'ariv*, 1996

8
THREE WEDDINGS

Marriage is a union between two deities that might bring a third deity on this earth. It is the union of two souls in valiant love, to do away with separation.

Kahlil Gibran,
The Wanderer

More than a hundred guests were looking at me in anticipation. Flowers and floating candles decorated every one of the elegantly laid dinner tables they were sitting round. It was a perfectly pleasant May evening, and the garden around the pretty "Green House" – once the home of the richest *effendi* of the village, Sheikh Muanis, now the staff house of Tel Aviv University – was in full bloom. I cleared my throat nervously and then said into the microphone that carried my voice into the sound system, "Will you, Avi, take Nechama to be your partner for life? Will you, in the presence of all the friends and family, promise to love her and to respect her, to give her your support in happy days as well as in hard times, and to always be faithful to her?"

Avi (the names of the couple have been changed) said, "I do."

I continued to read the marriage vows that the bride had prepared in advance: "Do you, Nechama, take Avi to be your partner for life? Will you, in the presence of all the friends and family, promise to love him and to respect him, to give him your support in happy days as well as in hard times, and to always be faithful to him?"

Small white flowers decorating her lavish blonde hair, Nechama said, "I do."

I asked the couple to repeat some more vows and promises, read them some lines on the importance of their new status as man and wife, oversaw an exchange of rings, and then made the final declaration: "As Avi and Nechama have made their vows... we shall now consider them husband and wife, a loving and committed couple, and wish them happiness ever after. Avi, you may now kiss your bride."

Fortunately, nobody in the room – except my then husband and my eleven-year-old daughter, who were quietly keeling over with uncontrollable giggles at a table in the far corner – seemed to find it ridiculous that I was pretending to be marrying people. It must have been the most surprising role I had filled in my entire life. Admittedly, I had to be fortified with two glasses of wine before I rose to my feet to perform the ceremony, in order to conceal my acute embarrassment. But then I sailed assertively through the proceedings, bravely ignoring my own family's disrespect. The sight of the beaming faces of the betrothed and their parents was a handsome reward.

Truth to be told, Nechama and Avi had already been legally married by the time of the wedding party. About a week earlier, they flew from Tel Aviv to the island of Cyprus, where, like hundreds of other Israeli couples, they institutionalized their marital status with the registrar of a romantic town near Nicosia. It was, however, a great disappointment that the photos taken during the registration were mistakenly destroyed, and they had no souvenir of the cherished moment. This gave rise to Nechama's idea to repeat the procedure during the party the couple was arranging to celebrate the wedding with all the many family and friends who had not been able to join them in Cyprus. Having decided that I was to stand in for the registrar, Nechama faxed me the carefully worked-out texts that I was to read, and sweetly made it clear that I could not possibly decline the bride's request.

In the regular Israeli Jewish wedding ceremonies, one hears mainly Aramaic texts dealing with the couple's joint commitments to the Jewish people and the Lord Our Father, lines commemorating the destruction of the Temple and quoting the sum of the bride's bond (*ketuba*) signed by the groom (representing the amount a husband must pay if and when the marriage is eventually dissolved). By contrast, in Nechama's ceremony the reading was all about love, romance, and future mutual commitments. The marriage vows were modelled on civil wedding procedures, which take for granted that bride and groom are partners of equal status in the marriage contract. Some guests came over to our table after the ceremony to tell me how much they enjoyed the simple procedure; two of the ladies revealed that they were moved to tears. The general view was that this wedding was "much nicer" than those we normally attend.

In fact, for almost all of the present company, this had been the first experience of a wedding that did not include the condescending pontification, often coupled with blatant male chauvinism, of the men in black suits who hold an absolute monopoly on the administration of Israeli Jewish weddings. The deprived tribe of non-Orthodox Israeli Jews is starved of simple, festive gestures that do not involve Orthodox clerics supervising our most vulnerable occasions.

The emergence and re-emergence of significant secular political movements in Israel did nothing to change the fact that the country is the only so-called Western-style nation where one may not become legally married without religious certification. Interdenominational marriages are therefore impossible. Nonreligious Israeli Jews have long given up complaining about this infringement of their personal freedom. In the sixties and the seventies, one could still expect the press to get excited about cases of people who were denied access to the marriage registry due to some obscure rabbinical regulation. In today's Israel, no story of hardships and humiliations inflicted by the rabbinical courts would provoke more than eyebrow raising. It is generally accepted that many people who live here may join the army and die for the state, but they cannot expect it to provide them with a marriage certificate.

Cyprus and Tuscany are the most popular destinations for the growing number – some say 20 percent – of Jewish Israeli couples (and obviously all mixed couples) wishing to or having to be legally wed without a rabbi officiating. The State of Israel recognizes foreign wedding certificates. A handful of these newlyweds also celebrate a non-Orthodox *Chuppa* ceremony with a Reform or a Conservative rabbi. Ceremonies performed by Reform or Conservative Jewish rabbis – some of them women – have no legal status, and their documents are not recognized for marital status registration. This is in contrast to the United States and most European countries, East and West, where non-Orthodox rabbis regularly and freely register weddings recognized by the state. In Israel, their ceremonies have only ornamental and sentimental value, much like the ceremony at which I officiated in the Green House.

In a country where state and church are fully separated, the state legislature's interest in marriage procedure is limited to the validity of the certificate as a contract for mutual commitment in the conjugal future. But in Israel the state – through its rabbinate, which is a governmental authority – imposes more than just the exact text of the vows its citizens should pronounce while they are getting married. Officials of the government also monitor closely the menu offered to the guests (kosher food only), the accessories (*Chuppa*, *ketuba*, a glass to be broken for the memory of the lost temple), and the dress code of the betrothed (bride must be modestly clad; bridegroom and participating male relatives should have the top of their heads covered). The ceremony would not take place and the certificate of marriage would not be administered without confirmation that the bride has taken part in several highly invasive prenuptial religious rituals. She must produce documents to prove that she has taken care of her personal hygiene on the eve of the important date (*mikve*[1] dipping, fully naked, in the presence of professional ritual female bath controllers). She also must attend a lesson on sex and relationships from a rebbetzin. It is up to the rebbetzin to set the date for the wedding, making sure it will not be too near – before or after – the bride's period of menstruation.

For thousands of Israelis, marriage abroad is the only way to institutionalize their relations, due to a variety of religious taboos. For a start, non-Jews may not marry a Jew. A Jewish man may not marry a divorcee or a convert if his name is Cohen, or Kaplan, or

---

[1] Ritual bath.

any other derivative of the tribal name of Jewish priests. Nobody is to be married if his or her father is not the man his or her mother had been legally married to at the time of conception. The lawfully wedded husband might have been absent for twenty years and more – deliberately or not; he may also simply refuse to divorce his estranged wife; but she is forever married to him, even if he is a wife beater or the common-law husband of another woman. The marital laws of the State of Israel make a maze of unintelligible instructions that might be mildly amusing were it not for the hassle and real pain they inflict on so many innocent people.

I was truly stunned, in 1975, when my friend Dahlia, who moved to the United States, sent me her wedding photos. The non-Jewish bridegroom Lance was wearing a yarmulke and standing under a *chuppa,* and the ceremony was officiated by a Reform American rabbi. For Israelis this procedure, so ordinary in Jewish communities all over the world who wish to keep members rather than alienate them after they find true love elsewhere, is still breathtakingly revolutionary forty years later. The Israeli state is oblivious to the growing number of foreign weddings and "common-law" couples. Nonreligious politicians make pathetic attempts to push forward a civil alternative for "refused" couples only (God forbid that they should be open to all who desire them). Even these efforts, meant chiefly to ease the pressure on the large Israeli-Russian immigrant community, have been effectively blocked so far. Wonders never cease. My friends and I were stunned, in the summer of 2016, to discover that clandestinely and without any public notice, a regulation was passed as a part of a new law in 2014, inflicting prison terms on anybody who "fails to register legally a marriage or divorce ceremony performed for oneself or for others". The simple translation of this rule is that people like myself who officiate a "marriage ceremony" are to be indicted and may be incarcerated. A Knesset member of the secular party "Yesh Atid" headed by Yair Lapid tried to change the law so that the required sanction will be "only" a fine, not a prison term, but failed to win a vote on her modest amendment. The issue continues to be debated as this book is put to press.

* * *

The Orthodox rabbinate sees it as a sacred duty to block any entry into Judaism of outsiders whose motives are not purely religious. As it happens, innocent mixed couples often come to the rabbis with a request to convert the non-Jewish party into Judaism, so that the two may start a "properly Jewish" new family. An Orthodox rabbi receiving a request for conversion that is motivated by love of a Jewish person is obliged not only to refuse point-blank, but also to document the interview so that the incriminating information should be stored for the benefit of all the other state rabbis. The computerized community registrar would make sure no rabbi would dare help with this particular conversion. Most Israelis are already wise enough to know that if a family member wishes to bring in a goy as a partner for life, he or she must rehearse a pack of lies in order to be able to fool the rabbis into opening conversion procedures.

And what a procedure this is. After the would-be Jew managed to convince a rabbi that he or she has decided to become an Orthodox Jew as a result of a spiritual transformation (and nothing to do with the desire to start a home with a particular Jewish person) the potential convert should be prepared for a period of learning of at least two years, consuming time and money, and including some humiliating and rather strange tasks. The convert might be asked to spend time living in an Orthodox household in order to study the proper ways to run a Jewish home, often in return for free housework.

By the end of this exhausting road, the candidate may expect a difficult final examination and the nerve-wracking worry of failing the test and not becoming Jewish after all. He or she must also vow to keep living an Orthodox life: keep a kosher home and make sure the couple's future children will receive Orthodox religious education, even if the partner he or she is hoping to marry by the end of the ordeal is a perfectly secular Israeli Jew who merely worries about the national identity and civic status of the next generation.[2]

---

[2] The late arch right-wing general turned politician Rechavam Zeevi (Gandi) boasted publicly that he had forced the rabbis to speed the conversion of his son's Scottish bride (*Ha'aretz* supplement, February 15, 2003). It is easy to believe exceptions are constantly made to people with leverage, which does nothing to help common citizens and residents.

Orthodoxy spares no efforts and puts enormous resources into making sure that children of non-Jews, or of so called "bastards", should not be allowed to infiltrate the Jewish people via the *chuppa*. Large databases, carefully collected and maintained, help the rabbinate officials spot any doubtful areas in the family tree. Suspicions that one is not a "proper" Jew would block any chance that the rabbis would let him or her marry.

Behind the extremely rigorous instructions of the Jewish religion stands the long tradition of abhorrence of mixed marriages, a sentiment not in itself a Jewish invention. For ages families in different parts of the world have been up in arms when children revealed a preference for a partner of another race, nationality, class, or denomination. Aristocratic families in Europe used to welcome marriages of first cousins, before the genetic toll incurred by this practice was understood. Traditional Arab families continue this unhealthy practice even today. Judaism is unique mainly in the efficiency with which it rejects newcomers, with the firm support accorded by the Israeli state.

Non-Jewish Israelis are equally denied access to civil and interdenominational marriage procedures. They at least need not worry so much if they wish to marry out of their communities. As long as they do not choose a Jew for a partner, Christian as well as Muslim priests welcome newcomers, and joining in with their flock is a negligible, instant formality.

So how does the state recognize who is a Jew? Ask this question, and Israelis will burst out laughing. Israel's history has been marked with vociferous struggles over the key to the definition of the national identity. The "who is a Jew?" debate traditionally ended with Orthodoxy's victory in setting ever-stricter criteria for the threshold into Israeli Judaism and into the automatic right to Israeli citizenship according to the Law of Return.

Still, Israeli bureaucrats had to stitch into the Law of Return some regulations administering the legal status of non-Jewish family members of Jews immigrating into Israel. Thanks to these administrative regulations, hundreds of thousands of non-Jews have immigrated to Israel, especially since the early 1990s from the former Soviet Union. They all automatically become citizens with voting rights and received the usual grand package of financial and other privileges. Currently, they are considered a powerful electoral group.

Toward the end of the 1990s, a strong lobby started to present demands that the conversion rules should be relaxed for the newcomers. Israel's mighty Defence Forces even started their own private rabbinical conversion courts for the benefit of young non-Jewish recruits.

One is tempted to fantasize how simple and good life might have been had this state allowed its citizens to choose their own national identity, respecting the "natural right for self-determination," without Big Brother of the state rabbinate watching over every detail of the fragments of this identity. The "Demographic Demons" Israel is so haunted by would have been far less menacing had Israel been able to adopt a secular nationality. But the state rejects the concept of an Israeli nationality, available to all citizens and not based on religion or ethnicity. [3]

Truly religious people, including the faithful ultra-Orthodox, understand very well the "catch-22" Israel is in. They can accurately point out that the unholy mixture of religion and politics is a product of secular Israeli Jewish sentiment. Rabbi Moshe Grilak, a *Ma'ariv* columnist for many years and a spokesperson for the *haredi* community, published a book that tries to open the dialogue between nonreligious Israelis and the ultra-Orthodox. His call is surprisingly in the spirit of the late Rabbi Weinfeld of Monsey:

"Why shouldn't all the secular members of the Knesset start a new initiative once and for all, and bravely decide to separate church and state in Israel? They should simply leave us in peace!" he cried out.

* * *

---

[3] The small association Ani Israeli ("I am an Israeli") headed by Professor Uzzi Ornan appealed in 2003 to the Supreme Court to demand recognition of an "Israeli Nationality" in Israel. The appeal (of which this author is a cosigner) was rejected by the Supreme Court in October 2013. The public discussion in Israel over this core issue continues to be marginalized (www.ani-israeli.org).

Less than two years after the pleasant wedding party in the Green House, my friends Nechama and Avi presented themselves at the Tel Aviv rabbinical court and requested to go through a wedding procedure for the third time – this time by a rabbi and under a *Chuppa* according to Israeli law. This was no case of born-again Jewish sentiment. The couple needed a rabbinical marriage certificate to secure the future happiness of their family, which was now focused on a beautiful baby boy adopted from Brazil.

To avoid any risk that their child would be an outcast, treated as a stranger in the Jewish state; to make sure that when it will be his time for marriage, he will not be rejected as a goy; and also in order to look him in the face and promise him that he is every inch as Jewish as his loving parents, Avi and Nechama knew that they must start the long, expensive process of an Orthodox conversion. Like thousands of other adoptive Israeli parents, they found the name and telephone number of an Orthodox rabbi who is known for his relative liberalism, one of the few who is prepared to convert babies with a minimum of trouble and insult to their families. But despite his leniency, and his exceptional readiness to turn a blind eye to the fact that the parents were not going to educate the boy in Orthodox lifestyle, as required, the good rabbi could not even start to take care of their case before they had been "properly" married.

The rabbinate was in no hurry to congratulate the two Israeli-born citizens who came to ask for a marriage certificate. To start with, they were required to prove that they are properly Jewish. For Avi this was no problem. He had been married before and divorced, and all his details were stored in the database of Big Brother of the rabbinate. Single, forty-three-year-old Nechama, however, needed to bring original documents, starting not with her birth certificate but with her own mother's *ketuba*. Things got really worrying when it turned out that Mum actually never had one.

Nechama's parents, both survivors of the Holocaust, were married in postwar Europe in a civil registration office and had never bothered with a rabbi. Displeased, the pious officials declared that it was necessary for Nechama's mother to prove that she is actually of Jewish origin and not a mere *Shikse* who plucked herself a young Jew in 1946 Germany. Should Nechama fail to prove the Jewish identity of her mother, she herself would have to start a conversion process before anybody would marry her to a good Jew like Avi. And until then, of course, her small son would continue his goyish existence; there would be no talk of his conversion.

The ultra-Orthodox registrar was sympathetic and had some tips up his sleeve for such predicaments, apparently not too rare. He suggested that the distraught Nechama and her elderly mother should embark on an intensive search for relatives who might be able to corroborate by oath that Nechama's mother's had not been falsely impersonating a Jew for the last fifty or so years. As it happens, she was a daughter of an ultra-Orthodox Belgian Jewish family. But most of her relatives had perished in Auschwitz, and the remaining few who made it to Israel had all died by now.

The search was at a dead end when Nechama's mother somehow located the address of a cousin twice removed, who she thought might recognize her even though they had hardly been in touch. Unfortunately, it soon transpired that the cousin had died two years earlier. The two women returned to the registrar in Tel Aviv to report the failure. Surprisingly, the official was kind-hearted enough to come up with a remarkable solution. He first of all made sure that the deceased himself was a proper Jew. With the help of his widow, it was established that their wedding had been duly registered in the early fifties in Naharia. Now Nechama's mother was asked to prove that she was truly related to the dead man. She was invited to a formal interrogation in the rabbinate. To everybody's relief, she was able to remember the names of her second cousin's father, mother, and grandfather.

All's well that ends well. There were no guests at the third wedding of Nechama and Avi, but friends received a digital photo commemorating the happy end of this particular saga: Baby Oron beams in Nechama's arms while his parents are starting, at last, a kosher Jewish home.

Few Israelis would find this story particularly funny or surprising. This is the way things are. If one's state is run according to religious regulations, and if the Jewish religion needs to exclude people unless they correspond to its requirements, then people might get hurt, or go through inconveniences. These are, after all, the rules and regulations that had kept us as a nation for the last two thousand years. We should not give them up or we might lose our unity, or our solidarity, or the unifying factor of our nationhood, and then how shall we survive the next two thousand years?

So with Jews putting up with so much inconvenience on a daily basis, it is hardly surprising that they expect non-Jews to be patient and show some understanding of the allowances they need to make. Bear in mind that there is only one Jewish state in the whole world. It's hardly surprising, really, all things considered.

9

TILL DEATH

The earth was a sleeping monster;
sometimes it rose a little and turned itself in
bed. They walked upon its back when living,
they were put into its belly when they died.

Winwood Reade,
The Martyrdom of Man

It is no coincidence that it was a Jewish comedian, Groucho Marx, who declared that he would never agree to become a member of a club that accepted people like himself. Anybody born Jewish according to the Halacha is automatically accepted into the exclusive group with access to the services of the rabbinical courts, not only for matters of matrimony but also for inclusion in the public cemeteries. The franchise for cemeteries is in the hands of associations belonging to the ultra-Orthodox establishment, who are very particular about the family pedigree of the corpses they put in their grounds. In the same way that Israelis may not get married or divorced without religious intervention, they are unable to be put to final rest without a rabbi's permission. (Some exceptions may apply if one is particularly prominent or affluent.)

My maternal grandmother's ultimate wish was that after her death, she should not be put in the hands of the burial society, the *Chevra Kadisha*, or at least that her funeral should involve no religious ceremony. This wish was not respected – not because we, her only relatives, did not try our best to fulfil it, but because we failed.

Throughout her life, Savta Chaya was contemptuous of all religious beliefs of any kind. This was her father's legacy, but also the legacy of the Zionist-Socialist upbringing she received in Bolshevik Odessa, the town she left in 1925 in order to realize her dreams elsewhere.

She arrived in Jaffa port together with Saba Shmuel on board a cargo ship. I have no idea when, or if, they ever bothered to be officially married. I had always known her by her maiden name, Chestnaya. At age twenty-one, she was planning an artistic career in the new Jewish homeland. Her expectations were based on her talent for playing the violin as well as her pretty voice and her eloquence in citing long Russian poems that she knew by heart. Additionally, she was academically qualified as a kindergarten teacher, having graduated in pedagogy in an Odessa Hebrew college.

Young Chaya in Odessa

She was the belle of the school. My Aunt Milka Lutzki was a classmate and remained a bosom pal long after the marriage between her brother Shmuel and my grandmother fell apart. When we were visiting the Lutzkis in Herzlia, Aunt Milla used to examine my face carefully and declare that I bore a resemblance to the young Chaya. "But then Chaya... she was truly *beautiful!*"

Being the class darling in Odessa as well as the beloved youngest child in the family was not a good training for the tough reality of 1920s Tel Aviv. Many good-looking Russian maidens, all well-educated and exceptionally talented, were competing for the very few good jobs. After the birth of her only child, Savta grew ever more bitter with her young husband, Shmuel, who failed as a partner and a provider. She soon became a single mother and supported herself and her daughter with odd cleaning jobs. One of her first employers was an important labour leader who had ginger hair and was known as Rota Rosa. Her husband was also a prominent member of the Zionist labour establishment named Nechemia Rabin, and they had a red-haired young boy named Yitzhak, who was a few years older than my mother. Savta loved to mention her modest contribution to the Rabin household that had produced such a great man. She died two years before Israel's best ever prime minister was murdered by a fanatical religious Jew.

Chaya and Shmuel with my mother Zahara, "73 days old"

She never really got over the fact that with all her beauty, intelligence, education, and musical talent, she was not able to develop any kind of professional career. Not that she was actively pushing for one. Mainly she innocently expected to be "discovered," as in fairy tales or the movies, and was madly jealous of artists and actresses she considered less talented than herself, but who were able to use their elbows on the way up, to swallow their pride, grovel, and ingratiate themselves with cultural bureaucrats on the way to success. When I was a child, she still hovered around the bohemian milieu and got all flustered when some minor actor called her by her name.

Her repertoire included long citations from Pushkin, Tolstoy, Shalom Aleichem (in Yiddish), and Maxim Gorky, as well as Russian folk songs. On the violin she had one virtuoso piece – a cadence by Sarasate. "The truth is," she once confessed to me, "I had been quite certain, all my life, that very soon the prince I had been waiting for would finally arrive and take me back to Odessa, so that I could see my father again."

Happy New Year card "Greetings from Eretz Israel" featuring Zahara, 9 months old

Throughout her troubled life, she was always surrounded by a cast of adoring female friends who were impressed with her penchant for drama and romance. Some of them made her beautiful clothes or took care to get her tickets to concerts and other performances.

Her old party gowns were kept for many years in a grey bag in our home. My friends and I used to put them on and pretend that we were great ladies or film stars. Otherwise, nobody ever wore lace and velvet in the fifties. Because my grandmother looked twenty years younger than her true age, people would tell me off in the street for calling her "granny" as they were sure she was my mother.

At some stage in her life, she found a permanent job as a switchboard operator in Nir, a powerful financial institution of the Jewish Israeli community. Before the state was established, Pinchas Sapir, a future finance minister, and Levi Eshkol, a future prime minister, ran Nir; it dealt mainly with funds that European Jews were moving to Palestine. When she was fifty-four, my grandmother was heartbroken when she was forced to take early retirement and give up her modest position. A few years into her pension, she experienced great happiness when Eshkol, by then a prime minister, arrived with his security guards for an early morning dip in the Mediterranean off Frishman Street beach, in front of the Dan Hotel. Time and again she would recall how he had called her name as he recognized her with a group of friends exercising on the beach, and how he had walked over to speak to her and to ask how she was.

She found a job as a babysitter with the family of young journalist David Lipkin, then a correspondent for *Davar*. Sara Lipkin, God bless her soul, was stunned as Savta came to work carrying her violin and played to the baby girl she was to look after. For years afterward, my grandmother was enchanted each Passover and New Year as the kind Mrs. Lipkin never failed to call and give her the season's greetings. "She always says what a good start I gave her child," she would proudly repeat. It was practically the only thing she could brag about in her dotage.

Holidays were special and very important. Twice a year Savta Chaya would come along with us to Savta Miriam's home in the Yemenite neighbourhood, to celebrate the Seder and Rosh Hashana with my father's extended family. Reading the *Hagada,* sampling the clay-like sweet *charosset*, and above all the set table surrounded by my many cousins, aunts, and uncles would bring her to an ecstasy that I found as exaggerated as it was embarrassing.

"Oh, these sounds of music – the prayers are so well sung!" she would say, daintily praising the monotonous Yemenite traditional humming. "The foods are so colourful; nobody knows these dishes even exist! This family is nothing less than amazing. Israeli television should come to film their annual traditional Seder night here! They go to different families every year, but none is as wonderful as this one! You have no idea!"

Savta Miriam, presiding over her large clan of at least four or five of her seven surviving children with their brood, was a perfect hostess to this particularly strange relative. The two women were about the same age, but they could hardly be more different: the son's endlessly chattering mother-in-law, with a dyed perm and deep low-cut fashionable summer dresses; and the lady of the house, her small body always wrapped in a worn-out housecoat and head traditionally wrapped and covered with a white shawl, gently but firmly running the feast. The fact that Savta Miriam could not read or write only increased our admiration for the fact that her sons never got away with short cuts in the reading of the long texts. She knew it all by heart.

Chaya was particularly pleased with Yemenite food. As a devout vegetarian, she had great faith in the potent medicinal forces of *hilbe, schug*, and other herbal supplements that were responsible – or so some learned doctors decreed – for the low occurrence of heart disease in the Yemenite population.

"You have no idea what a privilege it is to be here; this is one fabulous family," she would nag my aunts and uncles, who were all actually deeply divided by bitter family feuds. More than once I noticed the exchange of amused looks and raised eyebrows, but nobody had ever been unkind to Chaya. Granted, she was somewhat strange, but then every family has its *majnoon* .

In retrospect I understood that my resentment at what had seemed like a display of inverted intellectual snobbery was unjust. The truth is that the embarrassing grovelling was her way of trying to be accepted into what seemed to her like the warm heart of the tribe. For one evening she was dropping her solitary existence to become a part of a large family, longing for this particular feeling of well-being she must have experienced many years earlier, in the role of the most beloved, youngest sister of four siblings she had lost contact with many, many decades before.

* * *

With men she experienced a long list of bitter disappointments. She was attracted to intellectual types, scholars and authors who were always fighting their own cruel wars of survival and had nothing to offer her except their own misery and contempt. No wonder my own parents, who had to take care of all her earthly affairs almost from the day they got married, developed an acute distaste for artistic and intellectual pretences of all kind.

Her last companion and the one who treated her worse than all the others was a Yiddish poet-novelist-journalist with an American background. In the 1920s and '30s, Abraham Blei-Tzipori had been writing for the *Forverts* Yiddish daily in New York. His poems and short stories were well received, and he was considered a promising talent. But Tel Aviv, where Yiddish was considered anachronistic, was unkind to him, and he became a frustrated and bitter man. Some surviving Yiddish connoisseurs, including the important poet Abraham Sutzkever, were pleased with the short story collection *Arabesken* that he published in 1966; but there were no readers for this language any more. Most perished in Europe, the rest bullied by the young Hebrew-only zealots.

It was in the 1940s that Blei-Tzipori had deserted his family for Chaya. His children never forgave him, and he was cut off from his former life, but after about ten years of cohabitation, he had had enough of my grandmother and kicked her out of his Dizengoff Street flat. The distressed Savta landed with us and shared my room for almost a year when I was in second grade. She then managed to purchase a small apartment on Arlozorov Street. Twelve years later, when Blei was well into his seventies, he reappeared in her life and asked her to come back and live with him. Against everybody's advice, she immediately did, and this time it was for good. For the last three years of Blei's life, Savta took the bus twice a day for a ninety-minute trip each way to visit him in the geriatric institution where he was hospitalized, even though he barely recognized her any more.

It was on an evening in 1975 when she told us that he had died. Savta was depressed and worried that only a few people would show up for the funeral. To avoid this, I prepared a short press release titled "Author Abraham Blei-Tzipori has passed away," detailing his literary and journalistic achievements. I asked the night editor of the Yiddish language daily *Letzte Nayes* to publish it, which he kindly did. It was even easier to get the item into the appropriate section of *Ma'ariv*, as fortunately I was the night editor on duty that evening. Yiddish lovers and Palestine Communist Party veterans presented themselves in impressive numbers to pay their last respects.

Blei's death left Savta free of nursing and worrying about him, but ever lonelier in his bed-sitter that was now her home. She inherited half of it, as was her due as his common law wife of many years. My parents purchased the other half for her from Blei's estranged wife and children, who turned up to claim their part of the estate as sole benefactors of his will, in which Savta was not even mentioned. She tried to find some solace in joining the volunteer auxiliary support at Tel Aviv Hadassa Hospital in order to feel useful for the sick people, but soon got into trouble over her sharp complaints each time she heard racist remarks by the other volunteers.

There was, however, a bright spot at this stage of her life, as she embarked on a warm relationship with another lonely woman who lived next door to her tiny flat. The neighbour was a childless widow of Hungarian descent who could not read Hebrew. She missed the company of her deceased husband and was particularly sad on Friday evenings, as she told my grandmother, remembering him reading the Sabbath prayers to her over a festive meal. The widow was a diligent cook who adored feeding other people. It was a match made in heaven. Savta finally found an audience for her considerable talent for reading out loud. Every Friday night her neighbour hosted her to a sumptuous meal of vegetarian foods carefully prepared for her. Before and after the meal, Savta would eloquently read long passages of the Sabbath *siddur*, and sometimes she added some singing.

But as much as she had enjoyed her solos next door, my grandmother started to develop a strong aversion to the boring texts that are an integral part of the Sabbath evening ritual. Her literary criticism grew ever deadlier as she now could say the prayers almost by heart. Every Saturday, as she joined us for lunch in our kitchen, she would angrily report to us on the shockingly low quality of the *siddur* collection that she had read from on the previous evening. As far as she was concerned, the traditional Sabbath verses were overloaded with banalities and idle grovelling.

How can anybody take such a collection of mediocre prayers seriously? she raged. She found most of the service insultingly tedious, and now set herself a new task: to open up the eyes of her widowed neighbour – whom she truly liked – to the nature of religious bigotry.

"I tell her: You call this a prayer? What nonsense! What kind of a great God this is, who would have the believers ingratiate themselves with Him by repeating again and again that He is so great and so good? Does He not know it without being told? Has He no self-confidence? All this idle flattery. One needs to thank Him all the time: We thank You that Thou art our Lord our God and the God of our fathers and all their fathers before them; we should forever thank You and relate Your Glory... Thou art Sacred and your Name is Sacred, and the Pious will praise Your name every day *Amen Sela*, bless You the Lord the Holy Sacred God...You and Thou and You You You..." Savta was quoting from memory, making her voice rich with drama and sneering pathos. "How much of this can one take? I tell her: God must be sick to His stomach with this endless sucking-up, this overbearing nagging. I try to explain to her that this is an insult to the intelligence, all these 'Us You have chosen and Us You have made holier than all other nations.' When you compare it to the perfectly beautiful Bible verses, you wonder what these people had in mind. This mumbo-jumbo spoils everything!"

She really cherished the poetic biblical texts. Once a week, Savta Chaya would join the Workers Union choir at Beit Brenner, and whenever she had the chance she sang to us what they had been rehearsing. I can still hear her soprano, loud and clear well into her seventies, in her favourite Hebrew *lied* based on the book of Jeremiah and the music of Johann Sebastian Bach:

> *O that my head were waters and mine eyes a*
> *fountain of tears*

That I might weep day and night for the slain of the daughter of my people!

For the mountains will I take up a weeping and wailing, and for the habitations of the wilderness a lamentation – for I will turn their mourning into joy, and will comfort them, and make them rejoice from their sorrow.[1]

Savta Chaya died in 1993 at the age of eighty-nine, sick with the confusion of old age and shrivelled with osteoporosis that was made worse, I think, by the strict vegetarian principles she zealously adopted in the 1950s. As she grew older, my grandmother got ever more preoccupied with the increasing impact of religion on everyday life in her surroundings. She loved to start an argument each time she caught a nurse kissing the *mezuzah* in her room at the geriatric hospital, and doctors with a yarmulke were always in for a lecture. As old people go, she returned to the themes of her youth, and never stopped complaining over the bigotry and hypocrisy of religious professionals that she took as a personal insult. With Israeli politics growing ever more religiously inspired, her belligerence increased every time she listened to the news on the radio.

Chaya in her sixties

[1] Jeremiah 9: 1, 10 and 31: 12, King James Version.

"We left the Diaspora to get away from all this, to start from scratch a new land in Palestine," she would say to me. "We worked ourselves practically to death; our life was so miserable you cannot even imagine. Now these people, who came after everything was in its place, have the nerve to praise the Lord for handing the Holy Land to us, His Chosen People? Can you imagine anything more stupid? Has anyone ever heard of a greater Chutzpa?"

She would wander back to her own childhood and her beloved, long-suffering parents. How could she ever forgive the rabbis who had instructed her father's parents to brutally terminate his attempts to develop a musical career, condemning him to years of cooking Turkish Delight?

More than anything else, she passionately hated the effects of old age. "A person is better off unborn," she kept quoting to herself. She deeply detested her own wrinkled, small face and her thin, white hair, with nothing to indicate that this was once a woman in full blossom, and took special pleasure in informing my mother and me that the "horrors of aging" would catch up with us sooner than we expect. For years, in relatively good health, she claimed that she longed for an early death. She declared her life a total failure and was determined to end it in a sulk. All the energies that remained in her frail figure were now focused on the ultimate battle: to take control over the form of the exit she was about to make. She firmly and fervently demanded from us that after her death, we would not allow her into the hands of the pious Orthodox she hated so much.

This subject became an obsession that took all her attention in the hours when she was relatively lucid.

"I will not have them say their moronic nonsense over my dead body!" she would snap at my mother admonishingly, as if there were no other subject for conversation during her only daughter's regular visits at the old people's home.

My mother, who had bravely put up with the whims and escapades of this exhausting parent since early childhood, was more than willing to accommodate her last wish. When it seemed that it would soon be time to pay our last respects, we started checking the options. The fact that around that time Tel Aviv Burial Society was in the middle of a major corruption scandal, where it was alleged that its pious members managed to funnel millions of shekels into their private bank accounts, only increased our ambition to find an alternative, secular burial option.

It turned out that the only available secular burials, on offer by some kibbutzim, were a rare luxury, too expensive for ordinary people who did not have special contacts with the kibbutz or celebrity status. My unrelenting mother even called a radio talk show that specialized in finding solutions to any special problems people might have. She was put on the air and bravely gave her telephone number, hoping that someone would have an idea as to how to make sure her old mother would be put to rest according to her wishes. The only calls she received were from religious women who angrily scolded her.

When Savta Chaya died, her body was handed to the *chevra kadisha*, Jewish burial caretakers, and brought to the Yarkon cemetery. We asked them to drop the traditional Orthodox ceremony and to say no prayers over the grave. We explained that this meant a lot to the deceased and that we were bound by the promise we gave her.

Not surprisingly, they took no notice of the dead woman's last wish or of our own pleading. We were informed that the funeral service would be held according to tradition, and that all the required texts had to be recited as was the Halachic rule. A bitter argument started. It soon transpired that we had a very different understanding of what "respecting the dead" meant. My mother and I were convinced that to respect somebody means to accept their pronounced requests; for us there was no room for ambiguity. The *chevra kadisha* professionals had no doubt that putting a Jewish woman into the ground without saying *kadish* and singing "The Lord is all Mercy" would be such an insult that my grandmother's ghost might try to avenge itself against them, God forbid. Or maybe they worried they would lose their lucrative jobs if word came out that they had failed to perform the necessary rituals.

At the end of an annoying and exhausting exchange, we eventually managed to get them away from grandmother's grave. The three caretakers assembled a few meters away from our little group and piously mumbled their prayers for the wretched soul of the dead old woman. As far as they were concerned, this was the right thing to do. To us, the idea that none of us had any say even in the nature of our own funeral seemed as unjust as it was sad. Thus Savta was defeated even in her very last challenge against religious officialdom. Her thin bones will forever rest in perfect solitude in the enormous dead people's city next to the Yarkon River, yet another exclusive Jews-only zone like the ancient ghettos of Europe, the Israeli settlements in occupied Palestine, the kibbutzim, and the moshavim of socialist Zionism.

* * *

In death, as in life, Jews are supposed to avoid the company of people with uncertain Jewish identity. Non-Jews or unrecognized Jews may not be interred in the public cemeteries. Members of "mixed" families, friends, and partners are being separated after their death even if they had perished together in a terror attack. From time to time, public opinion wakes up with an outcry about these absurdities, and ad hoc arrangements are made to fit a particular need. Eventually, the fences of this macabre ghetto are slowly being eroded. Here and there the rabbinate has allowed special sections for non-Jews next to the general cemeteries. After all, non-Jews are in the habit of dying just like all others, and they should be laid to rest somewhere.

Jewish obsession with dead bodies dictates that the sanctity of Jewish graves is eternal. Thousands of years after a person has been buried somewhere, it is forbidden to build anything over the site. In an age of ever-increasing population, in the state with the highest density of humans per square mile, the short-sighted dogmatism of the Halacha becomes a real practical problem for the nation's *lebensraum*. Our "cities of the dead" mushroom alarmingly, and it is quite clear that in a few decades, there will be no room for more hundreds of thousands of dead people. The latest creative solution is multi-storeyed graves, soon to become high-rises. Or else Israel will need to embark on new wars to secure more territories to occupy.

The rest of the world has already grasped the fact that since humans have a devastating influence on the environment in their lifetime, efforts should at least be made to reduce the damage they cause after death. In most urban cultures, the process of turning dead bodies into ashes is seen as a desirable way of saying goodbye. Ancient cemeteries eventually get ploughed and built on. But when I ventured, years ago, the view that a funeral parlour with a cremating system would be an appropriate solution for most nonreligious Israelis, and could make a very good business for anybody who would care to invest in it, the stares I got from my friends made it clear that they considered my idea totally unrealistic.

"The religious people will never let this happen," secular people told me with a shrug. If truth be told, it is those so-called secular people who are not yet ready to forsake religious instructions in the matter of dealing with the dead. "It is too reminiscent of Auschwitz," many Israelis would tell you with horror. As if the Nazis did not dispose of masses of dead Jews also by burying them in the ground. At long last, in 2005 the first-ever Israeli crematorium was clandestinely started. The location is kept secret, but the enterprise has, nevertheless, been burnt down – appropriately – more than once, presumably by religious zealots.

10

THE BICYCLE REVENGE

On Yom Kippur Berl [Katzenelson] made a pilgrimage to Karl Marx's grave in Highgate. [1]

Anita Shapira,
Berl

Our neighbourhood gang consisted of five or six little girls. We did not go to the same schools but spent most our afternoons and weekends in the quiet streets of our block between Dizengoff Street and Ben Yehuda Street, next to the avenue that was once named after the Jewish National Fund and is now Ben-Gurion Avenue. We played *Klass* and Five Stones in the then-empty plots of Weiss and Ranak streets, and sat around chatting on the wide steps leading to Shalva high school. The other kids were a year or two older, but I was by no means the easiest to bully.

It was therefore quite unusual for me to storm up three floors back home to our flat sobbing loudly, as if my heart was broken. My alarmed parents had a hard time convincing me to come out with the source of my agony. Eventually they coaxed out the terrible secret. The gang had just declared unanimously that our family was not Jewish.

The evidence against us indeed was hard to refute. It was the evening of Yom Kippur, the holiest of all holidays in the Jewish

[1] Berl Katzenelson (1887-1944) is considered the father of the Israeli Labor movement.

calendar. In every flat in the neighbourhood, people were busy getting ready for the last great meal before the fast, dressing up to join the *Kol Nidrei* public prayer. My own father and mother did not take part in this activity. We had no intention of avoiding food for twenty-four hours, and nobody could remember ever spotting my parents attending the packed gathering in the nearby Byron Street synagogue during the sombre holiday season in September of this year, or the last. My peers cruelly counted the facts exposing the family's disgrace, triumphing with the distressing crescendo: "Everybody Knows about You People."

"Everybody" on our street, part of the area that was then known as "The North" of Tel Aviv, was not observant. The only grown-up man wearing a yarmulke regularly was old Mr. Bloomenfeld on the first floor, who actually quite liked us. He was pleased to come up once a year, on *Sukkot* (Tabernacles) holiday, to the traditional palm-roofed hut that my father used to erect on our small veranda for my sake. He climbed the stairs carrying his meal on a tray, in order to enjoy the privilege of dining in a *Sukka* and performing the prayer over the Four Species. Next to his plate, he carried an ornate silver box, perfumed with the traditional citrus fruit, as well as willow, young palm, and myrtle branches. Apart from Mr. Bloomenfeld, nobody refrained from cooking, smoking, or turning the lights on during the Sabbath, let alone using taxis to get about (only the two rich cats of the neighbourhood possessed private cars).

But Yom Kippur – the knowing little girls who I thought were my friends told me – was something else. Maybe not everybody fasts, maybe the ones who start the fast do not keep at it a whole day – but people would sit down to the "End Meal" and then present themselves at the synagogue wearing their best clothes. Only two or three of my friends' fathers actually participated in the prayer inside, wearing prayer shawls. For a proper seat inside, one had to pay an annual fee, which was a pity since most people only attended on Yom Kippur and Rosh Hashana. The rest of the neighbours just stood about enjoying a chat, craning their necks to catch the familiar tones of the *Kol Nidrei* prayer, which absolves us from last year's vows. Later in the evening, and deep into the warm September night, small card playing parties would be forming on the balconies, lit with yellow bulbs. It is hard to go to sleep on an empty stomach, and if you play cards all night and wake up at noon, the suffering needs to be endured only a few more hours.

All my friends' parents were at least ten years older than mine. They were all Eastern European immigrants who spoke Yiddish as their mother tongue. The gathering by the synagogue was a meaningful and important event in their social life. My own parents, who socialized with a completely different circle of friends, openly scorned anybody who spent time playing card games. The ideological ethos they were educated in judged such activity as intellectually degenerate. None of our family's many friends lived on our street, and the idea that I took offence because some neighbours told their daughters that we are not Jewish seemed ridiculous to both my parents. My mother instructed me to ignore the gossiping nonsense spread by little busybodies, wash my face, and calm down.

That was not a great help. To be declared a social outcast is a frightening experience at any age, and I was not even seven years old. There was every reason for a great panic. If my friends were right and my mother was wrong, I was condemned to the life of a pariah. I was no more part of the nation. Fortunately, my father sensed the measure of my distress. He was able to offer the antidote I craved.

"Come on," he said. "There is still time. Let's go and listen to the Kol Nidrei prayer."

For a moment I was stunned to think that he was actually going to walk with me to the local synagogue, but this idea did not even cross his mind. We went downstairs and he unlocked the chain off his rusted bicycle that he kept by the fence next to the entrance to our house. The sun was just about to set, and the streets were empty of cars. No traffic is tolerated on Yom Kippur in any Jewish town in Israel. I was used to the ride sitting on a small cushion on the rack behind my father, and we glided freely along a silent Ben Yehuda Street, turning right and left at Allenby Road into HaKovshim Street, all the way south to Kerem Hateimanim, the Yemenite Vineyard neighbourhood. Savta Miriam was just about to leave her home for the prayer in her regular synagogue, and was very pleased that we had unexpectedly come to join her for the holy evening.

My father picked up from his mother's cupboard the *tallit* prayer shawl that was given to him on his bar mitzvah and went to join his brothers at the main prayer hall. Savta and I climbed up the stairs to the women's section. I was given a prayer book and was able to watch the long service, which I found fascinating. There was no more room for doubt. We were as Jewish as one can possibly be. The other women up on the balcony treated Savta with respect, and all my uncles had allocated front seats in the hall. Furthermore, apparently the modern neon lighting in the synagogue was fixed by no other but my own father, who in those days made a living as an electrician. High above the Holy Ark, the heart of the synagogue, where the Torah parchments are kept, this modest prayer house boasted a large fluorescent Star of David, one of the first of its kind in the city. My father had actually wired the whole ancient building to put in a sophisticated Sabbath clock. This means that he had worked inside the Ark to put in a gadget that smartly turned the light on the parchments as soon as the doors were opened so that the congregation could bring out the holy scrolls. By the time we got on the bike to cycle back home through the darkness, I was free of any doubts concerning my family's national identity.

But there was something almost as dangerous to worry about now. All over the city, barricades had been installed by self-appointed guardians of the Yom Kippur traffic ban. In HaKovshim, Allenby, and Ben Yehuda streets, vigilantes were having a field day with piles of branches and junk that they dragged into the middle of the streets. Bicycles were considered a vehicle in those days, which meant that riding one on Yom Kippur was a serious sacrilege. The righteous youngsters' purpose was to stone anybody who did not comply with the ban.

My father had to use back streets and alleys. Instead of going due north from the Yemenite Vineyard, he meandered eastward. We managed to ride the length of Pinsker street all the way to the Tzina Dizengoff circle, still in its original form of an elegant round piazza with grass and a fountain in the middle. On the other side of the circle, Dizengoff Street was heavily barricaded.

Abba decided to take a chance on the quieter Reiness Street and stopped for a few minutes under the thick fichus trees, where the darkness was complete. There was a barricade in the Reiness and Esther Hamalka junction, but it seemed relatively flimsy, made of several wooden boxes arranged side by side with small spaces between them. "Hold very tight," Abba instructed. The obstacle was created for cars, and it was no problem for a bicycle to shoot through the middle. We shot through it a split second before the boys on both sides of the pavement managed to jump angrily toward us, cursing loudly, some holding up sticks.

Petrified, I held on to my father's hips. One of the boys was getting really close, but Abba was faster. It was all over in seconds; we were far away and safe, with the angry shrieks well behind us. How shaken by the incident my father actually was I could deduce from the way he related the incident to my mother when we eventually arrived home unscathed. An even more dramatic version of our encounter was used to entertain the guests that came to lunch on the next day.

Yom Kippur lunch had been a family tradition in those early years of my parents' marriage. My mother cooked a typically Jewish Eastern European festive meal of fish cakes, soup with dumplings, chicken as main course, and boiled dried fruit soup for desert. My father's younger and unmarried brothers walked all the way from Savta Miriam's home and were joined by some friends who also lived with families that did not serve food on the day of fasting.

This strong childhood memory probably explains my deep attachment to the present Yom Kippur tradition that has since developed in Tel Aviv and elsewhere. In present-day national consensus, the Sabbath of Sabbaths applies to engine-driven vehicles only. As all car traffic comes to a halt toward the time of the Kol Nidrei prayer, the streets become an enormous alternative transport celebration. Thousands of people of all ages move on self-powered wheels – bicycles, roller skates, roller blades, and roller boards. For many, this is the only day of the year that they would get on their bikes. For the rest of the year, cycling in Tel Aviv used to be almost suicidal. Bicycle tracks are a relatively new phenomenon in our city.

Israeli bicycle shops do half their trade during the ten days between Rosh Hashana and Yom Kippur, known as the Days of Awe when God is deliberating whether or not to sentence us to Life or Death in the New Jewish Year. The fasting masses all over the country are eagerly waiting the sunset of the Day of Atonement, signalling the termination of the self-imposed torture of hunger and thirst. Towards darkness – for me it is always too soon – car engines resume noise and pollution in our nonstop city. One has to wait another whole year for the next Green Day.

By the corner of Reiness and Esther Hamalka Streets, I am always reminded of our small victory over the thugs and their blockade. (Maybe some of them grew up to be the builders and planners of separation walls and check points elsewhere. It is agreeable to think that my late dear father and I were the pioneers of the tradition of bicycle riding on Yom Kippur.

11

SHAWLS OF DISCONTENT

Israel is no democracy. It is a religious dictatorship.

Dorrit Moussaieff,
ex-Israeli, wife of Oliver Grimsson, the president of Iceland, in an interview with HA'ARETZ WEEKLY Supplement, January 2, 2004

On my twelfth birthday, my parents invited their friends to mark my bat mitzvah with a dinner and dance to music from a record player in the "Soldier's Centre" in Dizengoff Circle, a smart hall of two floors that has since become a branch of FIBI Bank. Another party – with folk dances and modest barbecue – was organized for my classmates.

Nine years later, when my brother reached thirteen, he did the traditional bar mitzvah Torah reading in Savta Miriam's synagogue, and was greeted with the habitual shower of sweets that the ladies threw at him from the balcony. My fully secular family did not think twice about accepting and ritualizing Orthodoxy's gender discrimination. A bat mitzvah celebration in a synagogue, which includes the young girl addressing the congregation and being symbolically accepted into adulthood, is a rarity in mainstream Israel to this very day.

Forty years after my bat mitzvah celebration, I was invited for the first time ever to make a public Torah reading. The occasion was a bar mitzvah celebration that close friends had arranged for their son with the Reform Congregation of Ramat Hasharon. It was good to be with observing Jews who did not consider it unacceptable for a woman to touch the revered parchments, let alone participate in the reading. Bar mitzvah as well as bat mitzvah celebrations in the few congregations of Progressive Judaism that exist in Israel are heart-warming occasions for a first-timer secular Israeli Jew. Boys and girls as well as their relatives and friends are not forced to pretend that they accept the rigid Halacha lifestyle in order to receive a rabbi's blessing. Families may worship together, as the women – considered by the orthodoxy to be profane and destructive sexual objects that need to be out of sight in their special ward or balcony while listening to the men praying – are accepted as normal, equal human beings in the main hall.

Ramat Hasharon congregation had to use the entrance lobby of a local school, available on weekends, as its prayer hall. Plastic chairs are arranged every Friday and Saturday for the benefit of the worshippers, and then stored during weekdays.

For nearly seven million Jewish Israelis in this densely populated area, there is only a handful of such synagogues. In all the other hundreds of Jewish synagogues in the area (550 in Tel Aviv alone) the Orthodoxy rule on banishing women is taken for granted. Religious girls learn to wave lovingly at the Torah scroll and rejoice in the fact that once a year – during the Torah Festival following *Sukkot* (tabernacles) – they and their mothers may touch and kiss the covers of the holy scrolls.

The enormous system of state-sponsored synagogues, yeshiva schools, day learning centres for adults, and other religious institutions makes a robust infrastructure for the preserving of the patriarchal Orthodox way of living. Tens of thousands of families owe their livelihood to the strong bond of church and state. State jobs for kashrut controllers, slaughterers, *mohels* (circumcisers), day care teachers, yeshiva instructors and supervisors, rabbis, rabbinical advocates and judges are administered by community elders, highly experienced in handling government and local budgets; other jobs are secured for civil servants who administer the system. It is not merely about breadwinning. These institutions also provide a strong base for the men's leisure culture within the community. Yeshivas, synagogues, and *kollels* are areas of daily gatherings providing a social support system for the male congregation as well as a focus for spiritual inspiration.

Israelis, men and women, who do not comply with the Orthodox code of behaviour have no free access to a similar system. The spiritual and religious needs of Jews who are not Orthodox – throughout the world they make the absolute majority of all Jews – are not recognized by the State of Israel. The few who choose to be members of progressive Jewish congregations need to dig into their own pockets in order to pay for religious services. The state, while spending large fortunes on great armies of Orthodox religious employees, is unwilling to finance the salary of a single Reform rabbi, no matter how many followers he or she might have. Inviting a Reform rabbi to perform a wedding ceremony or a bar mitzvah is therefore a relatively expensive luxury, reserved for the comfortable middle classes.

And still, hundreds of families try every year to arrange a bar mitzvah for their children with one of the very few Reform or Conservative congregations. This "alternative" option is extremely popular with nonreligious middle-class families. One must, however, book two or even three years in advance.

While the Orthodox religious establishment is undisturbed by secular Israelis, it is greatly alarmed by the slowly growing popularity of the progressive, women-friendly movements. Their advances are fought tooth and nail.

Conservative and Reform Jews in Europe always belonged to the educated bourgeoisie. They were not attracted to the Zionist movement that drew its followers from the depressed masses in the densely populated poor Orthodox communities. Reform and Conservative Jews and their children did not emigrate to Palestine en masse. It was left to the children of Orthodox Jews, escaping hardships and oppressive environments, to realize the national dream. They carried with them the only version of Judaism that they were familiar with.

The Jewish Reform Movement is a real threat to Jewish self-isolation, so pivotal for the Orthodoxy. Unlike traditional rabbinical Judaism, Progressive Judaism is open to people who were not born Jewish. It easily and naturally accepts converts into Jewish communities all over the world. In the sixties and seventies, the piously converted Elizabeth Taylor and Sammy Davis Jr. were heralded and warmly greeted in the then-young

Israel. In the early 2000s, Israelis are flattered by the passion celebrities like Madonna and Britney Spears have developed for Kabbalah studies. None of these celebrities would have any access to a Jewish community in today's Israel.

The moneyed aristocracy of Jewish Europe never had any problem converting desirable attractive blondes into kosher mothers for their offspring. Reform and Conservative user-friendly conversions regularly inject new blood into the dwindling Jewish communities, making up for those Jews who complete their assimilation into the general population by severing all ties with their synagogue community. No wonder that beyond Israel, Reform and Conservative are the only vibrant Jewish disciplines.

Under the auspices of Israeli legislation, and lavishly financed by taxpayers, Orthodoxy is the only religious game in the Jewish homeland. Its monopoly is well sealed and its administrators perfectly able to veto any attempt to challenge their exclusive control on vital issues like personal status and nationality. Their relentless campaign makes a lot of sense from the point of view of the members of the closed system of *haredi* communities. Why secular Jews with strong national sentiment automatically support religious demands used to be a mystery to me. In later years I have started to realize that quite a few cynically help preserve the Orthodoxy as a useful tool to guarantee racial supremacy.[1]

* * *

The Orthodox establishment has a real – and growing – problem with women. Regulations concerning women's clothes (even three-year-olds' naked arms were declared offensive), women's voices (banned from singing in public), and women's participation in religious political assemblies are a constant source of strife. Attempts to force women to the back of public buses and even to allocate special "men only" pavement space in *haredi* neighbourhoods exasperate even the modern Orthodox. A famous

---

1 "The rabbinate represents an ideology that strives to preserve the genetic profile of the Jewish community and creates serious difficulties for those who want to join its ranks. Such an ideology must be called by its true name: racism." *Ha'aretz editorial*, July 26, 2013.

ongoing case relates to the rage of religious authorities over a group of observant, conservative women who insist on their right to worship publicly in the holy vicinity of the Wailing Wall in Jerusalem. Violent incidents occur each time a small group of Jewish women, clad in prayer shawls, gather there to say their prayers in a very traditional Jewish fashion.

The ladies never attempt to penetrate the "Men Only" praying area and have no interest in doing so. They had repeatedly submitted official requests to be allowed a prayer corner, where they may read the Torah and perform bat mitzvah ceremonies. But the rabbinical gentlemen are so alarmed by the subversive potential of this idea that they forced specific new legislation against it. In the year 2000, the Israeli parliament, the Knesset, spent considerable committee time discussing a proposed new law against women's prayer in the area of the *Kotel*. The proposal quoted a maximum of seven years in prison (!) for any woman who dared to put on a *tallit* and *tefillin*, blow a *Shofar* horn, or read the Torah loudly near the Wailing Wall.

The only reason this bizarre law's supporters did not manage to raise a Knesset majority was that some of the House members were worried about offending American Jews, a prime target for their fundraising efforts. Nobody worried about the reaction of secular Israelis. For them, women with prayer shawls are just a bit crazier than other religious *meshuges*.) (In October 2013, "The Women of the Wall" accepted – "regrettably", as they announced – a compromise that allows them to have their monthly service in a "specially new egalitarian prayer plaza ... subject to a list of conditions"). In early June 2016 Lesley Sachs, a feminist and a board member of Women of the Wall, was arrested by police for carrying a Tora scroll into the allotted prayer area.

A direct line leads from the women's balcony in the synagogues, via the status allocated to women in Jewish traditional public life, all the way to the other manifestations of blatant male chauvinism in everyday life in Israel. Our society has moved a long way from the projected image of gender equality that was cultivated in the early years.

It should be acknowledged that in the very midst of the Orthodox communities, an original version of Israeli feminism has actually started thriving. Women raised and educated in national religious or even in ultra-Orthodox homes are actively engaged in a campaign for internal reform, while officially adhering to the Orthodoxy. Traditional mothers in long skirts, long sleeves, and headscarves find ways to promote progress and more transparency without forsaking the commands of the Jewish Halacha. Some *haredi* women went as far as to assert a demand for the right to officiate in public prayer and take part in the daily running of the community. Some positions in the rabbinical courts that until a few years ago were reserved exclusively to men are now open to well-learned religious women. A few tried in vain to force religious political parties to include women in legislative positions.

However, waiting for these good ladies to achieve the necessary change in their communities and eventually bestow their benevolent influence over the rest of Israeli society means waiting for several generations. Their energies and resources are severely limited. With very large families to care for, material hardships, and little or no community support, the daily survival battles with rabbinical impositions seem a gargantuan task.

Patriarchal and male chauvinistic as it is, Judaism boasts also some regard for the position of (well-behaved) women. The ancient system of laws and regulations accords every wife special rights and secures her status within the family. As long, of course, as she does not try to change or bend the rules.

Discussion of Judaism's attitudes to females cannot be complete without contemplating the very special manner in which the male members are initiated into our religion. Viewed without prejudice, this particular ritual may also tell us quite a lot about the role of women.

Part IV – Cutting Down to Size

In any event, there is much festivity, with music, special foods, and many guests. While the actual event is taking place, one may hear praise of God, partly, as some observers have suggested, to drown out the boy's cries. But the procedure is relatively safe, and those who perform it are usually trained and experienced.

The Circlist, *website dedicated to the subject of circumcision, describing a celebration in Turkey*[1]

[1] http://www.circlist.com/rites/moslem.html

12
THE BLOOD BOND

Once taken away, it's very
difficult to put it back.

BBC World Service report on circumcision, July 31, 2000

My only brother was born a few weeks after the death of Saba Shmuel. Saba's widow, Chenia, as well as some other relatives, naturally assumed that the child would be named after his grandfather. The trouble was, the name Shmuel sounded traditional and old fashioned in late-fifties Tel Aviv. It was all right to give a baby a biblical name, but only if it sounded brave or at least foreign: Avner, Nimrod, Gideon, Jonathan, or Dan. My mother stood her ground under heavy emotional pressure, and protected her son's right to receive a trendy first name. Both my parents took the view that the choice of name should be made with the boy's future comfort in mind rather than the feelings of other people, or even the supposed expectations of the deceased.

A modern, pleasant-sounding Israeli name was chosen for my brother. As a gesture, my parents registered Shmuel as his second name, to be used in official documents only.

This blessed lack of interest in preserving the past at the expense of the new-born's welfare stopped short, however, when it came to the traditional ceremony of initiation to the Jewish faith. The ceremony is called *Brit Mila*, and it includes a public circumcision at the tender age of eight days. Without this removal of the foreskin, no male is considered Jewish. The *brith* is performed as a religious ceremony, by a specialized professional – the *mohel*. A reception and sometimes even entertainment including music and dancing may be offered to the many relatives, friends, and colleagues, who arrive laden with gifts and donations for the young family. Half-embarrassed crude jokes are always in order: "It's his party and everybody is laughing, while the one we are celebrating is crying his head off!"

* * *

There is nothing in the Israeli legal codex that even remotely obliges anybody to circumcise new-born male babies. Yet male circumcision is the one ritual of the Jewish faith that is upheld, with extremely rare exceptions, by every one of the Jewish families living in Israel, including those who are the most fervently, and vocally, antireligious.

My parents were tense and worried during the hectic days before the ceremony, which was to take place at our home. My ears pricked up at agonized deliberations concerning the question: who should be chosen to perform the delicate procedure. It needed to be a competent, very experienced professional. Horror stories about the potential for the procedure to go wrong, resulting in temporary – or even permanent – damage to the vital tiny organ in question were a major concern. The dilemma for the concerned secular parents was this: mohel or a medical surgeon? Mohels, the traditional performers of circumcision in the Jewish as well as the Muslim tradition, have no medical qualifications. They are devout practitioners, and like ritual slaughterers, pass the practice from father to son.

My parents much preferred a qualified medical practitioner, but older family members strongly rooted for a traditional mohel, claiming that experience guaranteed quality of the performance. With up to four baby penises trimmed every day of the week, mostly without a hitch, these people are pretty trustworthy. The physicians, by comparison, with all due respect to their theoretical knowledge of anatomy, are simply not getting enough practice in this area. One would not wish one's baby to be experimented on in this matter.

The most common problem that occurs during circumcision is overbleeding. An experienced mohel uses his own lips to suck the extra blood flow, which might lead to problems of hygiene and the wound going septic. What sealed the subject was information about a misfortune that happened to our relatives, a young and progressive couple. Out of concern over the quality of their son's operation and disgust with the mohel's primitive methods, this couple approached a prestigious paediatric surgeon who performed the circumcision in a first-class hospital. The baby sustained serious damage. One could only hope it would be reversible. The child was in terrible agony, the parents were devastated, and the potential hazard from inexperienced doctors was displayed in the most frightening manner. An old Yemenite mohel was summoned to take care of my baby brother.

There was nothing unusual about my parents' anxiety. People have fainted on these festive occasions, and it is normal for the father not to take an active part. A godfather is chosen to hold the unsuspecting infant. Even the most pious Orthodox Jewish mum, I am sure, feels the pain of her frantically crying baby son while the cut is being made on this highly sensitive piece of flesh of his new body.[2]

Our little apartment on the third floor in Graetz Street was packed on that early spring day of 1958, when my brother's *brith* ceremony took place. The living-room table was loaded with refreshments typical of those days of Spartan modesty – sponge cakes, sweets, and artificial juices. My late Great-Aunt Milla came looking for me out on the balcony, which was a narrow space open to the fresh air in the days before asbestos shutters turned most Tel Aviv balconies into small extra rooms. My girlfriends and I gathered there in excitement, intrigued and somewhat alarmed by the discovery of what new-born boys have to go through. Milla fought her way through to reach me for a big bear hug. "Congratulations, Ofrele!" she roared beaming, planting a great

---

[2] In July 2001 a court ordered Member of Knesset Nissim Zeev to pay NIS 800,000 (about $200,000) to a boy who lost most of his penis due to his malpractice as a mohel. The media sometimes carry reports of babies who suffered serious damage due to contamination they contracted from a mohel, or about dangerous bleedings.

wet kiss on my face. "Now you have a *Jewish* brother!" The new small Jew expressed his protest with a terrible yelling that was cheerfully received by all present.

Zahara and Mousa with daughter Ofra and baby Gilly, 1958.

In the 1950s, the medical profession was still united – or so we were told – in the view that circumcision is a good thing. Jews were not alone in supporting this practice. It is possible that their considerable prominence at the top of the prestigious American medical circles had influenced the verdict on this issue. Many American middle-class parents, and reportedly even the British royal family, chose the Cut. Arguments in favor of the procedure progressed creatively from one generation to the next. In the 19th century it was claimed that removing the foreskin could "cure" young males from the reprehensible habit of masturbation; that foreskins are bad for the health, increasing cases of epilepsy, diarrhoea, tuberculosis, bedwetting, venereal diseases and impotence. Pain from the cut was considered healthy and invigorating. In the 20th century foreskins were blamed for cancer in male genitals as well as for cervical cancer. As soon as AIDS became known, there have been renewed calls for preventive circumcision although the disease did not spare circumcised populations.

Since then, the medical profession has moved on a long way. The school of thought that supported elective surgery to remove healthy body parts that might become a source of trouble had lost out to the current belief that nature should not be interfered with unless there was good reason to do so. Circumcision of babies was only one such elective surgery. In those days, it was quite common to have polyps and tonsils removed even if they were not giving any trouble. Appendixes that showed no infection whatsoever were taken out, as well as the unproblematic wombs of middle-aged women. It was the same logic that suggested a daily enema to ensure regular bowl movement, and turned every birth into a caesarean section. But the decisive change of heart and practice concerning circumcision in non-Jewish medical circles is kept almost as a state secret in Israel. Dr. Penelope Leach has eloquently presented the case against circumcision in *Your Baby and Child* which has become the bible of millions of mothers throughout the world. In the Hebrew translation of the book the chapter on baby genitals has been rewritten. There is no mention of the negative effects of the procedure. Treatment of the wound is discussed instead.

Most Israelis have no idea that the procedure is no longer recommended in healthy infants. Newspapers rarely discuss it, but apparently the number of parents who choose to avoid the procedure is on the rise – from a few dozens in the late 1990's to possibly hundreds in the second decade of the millennium. A very lively forum of "giving up circumcision" is run as part of the popular Tapuz portal (Hebrew), and more information is offered by the Israeli Association Against Damaging Male Babies' Genitals which has a good web presence. The "Brit Shalom" group of US reformist Jews recommend "Brit without Millah" on their website[3].

Israeli born Danae Elon produced a documentary comedy on male circumcision titled *Partly Private* based on her own dilemma as a would-be mother. It premiered in the 2009 Tribeca film festival (winning Best New York Documentary award) and was shown in the documentary channel of Israeli cable TV. Although

---

[3] http://www.circumstitions.com/Jewish.html

she presents all the good reasons to avoid the procedure, Elon eventually succumbs to tradition: both her sons were circumcised. The film met with relatively little attention and generated hundreds of scornful web reactions.

Each time a newspaper carries informative magazine stories about the practice it is immediately bombarded with a storm of scornful letters from procircumcision Israeli doctors and other experts. Readers must conclude that opposition to circumcision is just another issue picked on by dubious extremists – anti-Zionists or fanatic environmentalists, or both.

Uncircumcised males are curious and worried about the idea of circumcision. They seem quite attached to their foreskins and consider them indispensable. They claim, for example, that the tip of the internal part of the penis – the glans – is extremely sensitive and moist. The idea that this part, unprotected by the foreskin, becomes dry and is constantly rubbing against one's clothes seems to them unacceptable and unpleasant. Circumcised males rarely refer to the condition any other way than by making jokes.

In the United States, the anticircumcision lobby is powerful and active. One does not have to be a medical expert to understand why removal of the foreskin is perceived by members of most western societies as having a crippling effect.

Searching the Internet, I soon came across the list below that was compiled from various sources:[4]

The foreskin has some known functions. They are:

- To protect the infant's glans from faeces and ammonia in diapers.
- To protect the glans penis from friction and abrasion throughout life.
- To keep the glans moisturized and soft with emollient oils.
- To lubricate the glans.
- To coat the glans with a waxy protective substance.

---

[4] http://www.cirp.org/pages/anat/. The site provides detailed graphics.

- To provide sufficient skin to cover an erection by unfolding.
- To provide an aid to masturbation and foreplay.
- To serve as an aid to penetration.
- To reduce friction and chafing during intercourse.
- To serve as erogenous tissue because of its rich supply of erogenous receptors.
- To contact and stimulate the G-spot of the female partner.

The first ten items concern the benefits and comforts that the foreskin affords men and boys. Only the last point is a claim that an uncircumcised male can offer more pleasure to his female partner.

Strangely enough, this particular argument of circumcision opponents is supported by none other than the Jewish Talmud. The wise men of Judaism, may they rest in peace, have decreed that women overwhelmingly prefer an uncircumcised penis.

Jewish sources express the opinion that the foreskin allows for better performance. Discussing the story of Dina – the unfortunate sister of the sons of Jacob, who according to the bible, was raped by Shechem, son of Hamor – the wise men indulge in some serious gossip. Apparently the young woman refused to be separated from the perpetrator, and her brothers could not get her back home because "said Rabbi Huna, '(a woman) having copulated with an arel (man with foreskin) finds it difficult to be weaned.'"[5]

If this is not enough, Orthodoxy's most prominent interpreter, Maimonides (the Rambam-Rabbi Moshe Ben Maimon 1135-1204), in his monumental work *Moreh Nevuchim* (Guide for the Perplexed) describes "that organ" that "lacks extra passion compared with need, as circumcision reduces (the) power of erection and occasionally pleasure is missing.[6]. As he looked

---

[5] Bereshit Rabba 80:26. Quoted from the publications of the Daat Emet association, which is run by ex-yeshiva scholars turned secular. www.daatemet.org.il.

[6] Part 3, chapter 49.

down on overindulgence in corporal pleasures, Maimonides used this argument to display the benefits of circumcision. A trained physician (so illustrious that he served for years as the personal doctor of Saladin), Maimonides also confirmed that removing the foreskin occasionally killed an infant.

This supposedly expert opinion on sexuality expressed by the great rabbis merely exposes ignorance in yet another aspect of daily life. Jewish and non-Jewish women have been living happily with circumcised men for generations, producing large families, and there is no real evidence to substantiate a claim that women prefer men with foreskins, or that the circumcised ones lack passion. It sounds plausible, however, that uncircumcised men may find self-gratification easier.

The Israeli Army, incidentally, recognizes circumcision as a minor medical handicap. A fully healthy Israeli male soldier can score a maximum of ninety-seven points on the health scale out of one hundred. All Jewish and Muslim soldiers lose three score points on the standard health chart due to the missing foreskin.

* * *

The baby boys generally recover quickly. The open wound heals. There is no evidence that the life of adult Jewish males, or of those members of the British royal family who were circumcised as infants, develop less happily or less successfully due to the removal of their foreskins. And yet one would have a job arguing that the painful, potentially harmful operation leaves no mark on the tiny infant's tender soul.

Modern infant development studies take early life experiences extremely seriously. Expectant mothers are told that peace of mind, as well as the sense of wellbeing and comfort of new-borns starts at the embryo stage. New humans absorb and register the world around them. They react with alarm, anxiety, and pain long before they emerge from their mother's womb. This view is warmly endorsed by the most traditional of religious people. Jewish, as well as non-Jewish, "right to life" sympathizers would have us resist abortions based on the belief that the foetus is a fully formed human being with feelings and a fragile, sensitive personality.

The "birth trauma" is considered a pivotal phenomenon in paediatrics and child psychology. Some psychiatrists believe that many of their patients are carrying painful long-term mental scars from the early traumatic experience of being suddenly pushed violently and painfully from the perfect environment inside the mother's body into the noisy, blindingly lit, unwelcoming world outside. Parents and professionals consider it important to keep babies secure and comforted, to soothe the impact of this heavy early punishment.

Sadly, the same parents and professionals do not apply this wisdom to new-born Jewish males. Hardly a week after he has learned how to breathe, a Jewish infant has a deliberate injury inflicted on one of the most sensitive areas of his body. A piece of tissue extremely rich with nerves and sensors is removed, in most cases without anaesthetic. Traditionally, Israeli mohels soothe the wounded child by giving him a hanky dipped in wine to suck. Another controversial practice of mohels was exposed in August 2012 when the Israel Ambulatory Pediatric Association called for an end to the "oral suction" technique used by mohels during the circumcision rite, in the light of fears that some cases of neonatal herpes had been caused by the technique. Mohels reacted indignantly.[7]

Esquire magazine published an article in the mid 1980s recommending the merits of circumcision with local anaesthetic. The idea is still a novelty for Jews in Israel and abroad. Mohels have no interest in recommending anaesthetic for the surgery, as this would bring physicians onto their turf. They are actually correct in claiming that narcotic drugs, for local or full anaesthetic, are in any case only a temporary solution. In one or two hours, the pain would return in its full horror, until the wound heals.

Anybody who has taken care of a baby after circumcision knows how difficult the period of convalescence is. The affected area keeps being washed again and again with the acidity of urine and could become contaminated with faeces.

Israelis are attentive to new ideas and fashions, fast to adopt modern trends. The concept that personalities are being moulded

---

[7] http://www.ynetnews.com/articles/0,7340,L-4265887,00.html

so early in human development has influenced our society and other western cultures in the same way. A whole industry geared to improve the quality of life for new-borns and would-be-borns is booming in our big cities and affluent suburbs. The more advanced and educated the expectant mother, the more certain you may be that a prime selection of Brahms and Mozart music will be played to their gradually bulging bellies. They will talk to their growing embryo and sing to it, so that it recognizes mummy's voice from the very beginning. They will attend expensive swimming lessons for the new-born, and will pay for music, dancing, and gymnastics workshops for a four-week-old. Their babies will be sure to hear the ocean humming and the song of whales reverberating in their well-designed nurseries. "Talk to your child," the learned expert books instruct the young mother. "Sing to him and hug him lovingly for as many hours as possible during the day. This is the way to build his (or her) future as a person secure in the love he is always going to receive, a person of emotional stability, positive thinking, and a deep belief that the world is a good place to be in, a place of pleasure and hope."

Well, if babies are such complex, sensitive, and emotional creatures as we are told, if indeed they are receptive to our efforts to make them happy at this early stage of their being, and if they benefit from the positive handling in the years to come – then what exactly is the impact of a sharp razor shearing the tip of their genitals unexpectedly when they are only eight days old? How do they feel about it? What sad memories are carried into the future from the days or even weeks of healing, from the treatment and dressing of the wound, from the soreness that comes with every wet nappy?

In 2001, a very small group of Israelis who started The Israeli Association against Damaging Male Babies' Genitals tried to convince Israel's Supreme Court that circumcision is in fact an act of corporal violence infringing upon a new-born's basic rights. The attempt was scornfully rejected by the learned judges. The media reaction, which consisted mainly of giggles, was in line with the level of public discussion reserved for this delicate subject.

* * *

In countries that are perceived as enlightened, it is no longer assumed that parents have full and exclusive rights over their children's bodies. Female circumcision (also known as female genital mutilation) has long been considered an abomination. Nobody would tolerate today the horrible tradition of tying little girls' feet to keep them small, which was practiced in China until early in the last century. Only the corporal injury to young males is well tolerated. There have been some attempts in Scandinavian countries to ban circumcision in minors. These are the same countries that also try to put an end to the slaughtering of animals without anaesthetic, a requirement of Jewish and Muslim slaughter rituals, so – predictably – one hears claims that the Nordic legislators are anti-Semitic.

Even among the most fervent secular Israelis, one does not find many families who avoid this elective surgery in infants.

We are talking here about people who have for generations been ignoring almost every other tradition of our religion: they pay no attention to the kosher food rules, to Sabbath regulations, or even to fasting on the Day of Atonement. But for some reason, circumcision is considered an integral part of the Israeli secular-Jewish identity.

Normally, most of us secular Israelis are quite comfortable with our secular national identity, and need not spice it with religion. We supposedly share quite a few cultural traditions: a language, a history, memories of school days and army days, the flag, and national sports teams, as well as literature, TV favourites, Israeli music, and lately even a very decent Israeli cinema. Our Jewish identity and national solidarity would have ample cohesive ingredients to keep it going even if we quit interfering with the way nature had created the bodies of male babies. It still surprises me to watch Israelis who react with holy rage each time they spot a Jewish mullah attempting to limit their access to bread on Passover or to pork the year round, but who take their sons and grandsons to the best mohel – now that you can find some that have actually qualified as doctors as well – to give them a proper circumcision.

A young friend told me happily that she was lucky enough to have her firstborn come to the world with no foreskin at all. All you need to do, the mohel in the maternity hospital told her and her husband, is to draw a drop of blood from the child's small organ, for the mitzva's sake. The parents rejected the idea with disgust, unwilling to hurt the boy. However, had he not been born thus, they conceded, their son would have been circumcised.

I bet men's devotion to this particular Jewish tradition would have disappeared very quickly had they been required to practice it as adults. Unfortunately for the Israeli male babies, nobody asks their permission to remove their foreskins.

Asked about the seemingly illogical devotion to this unpleasant habit, secular Israelis have no problem explaining. Foreskins are socially unacceptable in our society, and an uncircumcised boy should expect harassment. "One simply has to go through with it," parents say with sad resignation, as if they were discussing the pulling out of a bad tooth. The very word arel – with foreskin – means thick, brutal, and profane. By general consensus, the temporary ordeal of circumcision is a small price to pay, as the alternative is cruel ridicule at the sandpit for a toddler and the life of an outcast for a teenager.

The only uncircumcised Israeli baby I have personally met was the son of a non-Jewish Dutchmen and an Israeli mother. The father, who would not hear of an elective foreskin removal for his son, announced that he would teach the little boy to avoid exposing himself in front of other boys when he gets older, to save him from playground harassment. This, incidentally, is exactly what Jewish boys did in anti-Semitic Europe for generations. I often wondered if I would have had the courage to take the same decision as our Dutch acquaintance. Fortunately, we were blessed with a baby girl.

13

READY FOR ACTION

Americans fight because they wish to live and enjoy materialistic pleasures. We [Muslims] fight so that we may die for the glory of the Lord.

A Taliban leader,
briefing CNN in Afghanistan,
September 26, 2001

It was a mother of a school friend who enlightened me that there was an aesthetic aspect to the redesign of the penis by circumcision. She shared with me one evening a nasty experience she had endured earlier in the day in the nursery school that she ran at her home. A small son of a foreign diplomat who lived in the area joined her establishment that morning, and she needed to help him go to the toilet, as she did with all the other kids. "And then I noticed it," she confided. "Poor kid – it was disgusting; I nearly threw up."

I did not ponder this revelation at the time. It resurfaced in my mind a few years later, as I came across an adult's foreskin in its original form. Circumstances were friendly, and I was able to take a good look. My first impression was that in the unerect state, an uncircumcised penis seems less exposed – and therefore somewhat less embarrassing in its nakedness – than a circumcised one.

The top of the glans of the uncircumcised penis becomes visible in a state of erection, as the thin foreskin is pulled back. I was amused when an Israeli friend once informed me that in pornographic movies, the male performers are always circumcised, "because it makes it look better." It is an easy mistake to make.

In fact, there is often no clear visible distinction between a circumcised and uncircumcised organ in the erect position.

It is true however that a circumcised penis in the flaccid position retains the form of an erected organ, with the glans sticking out. Perhaps this aspect is reflected in Modern Hebrew. The Modern Hebrew name for a male organ is *zain*, which in old Hebrew means a weapon. This choice of a double meaning denotes a very particular line of thinking concerning intercourse. It might explain why the *zain* must always seem ready for action.

* * *

The archaic origins of most ancient rituals are supposed to contain practical and symbolic social purposes. Maiming and scarring the young of the tribe has been a common practice for a large number of ancient societies.

Compared to scarring youngsters, female circumcision, adult circumcision, or the no-less-despicable old Chinese habit of bandaging girls' feet, infant circumcision as ordered by the Jewish faith may be considered a trifling inconvenience. Its symbolic implications, however, are far reaching.

The *brit* – Covenant – marks the young bodies, branding and bonding them into a group that is characterized by a high degree of cohesion and obedience.

The symbolic meaning of circumcision denotes a symbolized castration. The new-born's manhood is physically reduced to make him part of the national group.

In the Bible, God commanded Abraham to circumcise all the males in his household at the age of eight days (Genesis 17: 19). It is the responsibility of every man to take care of his son's *brit*, to perpetuate Abraham's covenant. The father-son relationship, perhaps the most loaded emotional axis in any man's life, is marked for the children of Israel with this symbolic act of branding their genitalia, indicating ownership and absolute submission of the next generation to the previous one. It is no coincidence that the Jewish people are the most loyal of nations when it comes to our common past, our traditions, and our heritage.

The first circumcised baby son, the righteous Isaac, is commended by the Bible for only one merit: Isaac was the model obedient son to his father, the powerful patriarch. The most dramatic event in Isaac's life was when he was bound up by his own father, at a very tender age, over an altar. Abraham was about to turn his only son into a human sacrifice for his newly discovered God Jehovah.

* * *

An enlightened group of the ancient era, the Hebrews had never even considered the abominable option of female circumcision (for this it would be most appropriate to say, Thank God!) Women are therefore not included in the ritual that "turns one into a Jew," which is not too surprising considering that they are also free from abiding by most of Judaism's practical commands.

Only the sons are inflicted with the painful clipping, yet only women may bequeath Jewish identity to the next generation. A Jewish man may be as pious and as religious as he can possibly be, but his children would not be considered Jewish unless born of a Jewish woman. Every Jewish baby girl, on the other hand, is a potential mother to Jewish children, no matter how irreligiously she would live her life and who should impregnate her.

This one-way-traffic system into the Jewish people also explains the continuous "demographic" issue bothering Israelis, as well as Jews all over the world. Judaism might be described as a typical patriarchal religion, yet the males in this religion are not free to choose foreign partners. Choosing foreign partners becomes especially common in societies on the move, during migration and emigration. Jewish men may not follow this pattern if they wish their children to be part of the national-religious group they were born into.

The Jewish uncompromising position on mixed marriages greatly enhances the position of women in the community and their motivation to cooperate with the core ritual of Jewish initiation.

The very term "Jewish Mother" evokes total devotion to children. So cherished and praised by Jewish literature and popular culture is the Jewish mum, that some of us honestly believe that a mother's love is yet another original Jewish contribution. It is interesting to observe this highly extrovert devotion in the context of the trauma every Jewish mother needs to experience together with her baby boys at the very start of their relations. With an uncompromising efficiency, the *Brit* trauma turns young women into the most important agents of the national-religious preservation mission. Having once cooperated with the group of adult males that brands their baby as a member of their group, a mother is bound to continue and defend the unique identity that her child has acquired with so much pain.

The cutting of the foreskin ("one cut you can never paste!" as the anticircumcision Internet forums constantly repeat) allows another interesting reflection on mothers' relations with their baby sons. Supporters of circumcision point out that the minute surgical procedure allows for a more hygienic environment of the genitals. In the uncircumcised penis, excess excreted bodily fluids accumulating under the folds of the foreskin may become a hygiene problem and a health hazard. Circumcision's most important advantage, which once made the procedure appealing to the medical professionals, is its guarantee of cleanliness.

Mothers of uncircumcised children have to be meticulous about teaching them to clean this part of their bodies, by pulling the foreskin back during a bath or in the shower. Once the child is old enough to look after himself, he should be taught to take care of this part of his body, in the same way that he would be responsible for brushing his teeth and cleaning his ears. According to Dr. Penelope Leach, during the very first years of the baby's life, the foreskin is tight and separation happens only when the child is four or five years old. (Dr. Leach also makes clear that circumcision becomes sometimes medically necessary because of attempts to retract the foreskin forcibly before it was ready to retract of its own accord.)

Mothers of circumcised babies are exempt from the need to occupy themselves with their boys' genitalia as soon as the scar from the surgery heals. This excess intimacy is therefore avoided, while the boys are deprived of the easiest method of masturbation. Chopping off the foreskin is, in this context, another ritual of cleanliness and sterilization in a religion that must be the world champion for ritualizing hygiene.

* * *

The most powerful argument in favour of continuing the circumcision of Jewish males – when it comes to secular Israelis – is the emotional plea for solidarity, based on the horrors of the Holocaust.

The Nazis exploited the religious surgical customs to identify Jews who tried to escape their murder machine. The painful collective memory of these atrocities urges us to uphold the ancient custom. As we bring new-born babies into the covenant, we vindicate our national mark of self-determination. Even the most secularly inclined Jews cannot bring themselves to break up with the symbolic cut that sets our nation apart. Circumcision was a tragic vulnerability for thousands of innocent men and boys. Instinctively our emotions tell us that rather than abandon it, we should embrace circumcision as part of our new identity as a free people defiantly holding on to our symbols against all adversaries.

This line of thinking has only one flaw. We are presently in the Middle East, the region where our old traditions started in the first place. Back in the land where our national history had begun, forcing men to drop their pants cannot tell much about their religion. In this vast area, hundreds of millions of people – some of them our sworn enemies – circumcise their young boys (and sometimes, alas, their young girls as well).

Muslims continue to perform the painful surgery on their young males with the same relish as Jews. Like the Jews, they celebrate circumcision in large gatherings full of music and nice foods. The difference is that Muslim boys, unlike the Jewish babies, are supposed to be conscious participants in the ritual. It is traditionally performed when they reach puberty, and can fully appreciate what they are going through in this particular initiation test.

How this painful minor surgery affects Muslim young men one can only imagine. "The case against male circumcision" applies to Muslims as it does to Jews, with the added twist that sensitive young boys must surely be terrified before the act and traumatized after it in a way that is spared their Jewish counterparts who go through it a week after they are born. Israeli Muslim Arabs, incidentally, have overall adopted the Jewish method, and parents circumcise very young babies rather than boys.

Does the experience affect a sense of collective male solidarity for young Muslim males? Does it alter their outlook on violence, self-sacrifice, and the macho acceptance of great pains? Speculation might run wild in all directions. The cut the boys have to endure at this fragile state of their development surely touches on their natural exuberance and increases any tendency toward a violent nature. It is an exercise in tolerance of pain and aggression. It might even partly explain what seems like strained relations between men and women in Muslim society, or why it is harder for women in these environments to successfully achieve the equality they deserve.

One thing is certain: the covenant God started with the children of Abraham has not served to help Muslims and Jews realize how much they have in common, or to teach them how to live happily ever after on the same piece of land.

It only managed to guarantee, for many generations, the circumcised people's disposition for submissiveness and resignation – unconditional acceptance of fathers' superiority over their sons, grandfathers over grandsons, history over the future. It facilitated a depressing intellectual fixture that can be observed in the Middle Eastern religions. The ritual of circumcision does help to explain the passive acquiescence both Jews and Muslims display when it comes to putting up with oppressive authoritative hierarchies that manipulate them into acting against their own interests.

With all due respect to the spirituality, the morality, and the sublime inspiration that both Judaism and Islam bestow on the good believers, it is not too much to ask that both denominations find a new bonding method for their flock and stop maiming private parts for ritual reasons. If we must absolutely have a symbol of the national club displayed visually on our bodies, any exclusive magnetic card, silicon chip transplanted under our skin or fraternity ring would do the job. It is, after all, the twenty-first century.

In both societies, it is up to women to open this subject for discussion. They are the ones who have no reason to feel emotionally stressed and frustrated by the mere mention of the subject.

Part V – Brethren

Now, Brethren, as you are about to go Eastward now, you should always remember, that Eastern People you have been from your very beginnings; that while the whole of the West is preparing to go Eastward to inherit the legacy of the Dead, you must go there in order to bring the Dead back to life, and to start the building of the new society. Judaism's greatest foe had always been the West. Therefore I consider it unnatural that the Hebrew People, being an Eastern People, should draw lots over the East together with the people of the West. I do believe that the Hebrew nation will live and stand up on its own feet; I do believe that this great People, a People so great that one could not picture what the state of the world would be without this People's books and its great spirit, this People will once again be granting life to a society; But this society must be a society of the East. The great Orient should come out of its slumber and start to live a proper life, by that time the People should be leading the nations, heading the revitalized East...Therefore, Brethren, as you travel to the East, do not travel as the enemies of the Orient, but as its lovers and devoted children. Do get stronger in order to resurrect it, not to end its life [...] a new, lively generation must please rise, to walk in front of the People [...] If indeed the Nation of Israel has a mission, let it pack its bible and its scrolls and carry them into the Orient with it [...] Not just to the "Land of Israel" but to the Orient as a whole [...] It is then that my People should know that it is walking on a well-paved and natural road. Do not let this generation arrogantly pretend that it may complete this task in haste. Do inscribe on your flag, Brethren, "I shall see him, but not now; I shall behold him, but not nigh." To the East! Go Eastward!

The speech of "Mad Nachman" in *Le'an*
by **M.Z. Fierberg**, 1875

14

HOW THE STATE WAS STOLEN

The section of society which gets the most out of it maintains in itself, and for as long as it can in others, an illusion of security, permanence, order.

Doris Lessing,
The Memoirs of a Survivor[1]

People used to raise their eyebrows, expressing surprise and disbelief, when they heard that I was on my way to spend the weekend with my parents in Ashdod. "You are not *Ashdodian,* Ofra, surely?" they would ask in alarm, making it sound as if it had just transpired that I was related to Charles Manson. I had to explain that as my parents had moved to Ashdod after my graduation from Tel Aviv University I did not actually grow up in the southern coastal town that in those days did not produce many yuppies.

Ashdod was synonymous with troubles and riots. In the housing estates built on the dunes around the new deep-water port, large families of poor immigrants, mostly from North Africa, lived in tiny flats that had more children than beds. The misery bred fury, some delinquency, then some more fury.

In the late nineteen-sixties, a local charismatic leader emerged in the city. Yehoshua Peretz dared to challenge the authority of the almighty Histadrut National Workers Union over labour relations in the recently completed modern port. He was born

[1] Octagon Press, 1974.

in Morocco, but his children grew up in Ashdod – with two mothers, who (more outrage) accepted each other, each in her separate abode. It was Peretz's idea that the labourers who had been employed building the port should now be hired as tenured port workers. This was against the National Union's ruling, but under Peretz's leadership, the port was paralyzed by a series of strikes that blocked half of Israel's exports and imports for many months. Eventually the Labour government and the Labor Unions granted most of the demands of the Ashdod labourers, as they were powerless against the solid support for the local leader throughout the town. The words "Ashdod" and "Yehoshua Peretz" represented a nightmare coming true for established Israel, so fully identified with the Labor Party and its social politics. The bold, bearded leader and his shop stewards were people who spoke basic Hebrew with a heavy Moroccan accent and who preserved North African modes and manners. They took the liberty of making demands that were centred on their own private welfare, while rejecting all calls to consider collective responsibility. The state – that is, the media, the politicians, and anybody who did not live in Ashdod – was appalled with this selfish act of sabotage, unanimously condemned.

My parents were therefore not too keen when, in 1968, they received an offer to move into this infamous place. It was, however, hard to refuse the package of benefits that my father, then an electronics technician in an important defence company, was offered as a reward for the relocation. The Israeli government of the day wisely assumed that moving sophisticated workplaces to development towns was the best way of improving the social and economic fabric. Professional people who agreed to take themselves and their families to Ashdod received housing grants and mortgage loans. For our family, who for years had been living in a rented Tel Aviv flat (although with protected tenancy, as was common in those days), this was a unique opportunity to become homeowners.

The housing site we came to inspect was emerging on top of a white sand hill overlooking a beautifully clean beach with very clear water. A private constructor offered high standard flats, four in every block, with cute balconies and little gardens. It was a real estate deal from heaven. In the years to come, and to this very day, such housing finance packages are offered only to families who agree to move into the occupied territories of the West Bank (and previously also the Gaza Strip).

Unlike Herzliya, reserving its beaches for the rich and mighty, or Tel Aviv, which sealed the seafront with a wall of large hotels, Ashdod was well planned as a coastal city and grew to become a vibrant Mediterranean urban centre. The characteristics of the North African Levant, a mixture of French and Arab tastes, made it into a very pleasant living environment.

My parents had lived in Ashdod for more than twenty years. Each time I came to spend time with them, the place felt like a private resort. Twice, at the end of the 1970s, I took a long vacation from work and moved in with them and my Hermes Baby Typewriter for a few weeks to complete the editing of two books by Gerald Durrell that I had been translating for a large publishing house. The small room my parents kept for me was the perfect location to concentrate on the eccentric sun-loving family so beautifully featured in *My Family and Other Animals* as well as in *Birds, Beasts and Relatives*. My own Ashdod could be described as a local version of Durrell's Corfu: "Through the branches of our own lemon tree next to my window the glitter of the vast blue sea was beckoning. I would drop work for long swims in the easy warm September waves, and occasionally friends would join me for lazy picnics on the empty, freshly washed sand beach."

Having later visited the busy commercialized Corfu, I remained convinced that Ashdod's beach was even superior to it in some respects.

In 1980 I married and moved abroad. On a home visit, I was sorry to discover that the sea view from my old room had been lost. Down the hill from us a single three-story home had been built in defiance of local planning regulations. Its shades of dark yellowish green stood in unpleasant contrast to all the other white houses on the street, none with more than two stories, each housing four families. The new house was clearly a private villa.

My parents shrugged their shoulders. It belonged; they explained, to a relative of the minister of the interior, Mr. Aharon Abuchatzeira, the rising star of the National Religious Party. The young minister himself and his family had often been observed arriving in this house with the chauffeur-driven limo. Rumour had it that the relative was only a straw man and the minister was the true owner. Abuchatzeira, a direct descendent of a holy Moroccan rabbi who was believed to have supernatural powers, seemed to share our own appreciation of this pretty spot above the Mediterranean Sea.

The "Abuchatzeira House" became a famous Ashdod landmark. I have never met the honourable ex-minister, nor changed my negative feelings about his yellowish-green home. But during the early eighties, I found myself more than once raising my voice, red-faced with anger, arguing in his defence. The heated debates concentrated on the "Abuchatzeira Affair" that in those days was at its peak. It was also a turning point in the road Israel took towards ever more hard-core religious nationalism.

* * *

Israel had seen state corruption scandals before and after the Abuchatzeira Affair. Still, this case of an Israeli minister who was indicted and found guilty for misusing public funds was a unique precedent.

From its very beginning, the centralized nature of the Israeli economy had made it convenient for officials interested in lining their own pockets. Socialist Israel would ritually go through a collective shock wave over each new revelation of public servants' greed, but had actually developed a remarkable tolerance toward this human fallibility. It was the late Prime Minister Levi Eshkol who coined the incredible saying "Thou shalt not muzzle an ox while it is threshing,"[2] a piece of Jewish wisdom that was traditionally used to block attempts to punish corrupt community elders.

In the seventies, corruption and embezzlement were exposed in the national theatre Habima, in the government controlled company for oil shipments, and in the Labour Health Care organization, whose mighty CEO, Asher Yadlin, was on the point of becoming governor of the Bank of Israel before the "Yadlin Affair" sent him to prison for several years. Leaks from a police

---

[2] Deuteronomy 25: 4.

investigation of serious irregularities in the Housing Ministry that pointed to the minister Abraham Offer as chief culprit pushed that minister to suicide.

One sector of society remained completely immune to the unpleasant digging of internal as well as external comptrollers, and suffered no whistleblowing from frustrated officials. The money allocations for religious institutions remained for many years a realm that by definition could not be monitored. Who deserves to receive state funds that were budgeted for heaven's sake; what are these funds supposed to be achieving; and where does all the money actually go? Most Israeli politicians and their appointed civil servants were not too keen to find out.

Financial autonomy of religious institutions makes a lot of sense. For hundreds of years, Jews have been paying and contributing to their communities in order to keep rabbis, cantors, teachers, tutors, slaughterers, kosher comptrollers, bath keepers, and many other officials and community administrators.

Religious community elders need to be accountable only to themselves and the Almighty. This is what they did for two thousand years in the Diaspora. After all, if one did not like the way the community was run, the way out was easy enough, the alternative being starting one's own study hall across the street. But when the State of Israel, having declared the end of the Diaspora, took it upon itself to be responsible for the financing of religious services in the country, something very fundamental changed.

At a certain point two thousand years of communal responsibility ended as the rabbis and the religious administrators turned into civil servants.

From a religious point of view, having the state apparatus involved in the way God's worship is being conducted was and is unacceptable. The hard core of the *haredi* community still adheres to this purist ideological position, and enjoys the admiration of other ultra-Orthodox. Not surprisingly, the hard core is made up of only a handful of households.

The delicate task of creating a synergy between Zionism and the Jewish religion was taken on by the National Religious Party. NRP and its follow-up incarnations had always had the most compatible ideology for the State of Israel: both national and religious, with no hypocritical socialist-liberal camouflage. This conceptual achievement was coupled with efficiency in devising creative methods of allocating money to yeshiva schools, daycare centres for the next generation, other religious institutions, and endless functions for religious services. An unspoken understanding prevailed between all Israeli governments and the religious establishment: funds earmarked for religious purposes were not interfered with by any nonreligious authority. As the years went by, the ultra-Orthodox relaxed and agreed to climb on this gravy train, accepting handsome sponsoring for their institutions as well.

The potential for personal and institutional gratifications via job creation and project sponsoring was almost endless.

In 1980, following several corruption scandals involving high officials of the labour movement, the police could no longer ignore the pious sector. Stories started leaking about an enormous corruption case investigation that involved, among others, NRP's powerful leader and Minister of the Interior Dr. Yosef Burg. However, to nobody's surprise the "Peach File," as the delicate investigation was coded, had been quietly archived, following uncompromising government pressure on the police as well as on the public attorney's office. The seedy tangle of religion, politics, and money was far too loaded for anybody to wish it out in the open. Toward the end of the year, the police chief inspector, Herzl Shafir had to resign. Hardly surprising, as the chief suspect Dr. Burg was in charge of the police in his capacity as minister of the interior.

At the time this affair was making headlines, the NRP was in the middle of a painful crisis. Its veteran voters, the modern religious Ashkenazi, were getting older and dying out. Their children had partly lost interest in religion; others radicalized and became ultra-Orthodox or super-nationalist, spearheading the settlement movement.

Fortunately for the dwindling party, a new source for a fresh young blood transfusion was now available. Many emigrants from Arab countries and their Israeli-born children started turning their backs on the Labor party, the ruling political force that successfully secured their allegiance during their first years in their new homeland. Almost all of them came from traditional Jewish homes, and they felt comfortable in the company of other yarmulke wearers. For many of them, the NRP seemed a natural political home, with a message that struck a chord in their hearts. In the large Moroccan Jewish community, the young and talented Aaron Abuchatzeira stood out as a perfect and natural leader. A descendent of an illustrious rabbinic dynasty, Abuchatzeira proved a powerful magnet for voters during the 1977 elections, with the result that the NRP doubled its share of Knesset seats. His reward was the ministry of religious affairs in charge of the sophisticated system of money-pumping for the party's sympathizers and their institutions.

Aaron Abuchatzeira and his close circle had every reason in the world at that time to consider themselves the upcoming generation of the National Religious Party. The challenge to the dominance of the veteran NRP's apparatchiks was as assertive as it was blunt. The rising political star was determined to make his mark on the important ministry that he now headed. To his rival's amazement, he wasted no time and started a series of political appointments to key positions. The new civil servants were almost all of Moroccan origin, at the expense of some veteran faithful members of Eastern European extraction.

This was one move too far, too soon. The NRP Ashkenazi elite realized that only the heaviest artillery might put an end to the pretence of the cheeky young North African. Israeli police had mysteriously received incriminating information that meant they had to start an investigation into several financial deals that had benefitted the minister's household. The allegation was that a bribery offence had been committed.

Out of the blue, the whole of Israel's establishment was suddenly engaged in a large and righteous anticorruption campaign. Clear evidence that at least part of the allegations against Abuchatzeira had been fabricated did not disturb the indignant or their moral high ground.

On the receiving end, Israel's Moroccan Jewry, together with the whole of the group of Middle Eastern Jews in the country, were thunderstruck at the total revolution that seemed to have suddenly altered the whole of the organs of law enforcement. Israel's police, whose chief was on his way home because he had tried to poke into this forbidden taboo area of religion and state funds – were suddenly raising the flag for an all-out war on a new type of religious politician who was trying nothing more than exercising the well-established norms in favour of himself and his close circle of supporters.

Abuchatzeira's many supporters believed his case should have been set aside as a case of minor negligence. After all, only a few months earlier the multimillion Shekel Peach File against the party elders was resolutely sealed and archived. The young minister's confidantes, followed by all Moroccan Jews, screamed blue murder at what they perceived as foul play and demanded an immediate end to the proceedings against Abuchatzeira – who in the meantime had been promoted to the ministry of the interior. They probably had a point. Journalist Dan Margalit, then a senior correspondent in the newspaper *Ha'aretz*, described some disturbing dishonest methods the police used in what he called the "State Attorney and the government's" obsession with achieving a conviction in his book *I Have Seen Them All.*

State Attorney Yitzhak Zamir and the government seemed to be obsessed with achieving a conviction (of Abuchatzeira). It was quite obvious. For the first ever time in its history, the police had leaked false information, that alleged that six witnesses were already cooperating with the prosecution and would incriminate the minister in court. This was the culmination of the attempts to get Abuchatzeira, and as confirmed by Chief of Police Herzl Shafir, the (deliberate) mistake did not originate just with the police spokesperson's office but with senior investigators. The lie of the six witnesses was exposed almost immediately. [3]

* * *

But the vociferous Middle Eastern anger provoked genuine panic in the Ashkenazi flock. The Israeli veteran population, of Eastern European origin, got into a trance of holy fury. The Jewish Israeli ethnic schism, as well as the mutual disgust and mistrust of immigrants and their children based on their countries of origin, had never been so openly displayed and advocated.

---

[3] Published (Hebrew) by Zmora-Bitan, 1995. Author's translation.

In May 1981 Abuchatzeira was found not guilty in the bribery trial. due to lack of evidence. As was to be expected, a major celebration erupted spontaneously for all Moroccan Jews in Israel. The Ashkenazi establishment, however, was stunningly quick to preempt any idea that the North Africans would now be free to come back and exercise their new potential in the political arena. On the very day of Abuchatzeira's acquittal, State Attorney Zamir presented a new indictment against the minister. As Dan Margalit described it:

Even Prime Minister Menachem Begin, who was ever so careful not to interfere with juristic authority, could not hold himself from scolding Zamir. How could they not have let Abuchatzeira taste a single day of bliss, one outstanding night of unhaunted sleep? It was then, in 1981, that I lost my own innocence. Never again was I convinced that the prosecution system operates objectively, free of self-interest and personal scoring considerations; never again did I consider state justice as independent of petty vindictiveness.

Just like the senior journalist, tens and maybe hundreds of thousands of Israeli Jews of non-Ashkenazi origin had gone through the process of losing their political innocence. The sudden urgency with which the police, the public prosecution, and the media enlisted for the destruction of Abuchatzeira seemed to have too much to do with the fact that all senior echelons in all three venerable bodies shared an ethnic origin.

The suspicions against the ruling establishment were aired loud and clear, but all it achieved was an even greater Ashkenazi rage. Eastern European mythology now mushroomed, following an incredible logic. Journalists and commentators, fed daily by policemen, prosecutors, and politicians, eyeballs rolling, vowed it was now vital to "clean the stables" in one big sweep.

Alarm bells were ringing in full force: Israeli democracy and sovereignty was at stake! With deep self-conviction, it was claimed that if the Israeli justice system were to overlook the fact that Aaron Abuchatzeira had treated his home in Ramla to an extra wall and a large shutter, courtesy of the Israeli tax payer, our model democracy would metamorphose overnight into a populist dictatorship, based on the demographic superiority of Jews of

Arab origins (who scandalously had a higher birth rate than their Eastern European secular brothers).

The danger was, so the pundits instructed, in the so-called Oriental Mentality. *Mizrahi* Jews,[4] after all, came from Arab countries and carried the bugs of Arab underdeveloped cultures. The legacy that they carried with them could easily turn into a death blow to the only democracy in the Middle East and its European Standards.

Nobody took any notice, of course, of the fact that it was this very democracy that bred the group of youngsters surrounding Aaron Abuchatzeira. They all landed in this country as young children. Their political mentors and role models were all established members of Israel's ruling elites.

Never mind that "European Standards" never hindered the generous and uncontrolled sponsoring of institutions headed by the "European-Born" leaders of the NRP and the Agudat Israel religious political associations. Never mind the shady, dubious deals that so characterized the Ashkenazi religious sector. That the so-called dangerous mentality was in fact a mentality imported from the small towns of Poland and Lithuania, a recognized code of religious operators the world over. This one Moroccan who was caught with his hand in the small cash till had to be sanctioned and politically eliminated.

Nothing annoyed Mizrahi Israelis more than the learned analysis that interpreted Abuchatzeira's delinquency as an expression of inferior ethnic origins. Columnist Yoel Marcus's version of compassion for the ethnic gap typically represented the sanctimonious tone of the leading liberal influential daily, *Ha'aretz*:

> *We see before us a dangerous mix of a justified bitterness over the discrimination against Mizrahi immigrants in Israeli society (that may be overturned), together with an irrational inferiority complex related to the past and the history (which may not be altered). The fact that there are Jews who came to this country*

---

[4] *Mizrahi* = Eastern, meaning originating in Arab-speaking countries. These of course include Jews from the Maghreb (western) countries in North Africa.

> *equipped with a thousand years of western civilization is not the fault of Jews who came from primitive countries with no civilization whatsoever.*[5]

Aaron Abuchatzeira disappeared from the Israeli political landscape after being convicted, on April 19th, 1982, of the felony of paying with public funds for the conversion of the balcony of his home in Ramla. The magical reputation that his family enjoyed due to his illustrious grandfather, the holy Rabbi Abuchatzeira from Morocco, was not wasted, however. Aaron's cousin Baruch Abuchatzeira plucked it for himself very soon. After a short spell as a small-time delinquent, having served some time in Israeli jails, Baruch Abuchatzeira had reinvented himself as a miracle-performing rabbi, well known throughout the land as the *Baba Sali* of the town of Netivot and enjoying a national reputation that made him a considerable fortune along with some very significant political influence.

* * *

Eighteen years after Aaron Abuchatzeira meekly served his sentence for the Abuchatzeira Affair, Israeli society was again shaken and shattered as hundreds of thousands of fans followed another young and talented Moroccan-born politician who was sent to serve time in Ramla prison. The specially written anthem "He Is Innocent" had reverberated throughout the land. Rabbi Aryeh Deri, a true whiz kid of Israeli politics, seemed to have justly earned his three years "inside." The arrogance he had shown for years, refusing to cooperate with police investigators; his battery of high-class lawyers; and the hordes of sophisticated politicians, left and right, who had never tired of expressing their full companionship and support had proved that within less than one generation, North African Jewry and its leaders became an almost integral part of the Israeli establishment. (In fact, in 2015, thirteen years after he completed a three-year prison sentence, shortened to two, Arieh Deri again became a member of the Israeli

---

[5] "Ethnic Degeneration" by Yoel Marcus, April 23, 1982. Author's translation.

Government as Minister of the Interior, followed soon after in 2016 by new corruption allegations, still on-going as this book went to print.)

The lessons of Abuchatzeira's failed adventure were well studied and thoroughly absorbed. The Shas movement, the Sephardic Association of Tora Observants, a product of Deri's political genius with the staunch support of the great Rabbi Ovadia Yosef, was the most perfect natural creation of the Jewish state's melting pot.

Unlike Abuchatzeira and other Sephardi community leaders before and after him, Deri did not fall for ethnic politics per se. Shas was indeed built over a homogeneous social and cultural basis, but its ideology is first and foremost Jewish ultra-Orthodox. The movement was originally launched on its glorious political road by none other than the greatest and most venerable Ashkenazi rabbi, the illustrious late Rabbi Eliezer Shach, who for many years was the uncontested leader of all the Lithuanian (non-Hassidic) Israeli *haredim*.

Modern secular Israel is constantly puzzled by the seemingly incomprehensible *haredi* reincarnation of so many Mizrahi Jews. They seem to copycat the Lithuanian-Ashkenazi model that to this very day adheres to keeping a distance from Sephardi Jews. Indeed, the apparition of Yemenites, Iraqis, and Moroccans clad in the ancient traditional Polish attire is weird to the extreme. Still, this weirdness, observed from a distance, is but a minor logical contradiction, a sample only of the maze of illogical patterns that most Israelis seem to live by.

Just like the NRP that mothered it, Shas is the Real Thing if Israeli politics is being discussed. These two religious political movements are the only ones with a clear vision of what a Jewish state should be: Jewish, for them, means according to the Jewish religion. Champions of Israeli so-called secular democracy ritually get shocked and appalled whenever Shas (and the other religious right-wing parties) act according to their Jewish interpretation of subjects like citizenship and human rights, introducing blatant racist conceptions. These "shocks" are based on total self-denial, so well imbued that the righteous rage seems almost genuine. But surely, the morally flawed state apparatus that officially and positively discriminates against citizens on the basis of their ethnic-religious origins was not devised by ultra-Orthodox Jews or even by the national religious – and certainly not by the children of immigrants from Arab countries. The image and essence of the Jewish state was programmed and produced by the secular, Ashkenazi, immigrants from Eastern Europe. The aggressive ultra-Orthodox metamorphosis of Mizrahi Jews may be contemplated as a rather comical punishment, a kind of poetic justice, inflicted on the veteran, Ashkenazi, secular Israeli elite; it is the privileged section of the population that often sums up its depressed mood over the country's political deterioration with the melancholic phrase "The State has been stolen from us!"

In other words, the ruling elite of the past is waking up to discover that its presumed secular identity is seriously challenged. It now conceives of itself as an elitist minority.

Sociologist Baruch Kimmerling nicknamed the veteran Israeli elite *Ahusals* (for "Ashkenazi Secular Socialists") and dedicated a book to the twilight time of their hegemony.[6] Personally I had always wondered how it is that the *Ahusals* never seemed to come to terms with the fact that their own roots in the Ashkenazi ultra-Orthodox segment of Judaism supplied the breeding ground for the unsophisticated Israeli nationalism they profess to so strongly detest. How it is that they are so sensitive to the obvious similarity between Jewish Mizrahi-*haredi* fundamentalism and Arab-Muslim fundamentalism, while they remain oblivious to the stubborn, entrenched aversion to non-Jews of the Ashkenazi-ultra-Orthodox population, and the way this aversion still affects the secular descendants of this segment – namely, themselves?

Jews of Arab origins in Israel eventually found their own version of the orthodoxy. The antiliberal forces of religious culture are accentuated by their everlasting aversion to what they conceive as the hypocritical attitudes of the established Israeli Left that so openly despises them.

With third and fourth generations of immigrant society, and many "mixed marriages," surely the cultural gaps between

---

[6] Baruch Kimmerling, *The End of Ashkenazi Hegemony* (Keter Publishers, 2001 [Hebrew]).

Israeli Jews of Middle Eastern and Eastern European origin are disappearing. Sometimes it is easy to assume that the whole ethnic subject is becoming passé. But occasionally the Ethnic Demons make a comeback, releasing heavy loads of passions and resentment over past and present, real and imagined wrongs. Israelis never stopped referring to themselves as "blacks" and "whites." In fact, our picture is made of different colours altogether.

15

WHAT COLOUR ARE JEWS?

But they always call themselves white men,
however black their skins may seem to be.

Winwood Reade,
The Martyrdom of Man

The mother of one of my friends – we were both about six at the time – was questioning me about my family. First the inquiry concentrated about what my parents did for a living.

Dad is a radio electrician, mummy is a teacher, I answered dutifully.

Then she wanted to know where they came from.

I answered proudly that my parents did not come from anywhere. They were born in Tel Aviv.

In the mid-1950s Israeli-born parents were uncommon for Tel Aviv children. Most of us in the comfortable residential area between the sea and the Zoo (near today's Rabin Square) were *sabra* – a nickname for Israeli-born people.[1] But in my overcrowded school class of more than forty children, I was the only pupil with a full set of sabras for parents.

The majority of the other parents were people who managed to escape Europe just in time, some as children themselves. There were a few who actually lived through the Holocaust and survived. In the summer you could notice blue numbers

---

[1] See chapter 20.

tattooed on their arms, but this was not something to mention in conversation.

Yiddish, Polish, German, and some Russian were spoken on a daily basis by parents and grandparents in other kids' homes in these good areas. The children, the same as immigrant children all over the world, were uncomfortable with the foreign sounds. That my parents spoke Hebrew as their own mother tongue was unusual where we grew up.

In the egalitarian Spartan midstream Israeli society of the 1950s, when most people lived in one-bedroom flats, travelled on Egged buses, and dressed very plainly, young native parents like mine, with their history of active military service, were as good a status symbol as could possibly be. Sure, some families in the neighbourhood were more affluent, and had nicer furniture, but my parents, graduates of the socialist Working Youth and the Young Guards movements, held the whole of the merchant class in contempt.

As a veteran ex-Palmach[2] fighter with war wounds, my father enjoyed several privileges, which mainly included invitations to the ceremonies and functions of the young Israeli Army. We had reserved seats for the IDF's military parade on Independence Day, and once I joined my parents at a reception with State President Yitzhak Ben Tzvi and his wife, Rachel Yanait, in the Ministry of Defence Rose Garden. I knew very well that no other child in my class had experienced such a treat, and I felt really comfortable about my family's credentials.

With some of this in mind, I thought the inquiry about my breeding was terminated, but the mother of my friend was not impressed with my obvious smugness. She was determined to discover who I really was.

"So where did the parents of Mummy and Daddy come from?" she continued the questioning.

I had a trump card answer for this one too. I already knew that our family was made of a very special combination. "My mother's parents came from Russia, and my father's parents came from Yemen," I said, showing off, prepared to savour the

---

[2] Prestate paramilitary units

expected effect. It usually came with a compliment like "So this is why you are such a pretty little girl!" To this day – over half a century later – people make a point of being impressed with my "unusual" ethnic mix.

Not this lady. The woman surveyed me with kind concern and then said, in a comforting voice, "Well, never mind; luckily it does not show on you."

What she meant was crystal clear to a six-year-old. Had it "shown" from my looks that my grandfather and my grandmother were Yemenite born, I would have been in trouble in the Old North of Tel Aviv.

For the first time in my short history, I encountered a person who was not beating around any bush of ethnic discrimination. "*It* does not show on you" is an ill-meaning encouragement I have heard on more than one occasion since.

I cannot claim to have been traumatized by this personal insult. The society I grew up with had a pejorative label for every ethnic origin. Romanians were supposed to be thieves, Polacks were people who did not wash often enough, *Yekkes* – immigrants from German speaking countries – were synonymous with pompous nerds, and Hungarians were *Eagen Mieagen*. Still "Darkies" like my father were at the bottom of this pecking order. There were hardly any non-Ashkenazi in our "Northern" bourgeois neighbourhood. There was no way I could ignore the fact that had my complexion been a bit more obviously dark – or even worse, had I spoken with a guttural accent, as did my cousins who lived on the other side of town – it would have been quite a job to maintain a comfortable social position.

In those years before political correctness was invented, kids and grown-ups would openly display their collective dislike of anybody who was not of Ashkenazi origin. Most remarks were made behind the backs of their targets, part of the private code of the cohesive community. Because I did not "show" my family origins, nobody hesitated to express in my presence degrading remarks about *Schwarzers* (blacks), or *Frenks*.[3] In the all-

---

[3] Probably a derivation of "Francs" – French speaking, to indicate early Sephardy Jews in Palestine.

Ashkenazi milieu, the Israelis who arrived from Arab countries were often talked about as *Schwarzer Chayes* (black animals); Morocco-Knives; Iraqi-Pajamas, and later simply the *Chach-Chachs* and the *Aarsim*.[4]

Those were our lovely, innocent years. In those days of "Little Israel," presently talked about with so much longing, there was no social ban on publicly mocking the different and the dispossessed.

It was common practice to warn colleagues and neighbours about newcomers whose ethnic origins were not obvious enough. "*Er ist nicht fon Unsere*" ("He is not one of us") would be a sufficient indication that a would-be employee or resident on the block, or a bank clerk, did not rightfully belong to the Ashkenazi Eastern European Jewish clan. Interestingly enough, in the Diaspora the phrase "*nicht fon Unsere*" was coined to identify a non-Jew (and if this is not complicated enough: originally the Hebrew term Ashkenazi referred to a non-Jewish German, *Ashkenaz* being the old Hebrew name for Germany).

Well-behaved children were under clear instructions not to socialize with *them*. During adolescence scandals and heartbreaks occurred when some of the best of girls were attracted by the wild charms of young men from the unworthy social-ethnic groups.

* * *

The terminology of "whites" versus "blacks," echoing racial discrimination that had been a norm in other parts of the world for generations, is still commonly used in Israel today. Colour, however, is often just a code for something else. Many of the kids in my class actually had complexions darker than mine, darker still than the skin colour of children whose parents came from Iraq or Morocco or Turkey. This by no means turned them into "blacks," as they had parents who spoke Yiddish or Polish.

Ashkenazi Jews are a fairly mixed ethnic group when it comes to shades of hair and skin. Judaism originated in the Middle East, but throughout the generations, quite a number of fair-haired people

---

[4] This particular derogatory term is Arabic for "pimp" but stands for "greaser."

were assimilated into the Jewish population, bequeathing their genes to their kosher offspring. The assumed mass conversion of whole Slavic clans has imported lots of blonds and redheads into Judaism.

Still, a great number of Ashkenazi Jews have preserved the genetic heritage of their Mediterranean past.

Non-Israelis find it hard to distinguish between the different ethnic brands. British journalist Brian Whitaker once summed up the question of Israeli appearance in a witty article in *The Guardian* about the profiling system developed "for security purposes." One of his friends was getting annoyed with the cross examination he was subjected to at Ben-Gurion Airport.

"Have you met any Arabs," the selector[5] questioned him, following the well-established routine.

"How should I know? You all look the same to me," the Englishman snapped.

Most of us could easily be mistaken for Italians, Greeks, or Arabs. In the 1980s, when the "Ethnic Demon" arguments were shaking Israel on a daily basis, I lived in Bonn, then the capital of West Germany. Some wives of Israeli diplomats in the embassy – almost all of them of Jewish Polish extract – were appalled to be insulted by locals who took them for Turks.

In a small German Schwabish town, I came across the pejorative term *Weisse Jude*, used exclusively to insult Christian Germans considered too smart (or too greedy) in their trade. For the local Germans, real Jews did not seem white. During the Holocaust, "Aryan-looking" Jews had better chances to survive, hide, and escape the death camps. Millions of Eastern European Ashkenazi Jews who were murdered by the Nazis were mostly people who did not look Aryan. Our common Middle Eastern dark appearance gave them away all too easily if ever they tried to escape their persecutors. In 1960 Hollywood chose the ravishing Paul Newman, a typical *sheygetz*, as the chief Israeli protagonist in the filming of Leon Uris's monumental *Exodus*. The golden-haired, enlightened Ari Ben Canaan character was juxtaposed against the dark complexion of his opponents: Jewish nationalist radicals and Arabs.

---

[5] This is actually the job description.

The elegant Viennese Dr Theodore Herzl, with his dark, curly beard and piercing, dark eyes, could easily pass for a young Iraqi rabbi or even a Hezbollah dignitary. The most influential Israeli Mizrahi leader, jailbird Rabbi Aryeh Deri, has a fairer complexion than that of former Prime Minister Ehud Barak, who (justly) found it necessary in the 1990s to make a public apology in the name of the Labor Party over past discriminations against the Jews from Arab countries. Blue-eyed former government ministers Professor Shlomo Ben Ami (Labor), Eli Swissa (Shas), and Meir Shitrit (Likud) are all three Morocco born, and therefore belong with the "blacks"; while Shimon Peres, who has been personifying the Israeli left wing for as long as any of us can remember, has looks that enabled his arch-political enemies to claim that he was born of an Arab mother(!), hoping this would disqualify him as a Jewish leader. In May 2016 Israeli Prime Minister Netanyahu found it necessary to announce that his DNA includes indication that some of his ancestors were Sephardic Jews, like a large segment of his most loyal supporters.

Presently some second- and third-generation Arab Jews in Israel proudly like to call themselves "blacks," following American blacks who eventually became proud of their colour and heritage. An Israeli "black" can easily have red hair.

The 1950s immigrants from Arab countries were condescendingly called "the Second Israel" by the veteran Israelis of Eastern European origins. In fact, "Second Israel" was completely synonymous with a lowly social and economic status, large and condensed families, and a below-standard educational system. An Israeli-born friend of my age group who is of Polish origin once confided to me, "On my first trip to Europe, I was quite stunned to see blond-haired garbage labourers."

* * *

Most unfortunately for the new immigrants from North Africa and the Middle East, their mother tongue was the language of the enemy, and their cultural characteristics bore striking resemblance to those of the local Palestinian Arabs. So while the colour terminology of the Israeli ethnic gap is in fact colour-blind, it had never been deaf. Our rigid class discrimination was based first and foremost on universal criteria well known to many societies: accents.

Arabs and Jews from Arab countries evoke specific prejudices: poverty, ignorance, uncontrolled tempers, and an above-average delinquency. Israeli comedians, just like their British counterparts personifying Irish or Cockney characters, built great careers on their ability to ridicule the accents of the less affluent, before and after political correctness was invented. Young Mizrahi intellectuals with trendy class awareness started making a point of cultivating guttural accents as an act of defiance against the stigmatic norm in the 1990s (alas, these days most of them are not native Arabic speakers, and they often get the accents wrong).

In 1950s Israel, you could hardly hear Hebrew spoken free from a foreign accent. The heavy intonation of immigrants from Germany and Hungary were constantly mocked and jeered at. But when you sound like the enemy – and listen to his quarter-tone music – this is not merely funny. The speech of native Arabic speakers in Israel instinctively evoked scorn, repellence, fear, and hatred.

Our chemistry teacher in high school, an immigrant from Iraq, was in big trouble facing a class of merciless teenagers who roared with laughter whenever he opened his mouth to say something. During school breaks we would savour excellent imitations of his Arabic accent. The most talented jester was himself a son of an Iraqi family, who already mastered the standard pronunciation mode of the Ashkenazi Elite.[6]

Our biology teacher, of pure Polish extract, had a reputation for bullying pupils. One of her favourite victims was a dreamy Yemenite girl called Chavatzelet Chavashus, who was in the class below us. Chavatzelet's crime was a tendency to emotional, superfluous language even when she was describing laboratory experiments. Mrs. L. used to come to our class furious, exclaiming that she has "no idea what these kind of people" are doing in this school. Years later, when Chavatzelet, who became a poetess,

6 Standard Hebrew pronunciation has been heavily affected by the intonation and modes of speech borrowed from Yiddish, as shown by linguist and literature expert Professor Itamar Even-Zohar.

committed suicide, which was connected to her miserable love affair with the much older author and guru Pinchas Sade,[7] I bitterly blamed the biology teacher who never gave her a chance during her tender, fragile, teenage years. Eventually and posthumously the diaries of the author were published. Reading his ruminations I was not too surprised to discover that when one of his friends and followers told him that he was considering getting married to a young Yemenite woman, the icon of Israeli free thinkers advised him "to avoid" making this move.[8]

* * *

Hurt pride and awful prejudices are things one must get over eventually. But the discrimination against the immigrants to Israel who came from Arab countries was not merely social and cultural. They were, first and foremost, economically disenfranchised and pushed down the class system. The only controversy is whether the discrimination was deliberate and maliciously calculated, as Mizrahi militants claim; or whether it was the tragic outcome of unfortunate circumstances, as most Ashkenazi and their descendants fervently believe.

The truth is that apart from the indigenous Palestinians, Arab Jews have paid the highest toll for the Zionist State's chief basic ideological flaw: the decision to build the Jewish Vision over the foundations of the Jewish Orthodoxy.

---

[7] The much-admired Sade (1929-1994) published the uncensored, erotic love letters that he had received from Chavatzelet Chavashus, following a relationship that started when Chavatzelet was nineteen. The publication was devastating for the young woman.

[8] This diary entry of May 7, 1969, was published as part of an article in *Yedioth Aharonot*, January 30, 2004.

16

THE SHORT CUT

Possibly this is the way the world has always been, a kind of ladder, whichever creature is up on this ladder is unlikely to cast an eye on those underneath.

Mordechai Tabib,
A Dirt Road[1]

Savta Miriam never forgot the lone Turkish soldier who entered the yard and put his hand on her hair while she was playing alone near the family's home in Yemen. The soldier was wearing rags and seemed dirty, weak, and famished. He crouched exhausted next to the little girl and started talking in an incomprehensible dialect.

"My mother came out of the house screaming murder. She shouted at him and yelled loudly, 'What is this supposed to be? Get away – shame, disgrace!'" Savta told me twice, sixty and also seventy years after the incident. No culture can be tolerant of a strange man touching a child.

The soldier's reaction was totally unexpected. He broke down in bitter sobs. He begged Um Miriam's pardon and asked for her understanding. "He said that back home in Turkey, he had left a small baby that must be exactly my age now. He was convinced that he will die and never see her again. He actually told us he was dying."

---

1 Am Oved Publishers (Hebrew) 1953. Mordechai Tabib (1910-1979) was an Israeli Yemenite-born writer.

Savta's eyes would fill with tears at the memory of this unhappy scene. Her mother's heart softened. She might have been thinking of her own husband, also driven by the demands of an uncertain life away from the modest home and his pretty little daughter. "She gave him milk and calmed him down. She blessed him, that he will see his family again. He was just a miserable man, a human being. My mother later told me that he was a good man, even though he was not Jewish."

These were years of wars and famine, the twilight years of the Turkish Ottoman Empire. For many months, eventually two years, Um Miriam had been living on her own, depending on relatives' charity, her big boys' labour, and meagre savings while waiting to hear from the family's father. Her husband had left their home in the town of Eub to inspect the possibility of resettling in the Land of Israel. He was a *morrey* (teacher) who was not taking Zionist promises at face value. Carefully calculating his moves, he had left behind his wife and youngest daughter (Savta was presumably born about 1900) under the care of the older boys, ten and twelve years old, who could get jobs as day labourers. He set out on his own, maybe even as part of the famous convoy of Yemenite Jews who walked all the way to Jerusalem.[2]

It was long before word came with the instructions that the mother and the little girl should set out to join the family's father. Savta had no idea whether the message came by letter – women could not read or write anyway – or with somebody who had returned. I have no idea how my great-grandmother came to figure out the travel arrangements, but it was made clear that the elder boys were not allowed to join at that stage. The prudent *morrey* was reluctant to lose the home base in Yemen, just in case Zion would not turn out to be a good place after all.

Family history had registered that the big brothers' reaction to this was an outburst of frustration and jealousy, taken out violently on the young sister. As a penalty for being Daddy's favourite, Miriam was furiously shaken and pushed to the ground.

---

[2] In 1907 this convoy of 220 was supposed to have made the way in two months. Later the immigration was institutionalized and organized by the Zionist movement.

Her mother barely managed to stop the boys from beating the child further. Savta never forgot the hostility or the humiliation, and neither did the brothers. My father and his siblings hardly ever met their uncles, who eventually made their way to Palestine as grownups and settled in Petach Tikva.

A kind neighbour – a Muslim – volunteered to escort the single woman and the little girl on the long journey from Eub to the port city of Aden. They walked in the evenings and very early in the mornings, resting at the heat of the day and taking breaks during the cold nights on the hills. The neighbour helped carry the few possessions and the water. Um Miriam protested that it was too much, but from time to time he picked up the worn-out child and carried her as well. This is the only detail of the journey that Savta remembered from the exhausting trip. She could not even tell whether or not they were in a group with other people. But she would never forget the kindness of the robust man who ended up making most of the walk with her sitting on his shoulders. Sixty years later, in her Tel Aviv kitchen, she felt moved just by talking about him.

"I cannot stand it when people say that all Arabs are bad," she would say incredulously. "If only there were many Jews as kind as that Arab neighbour of ours, *allah yirhamo*."

She had a really strange story about what happened to them after they arrived in Aden. Her mother, for some reason, was unable to receive a permit to leave Yemen and travel to Palestine with her child. Long after everybody else (from their group, presumably) was gone, the two hung out alone together in the port city. My grandmother told me that for weeks her mother would go every morning to the main street, waiting for the passage on horseback of the local Jewish *Malik*, who was the only one to issue the exit permits.

"What are you talking about, Savta?" I tried to understand. "Nobody heard of a Jewish 'king' in Yemen." I was very interested in her memories and even brought along a tape recorder to store them. But what she said made no sense at all. We all learned at school that the status of Jews in Yemen was so lowly that they were not even permitted to walk on the pavement when a Muslim was coming toward them.

"Yes, yes, I don't know myself, but I remember it very well," Savta insisted. "There was this one, he was a sort of king and the Muslims respected him too. Surely he was Jewish. And whenever he would ride out on the street with his horse, people bowed!"

So my great-grandmother apparently went out every day to stake out the *Malik* with the intention to throw herself at his feet. Eventually she did, and holding up her terrified, trembling daughter, she started to scream. She explained to the important person that she was a woman alone, that her husband was expecting her in Palestine, and that she was in a desperate position. Left alone in Aden, they were both as good as dead. Her bold move was successful, and (luckily for me) my grandmother and her mother managed to leave Yemen.

I often wondered about the meaning of this incomprehensible event. Savta Miriam was not a person to make up stories, and it was obvious that this incident left a tremendous mark on her as a child. Her understanding was that a very important Jew had the power to make her mother's trip out of Yemen possible. I can only guess that the seemingly royal personality that so impressed Savta was somebody who had the authority to issue travel tickets for the boat journey from Aden to Jaffa via the Suez Canal. Perhaps he was an important Zionist official – it might have been the well-known initiator of mass Yemen Jewish immigration to Palestine in those years, Shmuel Yavnielli.

The *morrey* and his family made their home in the Yemenite neighbourhood of Petach Tikva, the first-ever Jewish agricultural colony in Palestine. When Miriam was fifteen, she went through a trauma that Jewish girls in Yemen could expect at a much younger age.

"We were playing on the street. Suddenly a friend of mine came running and calling, 'Miriam, Miriam, they got you a bridegroom from Jaffa, Waaa Miriam! He is here! – '" Savta was telling, perfectly mocking the typical Yemenite mode of joyful yelling.

"They all started laughing at me," she continued, half annoyed, half amused. "'Hi Miriam; he is good looking; he is very tall; lucky you!' I got mad. Why shouldn't I pick up a large rock, throw it straight into this one's head? She really bled a bit.

Everybody was shouting and screaming. They said, 'Watch out for this one, she is completely crazy!'"

The savage nature of the would-be bride deterred neither the chosen groom, a distant cousin with the same family name, nor the parents who initiated the match in a perfect Arabic preference to inbred. The teenage revolt was quickly strangled. Nine months after the wedding, the girl was giving birth for the first time. The baby was stillborn. It happened again a year later. In the third year, there came a third stillborn.

My grandmother made a point of describing the miserable beginnings of her family life and the death of her first three children in order to arrive at the moral of the story that had a religious conclusion. Having approached almost every rabbi and wise man in the Yemenite community, asking for help and advice but with no improvement, the family finally found a healer who knew exactly what to do in order to keep the bad luck away. The healer gave his blessing to the young woman and instructed her to donate a few coins every week to the charity box in the synagogue, as "charity saves from death."

It turned out to be a very efficient cure indeed. Or perhaps my grandmother had in the meantime grown older and stronger, and her diet might have improved. My aunt Mazal, her eldest daughter, was born in 1919. Then at long last she had her first son, Israel, then Moshe, my father. Not all her pregnancies ended successfully. She must have gone through at least fifteen childbirths, including twins, only one of whom, my uncle Yitzhak, had survived. His baby sister Rivka died a cot death. Another son, perhaps her favourite of them all, Meir, died of a serious illness when he was sixteen. When I was born, as her fourth grandchild, my father had three brothers and three sisters, and Savta Miriam had every reason to consider herself blessed with so many healthy children of which the majority were boys. She never failed to make the weekly contribution to the synagogue's charity box, even long after her legs were too frail to take her there personally. She had seventeen grandchildren and lived the tragedy of the death of one of them, the sweet natured Nir, as a soldier in the first Lebanon War in 1982.

I heard very little from her about our Saba David Yeshua, "God rest his soul." He died from cirrhosis, the illness that destroys the liver of alcoholics, when I was only a few weeks old. For most of his life, he made his living by casting and selling building blocks and staircases. It was an exhausting physical task, poorly paid by contractors according to the number of units produced. Saba was able to pick up the heavy blocks from the casting moulds by himself, but in order to pick up the large staircases, he needed the help of one of his sons. The boys would reluctantly come and give him a hand when summoned from the home to the builder's yard at the end of Zrubavel Street, very close to the beach. They all learned from him the art of making the mix for the concrete "mosaic," but only my uncle Israel continued in his father's trade for several years, then dropped it for the job of a cashier on the number four bus of the Dan traffic cooperative, where I often met him on my way to school.

Before and after working hours, Saba David never missed his prayers and the reading of the weekly *Parasha*. Like most Yemenites of his generation, the only education he had was religious learning, and as he had no gift for either commerce or peddling, physical labour was all he was able to do for living. My Aunt Mazal, God bless her soul, had tender memories of her father as a loving, gentle man, who allowed his small children to devour the nourishing breakfast his wife would prepare for him every morning to make sure he had enough energy for his work. He might have lost his appetite at some stage. I have no idea if he ever expressed frustration, anger, or bitterness over the humiliating system that put him at the bottom of the social-economic scale of thriving Tel Aviv of the twenties and the thirties of the last century. The only person in the family who ever discussed his chronic drinking problem was my Aunt Esther. Her own husband, a Romanian-born theatre man, had a similar weakness as did some other members of our family.

During his last years, Saba David Yeshua did not live at home any more. His presence in the two crowded rented rooms that housed the family of seven growing children became impossible. When it turned out that the family's meagre savings had evaporated into his drink, the elder sons demanded that he should find himself a place somewhere else and leave their exhausted mother alone. He rented a tiny room up in the nearby Carmel Market, and Savta

Miriam would send her younger sons to bring him cooked meals. He would turn up for the holidays, and when his son Meir died, he sat for the mourning period (*Shiva*) with all the family in the flat on Malan Street, that was later renamed Pduyim Street.

Savta had a photo of her late husband on display in a *vitrine* at the top of a small cupboard in her living room. Whenever I see a picture of the founder of the Al Qaeda organization, Osama Bin Laden, who was also of Yemenite extract, it makes me think of the gentle features, the grey beard, the beret, and the joyless eyes looking out of the photo of my paternal grandfather.

David and Miriam Yeshua

* * *

A Yemenite Jewish community already existed in Jerusalem by the mid–nineteenth century. The dark-skinned community members were hardworking and easily disciplined. Just like the local Arabs of all denominations, they were keen to do any jobs for a ridiculously low fee in the service of the new settlers who paid in hard currency. They were also piously religious Jews. The Zionist movement warmly adopted the Yemenites at a relatively early phase of its history. The early Zionists were happy with this peculiar segment of the population, which provided a heavenly solution of cheap, urgently needed workers, on the one hand, and a way to avoid too many non-Jews around them, on the other. The Yemenites' "humility" charmed the settlers from Eastern Europe. As soon as it was realized that an almost unlimited supply of such adequate people was available to be imported from the faraway land of Yemen, organizing their immigration into Palestine was recognized as a prime Zionist goal.

Before embarking on this mission, the Zionist activists had to take care of the fierce objection of Ashkenazi rabbis, who initially would not hear of black Jews and showed stubborn resistance. The Yemenite Jews and their accommodating rabbis had to go through tough tests and thorough investigations. Ultimately the rabbinical Ashkenazi establishment had to admit, with some surprise, that the Jews of Yemen were as strict as any Jew could possibly be. The segregation of the community from any non-Jewish infiltration was meticulously observed. Just like the *Frum* Ashkenazi Jews, the Yemenites took great pains to instruct their children that any contact with a non-Jew is an abomination. To avoid any risk of mixed marriages and to prevent surprises and adolescent rebellion, it was customary to marry girls to suitable bridegrooms of all ages at a very tender age. Indeed, after the marriage, the child – seven or eight years old – was often allowed to stay with her own parents until puberty, when she was handed over to the man she was already married to, to be disciplined mainly by his mother in case he, too, was a young boy.

So I owe my presence in this world to the first-ever import of Arab Jews into Palestine for economic and demographical considerations. The Yemenites who came to the country at the beginning of the last century were willing and enthusiastic immigrants into *Eretz Israel*. Nobody promised them a rose garden. Religious motivation was there, but their basic drive was the expectation of a higher standard of living. Just like guest workers today, and in line with the historical pattern that made Jews migrate from country to country throughout the generations seeking political and economic havens, the Yemenite immigrants were careful to have scouts scan the would-be Promised Land in order to find out what was in store. They were not all pleased with their findings, and some were enticed with deliberately false information, mainly by their own relatives. In our family the story goes that Saba David, who arrived in Jaffa as a young orphan with his recently widowed mother, was personally responsible for one such deception. Having fallen on very hard times as a sole provider to his young brothers and sisters, he figured out he would be better off if a large support contingent from the clan in Yemen would join his family. He sat down to send enthusiastic letters to his relatives in *Eub* describing the situation in the Holy Land in rosy colours, and urged them to drop everything and follow the example of the early immigrants. By the time his uncles and aunts landed in Jaffa with all their brood and found out that there was nothing but hard labour for them, their bridges back to the old country were already burnt. For many years these relatives – who included the parents of my Uncle Shalom Yeshua, the husband of my Aunt Mazal – bitterly blamed my grandfather for their miserable circumstances in Tel Aviv.

The great winners of the passage to Palestine were, apparently, the Yemenite women. Just like my grandmother Miriam, they had discovered the benefits of going out to work, cooking and cleaning for Ashkenazi households, gaining a precious economic independence. For the men, the transfer to Zion meant more than merely a drop in social status. They also suffered a painful fall from the position of total authority within the hierarchy of the patriarchal family.

* * *

Zionism is often described as a colonial movement. In fact, Zionism was making its first moves in the era when colonialism was considered an act of progress, which is why it was such a source of inspiration for Theodore Herzl. The father of modern Zionism was convinced that the tragedy of the Eastern European Jews would be solved if these people were to reinvent themselves as an enlightened colonial people. There was only one problem: the Jewish religion blocked any chance for colonial dynamics of the kind that might have been beneficial for the indigenous inhabitants of the new territories.

Just like their parents in the small towns and in the allocated Jewish regions of Poland and Russia, the Jewish pioneers of Palestine were committed to the legacy of self-segregation.

National and ethnic groups moving to new lands – Greeks or Romans, Muslim occupiers, or European empire builders – never failed to make efficient use of their deities on the way to achieving control over, and preferably also cooperation with, the indigenous population. Priests and missionaries always came along either with armed forces or settling civilians, effectively supporting the territorial takeover with the word of whatever god they had on offer. Judaism, a religion that for hundreds of years has dedicated most of its energies to fending off the "danger of assimilation" could never offer even the pretence of opening arms and ranks for newcomers. The new, dynamic, ambitious ethnic-national group that landed in Palestine with the Zionist message was hermetically sealed to outsiders. It had nothing to offer the veteran inhabitants of the land or any newcomers who were not Jewish.

Zionist ideology adopted the view that Jews are the "true natives" of the land it settled, and managed to regard the non-Jewish natives as invaders; with the great taboo on any social mingling, the Zionist paradox started its unholy, precarious road.

The first Jewish colonies that preceded political Zionism in the 1880s were quite similar to German and even American colonies that were started some time earlier. Based on agriculture, hard work by cheap labourers was constantly in demand. Palestinian Arabs were natural candidates to supply this demand. The first Jewish landowners – later nicknamed the *Boazes* – had no problem finding hardworking local farm hands who were only too pleased to make the new estates bloom in return for a meagre fee.

Villagers – the *fellahin* – were the builders, the gardeners, and the maintenance workers of the settlers. With the capital and technology imported by the newcomers, standards of living improved dramatically also for the locals. Better medical care and sanitation and more food brought down baby mortality. The economic boom attracted into Palestine even more dispossessed farmers from the nearby regions, mainly from the Hauran of Syria. But the massive immigration of guest workers, together with the increased natural population growth, alarmed the settlers' communities. Thus the "Demographic Problem," the most worrying topic for the Jewish-Zionist thinking ever since, was born.

The Jewish settlers could not even conceive of an apparently simple concept: opening the new Jewish society for the devoted workers and their offspring who might show an interest in joining the settlers' culture. Although many romantic descriptions depicted the locals as descendants of the ancient Israelites, never did anybody consider encouraging at least some of them to reinvent themselves as new Jews. Such a concept is contrary to the very essence of Orthodox Judaism, ever so obsessive about its (fictional) hereditary purity.

So while some children of Eastern Europe's *shtetls* were enchanted, and quickly imitated some of the Arabs' more exotic habits of nocturnal meat barbeques on open fires, galloping with thoroughbred horses, and making strong, sweet coffee in small tin pots, their romanticism stopped short at the basic mentality of a homogeneous closed community as adopted by all the ideological segments of Zionism. Even the most radical socialist Zionists, who openly despised the "Diaspora" Jewish way of life and scorned the traditions of the Jewish European ghetto, were very careful not to allow "assimilation."

In the Israel of the third millennium, every attempt by a local Arab to adopt the language, the norms, the habits, and lifestyle of the Jewish Israelis or – God forbid – to try and live in a Jewish neighbourhood, is seen as an existential menace. The Jewish religion, so well used to running successful minority communities in the hearts of estranged populations, has no facilities to cope with groups of a population who show an interest in joining it on a nonreligious basis. Most Israelis feel more comfortable with the more fanatic, violent forms of Islam than with Hebrew-speaking Arabs, many of whom – Bedouins, Tcherkessians, Druze, and recently Christian Lebanese – even serve in the Israeli armed forces.

It is against this background that early Zionism opened its arms to the Yemenite Jews – up to a point. The dark, extremely poor ethnic group with rich Arab heritage and culture found its humble dwellings on the margins of the new colonies and the new suburbs. While the Eastern European settlers had no intention of mingling with them, the Yemenites, however, were fast to identify the shortcut offered by Zionism from life in one of the world's most backward regions into the new Holy Land bonanza. They willingly and diligently adopted the rules of the game as set by their Ashkenazi brethren. They were labour immigrants, and they worked hard to make their endeavour a success, mainly for the next generation. Some, like my own grandfather, did not cope too well and needed large amounts of *arak* to drown their depression over a lost social status. Others soldiered on. Eighty or ninety years later, hundreds of thousands of people continue to arrive with the same logic in mind — from the former Soviet Union, from China, Africa and the Philippines. They, continue to stream into Tel Aviv, to work as supermarket cashiers, brick layers, street cleaners and nursing workers in order to ensure a better future for their own children.

* * *

I can remember feeling deeply insulted when a strange woman tried to enlist Savta Miriam to become her cleaner.

We were sitting on our balcony during one of her rare visits to our flat – she came to spend time with me while I was too sick (or pretending to be too sick) to go to school. I enjoyed the visit because she was a little woman with a natural gift for storytelling, a delicate sense of humour, and a very good understanding of human nature. Her neighbours adored her wisdom and the family hung on her every word.

From a balcony on the other side of Weiss Street, a woman I did not know spotted us and started waving her arms toward us energetically. I immediately knew what she was after and was mortally worried that Savta might be hurt to discover that this woman considered her a home help, just because she was wearing the customary Yemenite white scarf for head cover. I hoped that Savta, with her back to her, would not notice the summons, but the woman could not be ignored as she started shouting, "Hello, hello!" to attract our attention.

"What does this idiotic woman want?" I said nervously, although there was no doubt about it.

Savta explained to me patiently, "She must be looking for a cleaner." With a friendly gesture, she indicated to the desperate housewife, "Not available, sorry." Having spent all her life cleaning other people's homes to support her children, she did not think there was anything unusual with the assumption that the only explanation for a Yemenite woman's presence on a North Tel Aviv balcony is that she has come to do the washing and to mop the floors.

17

HELPING HANDS FOR LABOUR AND WAR

Any Yemenite who so wishes may get one of my canvasses for free... Why? Because in these people's culture, the very concept of having an artwork hanging on the wall at home is missing. A Yemenite might have saints, he might have rabbis, and he would probably prefer needlework anyway. But he would not have a picture of landscape or a social [event]. I also know this is a matter of tradition. *Though shalt not make unto thee any graven image, or any likeness of anything* – most of them are traditional."

Painter **Uri Lipschitz** *explaining the cultural gap in an interview to a Tel Aviv weekly, September 27, 2002*

Saba David's children, all born and bred in Tel Aviv, made a better living compared to their father. They all acquired some professional expertise. Even the oldest daughter, Mazal, who was sent out at a very tender age to work as a cleaner in order to supplement the family's meagre budget, very soon found her vocation in cooking and worked for some top-tier Tel Aviv families. She became a master of Ashkenazi cuisine and ran a production line of *gefilte fish* and *apfelstrudel* cakes with *schlagzahne* (whipped cream), which was going strong well into her eighties. One of my father's younger sisters and one brother managed an academic education. His own formative years were spent with his "Ameliorating the Sea" mates in the Palmach paramilitary organization. Three years after the draft, aged twenty, he came back to Tel Aviv and started looking for a job. Sister Mazal at that time was employed with the wealthy Fromtchenko family, who co-owned the Elite chocolate factory. She asked them to help her brother, and Mr. Fromtchenko was most accommodating. My father was invited to come and see him in his office.

Having reported to the chief's secretary, he was asked to fill in a form with his personal details. When he handed the form to the woman, she nodded her head in disapproval and pointedly started to correct his writing.

"These *schvartzes*," she blurted in Yiddish to the other clerk in the office, "they cannot even spell their own name properly."

Instead of our family name, Yeshua, she wrote Joshua in large letters.[1]

My father thought this was funny. As a graduate of a Talmud Torah religious school, his Hebrew was flawless. As a Tel Aviv native with both mother and sister in service and a history of working as an errand boy, his Yiddish was good enough; in fact, he developed a real fondness for the German that he learned from his friends in the Palmach, who were young refugees from the Nazis.

My Parents Zahara and Mousa Yeshua on their Wedding Day, April 19, 1948

---

[1] In Hebrew Yeshua means salvation or deliverance, only remotely related to the biblical name Joshua.

The secretary at Elite, herself a new immigrant with poor Hebrew, was not the only one with prejudices. When my parents announced that they were getting married, Savta Chaya was tactfully asked by her friends whether her daughter chose a Yemenite husband because "she had to." My energetic parents did not let any of this nonsense, including the bride's father's avoidance of the wedding ceremony, to interfere with the institutionalizing of a model matrimonial relationship that would last for sixty-two years, until the death of my dear father in 2009.

They got married in April 1948, one month before and few blocks away from the historic declaration of the Israeli State. The ceremony took place in a wedding hall that a Yemenite rabbi used to rent out on Pinsker Street, next to the Mugrabi Cinema, another landmark that Tel Aviv has since allowed to be erased for the benefit of more office and shopping space. The bridegroom was an hour late: he arrived directly from the trenches in the Modi'in area to find the bride sobbing and the guests embarrassed, but this soon became just another family anecdote. The young couple sublet a room from a tailor and his wife who raised four girls in a compact ground-floor apartment in Schatz Street, off the fashionable Dizengoff in Tel Aviv. The War of Independence, otherwise known as the Palestinian Nakba, was still going strong, and my father was seriously wounded in combat a few months later. When I was born, about one year after he made what was described as a miraculous recovery, he converted the small balcony of the rented room into a kitchen area.

These were the days of rationing. In our family photo album, my young parents are featured displaying a tomato, a rarity that was acquired on a complicated barter deal. For a while we kept a rabbit hutch in the yard next to the kitchen balcony. These were my first and last pets ever, much admired by all the children in the neighbourhood. Their real purpose, as I discovered with dismay some years later, was to enrich the poor diet offered by the rationing coupons with fresh meat. My father had gained his expertise in slaughtering and skinning rabbits during his years in the Palmach prestate paramilitary. In the early forties, he and his mates trained for the "Carmel Mountain Program," which was a plan to have all the Jewish population of Palestine barricaded in the countryside in case Field Marshal Rommel managed to win the war against the allies in North Africa, take over Egypt, and then march into Palestine. When ninetysomething Rabbi Eliezer Shach disdainfully called the Israeli seculars "Rabbit Eaters," we knew very well that he was referring to our family.

In the summer of 1952, we moved to Ramat Hachayal ("Soldier's Heights"), at the far end of Tel Aviv. As a handicapped war veteran, my father was eligible for housing in the estates that were just completed for the ex-soldiers. We had thirty-five square meters with grey concrete tiles, and at last a private toilet that also had a shower rose on the ceiling and a drain in the floor. My mother's kitchen boasted the only electrical refrigerator in the estate. It was an almost scandalous luxury that stunned her neighbours in Schatz Street when she decided to buy it second-hand, to avoid the twice-a-week service of the ice trolley. She was a dedicated working woman who went back to her teaching job very soon after I was born, leaving me in the care of the tailor's daughters. During the school recess, she used to run home to breastfeed, ignoring some pedantic older ladies who scolded her for this primitive, outdated mode of feeding human cubs.

Ramat Hachayal was surrounded by wilderness. At night we could clearly hear the jackals howling. On the Saturdays, during winter, one could venture on long walks hunting for cyclamens, anemones and white daffodils. It was a haven for the many children on the estate, and my own childhood was particularly blessed: in our first year there, my mother started a kindergarten in our tiny flat. The range of toys at my disposal was legendary for those days.

Business-wise the kindergarten was a total failure. By the time the year ended, my mother accepted a job as a teacher in the local school that was still being built. I was sent to the Working Mothers' Nursery School, a twenty-minute walk from home, over burning sands in the summer and in deep mud during winter.

* * *

There were about two hundred meters of sand and at least one light year between our housing estate and the *Maabara* temporary camp, on the other side of Ramat Hachayal. The tarpaulin-coated shacks were a little bit newer than my grandfather's shack in Nordia, in the centre of town, but unlike Nordia these shacks were not built on sticks that prevented flooding whenever it rained. The sanitary arrangements of open-air water faucets and common privies were identical. The *Maabara* – some years later I thought I recognized it as the film set of the movie *Salach Shabathi* by Efraim Kishon – inspired a feeling of fear and discomfort. Shocked neighbours reported that some men and boys who lived there were observed picking vegetables from the plots that belonged to the apartments in the housing estate.

The children from the *Maabara* did not attend the Working Mothers' Nursery School, and it is doubtful whether they had any kindergarten at all over there. Actually their mothers and sisters were quite keen to find work, any work. They used to hang around the estate looking for odd cleaning and washing jobs. The young housewives on our block, some of them employees like my own mother, could afford the few *grushim* that the *Maabara* women charged for their services. All Israelis were poor in the fifties, but poverty is a very relative concept.

I learned how to read the clock together with women who were the same age as my grandmothers. My mother patiently informed every new cleaner how time was to be measured. She would draw a large circle on paper, with digits and hands, and explain that remuneration was directly related to the number of full rounds the large handmade, as well as the number of digits that the small hands pass.

A girl of about ten years old once arrived from the *Maabara* to the block. She was wearing a tattered dress and held in her hand a bottle of *Amma*, the only detergent available in those days. I watched her from the small playground in between our plots. She was knocking on doors: most opened then closed after a few minutes, leaving her outside. I thought it was strange that she was carrying the *Amma* with her, as surely everybody had detergents at home. She might have tried to advertise her trade; perhaps could not even speak Hebrew. She was about twice my age, but I knew for certain that she was too young to be begging adult jobs from total strangers.

My mother still remembers this child and the guilty conscience she left her with. She did employ her, mainly out of a sense of charity or duty, for about two hours. She taught her how to read the time and allowed her to come back for more washing. In the evening I eavesdropped on the young housewives who discussed the new cleaner. They unanimously condemned her irresponsible parents who sent their daughter to clean floors and staircases rather than go to school. It seemed cruel, on the other hand, to refuse her. Maybe she would be beaten up back home if she returned without any money. At least she was fed by her employers.

The families of the *Maabara* in Ramat Hachayal were lucky, compared with the lot of the new immigrants who were sent to the new *moshavim* in the Jerusalem Corridor up in the hills or in the far south. My mother came back with woeful impressions after a teachers' trip to the area. The school's wooden shack was not sealed from the rain and the wind. Some of the pupils did not have shoes. Some sat on the cold floor tiles in a particularly cold winter, as there were not enough chairs for everybody. The teacher was a female soldier with no teaching qualifications. Hardly any of the new immigrant settlers had any experience in agriculture, but they were expected to make their living off the land that had (deliberately) lost most of its Arab farmers.

"It was really horrible!" my mother used to insist many years later, when the subject of the ethnic gap and accusations of neglect and cynical exploitation of the new immigrants from Arab countries became a burning political issue. As a devoted member of a socialist Zionist movement, she assumed that a motivated educator like herself could have made a real difference in the quality of life of these children. "It seemed obvious at that time that the military received fantastic perks – larger salaries and housing conditions – in return for relocations," my mother complained. "How come teachers did not get similar offers? I would definitely have moved if such a challenge was on offer." It never occurred to her – or to anybody else in those days – that the state was not at all keen on producing too many highly educated newcomers. Teachers, in the years that followed, saw their remuneration drop sharply compared with army officers and non-commissioned officers. In 2003 an Israeli NCO earned three times the salary of a high school teacher, according to a September 18th report in Globes Money Supplement.

At the first opportunity they had, my parents sold their small flat on the estate and instead purchased a protected tenancy agreement over an apartment in the respectable "North" of Tel Aviv. They correctly assumed that the well-established school of the Labor movement in the neighbourhood would be a better starting point for the five-year-old that I was in order to begin my education, away from the estate, the *Maabara*, the poor *moshavim*, and the development towns, where the second generation of distress was making its first steps.

* * *

Angry criticism is hotly aired over the victimization of the new immigrants from Arab countries and their children in those sad, harsh days. But each time the subject matter is discussed, a tidal wave backlash is raised by Ashkenazi Israelis and their offspring. How could anybody accuse them of being even remotely responsible for unfair treatment of the Mizrahim? Did new immigrants from Eastern Europe not endure incredible hardships in the forties and fifties? "Everybody suffered here," goes the common wisdom. "There was nothing special about Moroccan grief. What gives Moroccans the right to always be so belligerent?"

The true nature of the mass immigration calamities is difficult even for the third generation of Israelis to grasp. It is hard to fathom that this immigration was not only an experience of poverty, unemployment, miserable housing conditions and the lack of adequate social and educational services. The cruel mass movement all the way down the social and economic ladder had everything to do with ethnic origins.

By the early fifties, most Ashkenazi Jews who started off as labourers in Israel had already acquired professional skills and had become homeowners. Even the veteran Yemenites were a small minority well on its way to joining the middle class. The true labouring classes were made up of Arabs, peasants on the land and workers – skilled and unskilled – who were making ends meet in the cities. After the 1948 war, the Arabs were gone – driven out of the land during the war, paying the price for the Zionist-Jewish concept of a "Jewish state" with a Jewish majority. At the same time, a few hundred thousand Jews who survived the European inferno landed in the new country. Facilities for their integration in Israeli society were urgently needed: food production, housing, and basic needs had to be provided.

The newcomers from Europe were mostly merchants or skilled workers, natives of a Jewish class tradition of many hundreds of years. They were unable to supply the need for industry, road, and agricultural labour for the growing population. The Jewish state, having just been created with much pain and agony, having just brutally removed most of the non-Jewish inhabitants from the areas under its control, had an acute need for more human resources, of the kind that might replace the former natives of the land. The state dispatched its best sons and daughters, supported by a highly motivated secret service, to Morocco, Iraq, and other Arab countries. They were to start a mass import of badly needed Jews.

A mass of Arab Jews was expected to immediately solve a series of essential problems: tip the demographic balance in favour of the Jewish population; supply the necessary class of productive labour; and of course contribute additional young men to be drafted for the Israel Defence Army.

"The Jews from the Arab countries were needed as helping and fighting hands," historian Tom Segev accurately summarized.

In the targeted countries, the Zionist message had worked well, exceeding expectations. The Mossad delegates had a messianic message about the resurrection of the people of Israel in its historic land. Under community pressure nobody could stay behind. A powerful anti-Jewish sentiment that rose following what was conceived as unjust and cruel treatment of the expelled Palestinian Arab population did miracles to enhance the Zionist message. A mass transport system transferred hundreds of thousands of men and women, children, babies, and geriatrics over the Mediterranean and the deserts.

Recently some sinister aspects of this organized mass immigration have come to light. Researchers point at the incredible callousness with which the immigrants were handled. Dr. Esther Meir Glitzenstein documented mass starvation and death in the

Yemenite deserts, which were ignored and erased from memory by the enchanted "Flying Carpet" myth that officially described the transfer of almost all Yemenite Jews.[2] When scores of thousands eventually were flown in, famished, sick, and confused after weeks or months without proper shelter, water, or nourishment in the blazing summer at the south of the Arab Peninsula, quite a few of their new-born babies disappeared, reported dead. Evidence suggests that a number of these babies were actually secretly given up for adoption by childless well-to-do couples. It was claimed that their own families failed to care for them. [3]

In 2013, Dr. Yigal bin-Nun of the Sorbonne in Paris produced stunning circumstantial evidence that a much-lamented maritime disaster in which dozens of Moroccan immigrants lost their lives was actually deliberately induced by the Mossad and the Israeli government in 1961. In his lecture in Jerusalem and media interviews under the title "Did the Mossad and the Israeli Foreign Office desire the sinking of the Egoz in 1961?" bin-Nun presents period documents expressly suggesting that an "accident" might come in useful as a means to force the King of Morocco to ease the mass exit of Jews.

By the time the newcomers found themselves in the large tents and tin shack camps that were hurriedly prepared in the dunes next to the cities, it was too late to regret the move to the Promised Land. Research has revealed that in that period, the Zionist establishment mode of operation involved censoring the private letters of new immigrants from Morocco to make sure they did not discourage family and friends from joining the exodus of all Jews from Morocco. Immigrants who were found complaining in their personal correspondence were reprimanded and told to produce nicer letters.[4]

* * *

---

2 *The Exodus of the Jews of Yemen: A Failed Operation, A Seminal Myth* (Reseling Publishers, 2011).

3 *Ha'aretz*, Decades later, disappearance of 1,000 children in Israel remains a mystery, June 9, 2016

4 "The Postman Came Upstairs and Said I Should Not Tell a Thing," *Yedioth Aharonot*, March 29, 2010.

The curse of the "upside-down social pyramid," a term coined by the Russian-Jewish writer and activist Dov Ber Borochov, (1881-1917), was discussed at length by early Zionist thinkers. It was that, many believed, which had driven the Jewish people all the way to Palestine. Certainly since the middle ages, the Jews were closely identified with the middle classes. Socialist Zionism's prime goal was to turn the pyramid over in order to build a healthy, normal society based on a Jewish working class. In practice, this new concept could only last as long as there were enough poor Jews who were not able to make a living by easier jobs than hard physical labour.

The reason is simple enough. By its very nature, Judaism pushes its children to educate themselves and seek excellence – a basic principle of the middle classes in all modern societies. In Europe Jews have always been identified with the bourgeois class of tradesmen and liberal professionals.

This is how Jews lived in the small towns of Poland, Russia, Romania, and Hungary. This was also how Jews lived in the Jewish quarters of North Africa, Persia, Yemen, and Iraq.

For many generations the Jews of Arab countries lived – just like Jews all over the world – within a non-Jewish population. It is commonly accepted that they lived in satisfactory harmony within those communities, making – just like the European Jews – a vital part of the middle classes. Just as the Jews of Germany regarded themselves as loyal Germans for all intents and purposes, except that they had a different religion, so Moroccan Jews also regarded themselves as good Moroccans. The French colonial occupation too regarded the Jews as natives (*indigene*), while allowing them to continue with the process of Europeanization that made it possible to join the French educated group and its special privileges.

The young Israeli society, which had been nurturing a dream of national unity based on cultural roots and ethnic identity entered, eyes open, into one of the deepest conflicts that would continue to harass it for decades. A Jewish concept of nationality was declared to be completely in line with the Jewish concept of religious identity. This completely fictional "national unity" was to be accepted by all immigrants who came from totally different national and ethnic backgrounds.

Impressively, the Eastern European immigrants managed to reinvent themselves. It helped that they were composed primarily of Yiddish speakers and their children, and that they had supporting financing institutions and many years to build a good educational system. But statehood injected into this relatively cohesive community a large mass of Jews who were as different as could possibly be from the traditional Eastern European model. They spoke Arabic in a variety of dialects, dressed as Arabs, ate Arab food and ran their weddings and other family ceremonies in a very Arabic style, which was fully integrated with their Jewish religious rites. They were Arab Jews in every aspect of their being, the same as my Yemenite great-grandparents. Yiddish to them was a foreign language.

Unfortunately, and disastrously, the community that was supposed to absorb these newcomers did not for a minute consider that this Arab identity could actually be a great asset, something that might facilitate the integration into the Middle Eastern realm that the new state supposedly desired. As far as the veteran Israelis and the Israeli establishment were concerned, the new immigrants were human material with inferior qualifications. With a lot of good will, many spades, and many trowels, this "material" had potential to be useful in the fields, on building sites, and in industry. Their children, at best, might be integrated into the canonized Israeli culture and quietly drop all the embarrassing indications of their Arab origins.

Later, when social unrest had begun and social protest movements started crystallizing around ethnic issues, nobody could understand why the Moroccan tradesmen and craftsmen did not agree to become friendly and accommodating labourers "like the Yemenites of many years ago" – why they so resented being cast in the role of the working classes that the new country so needed.

* * *

As Arab Jews had no experience of the turbulence that had shaken the lives of European Jews in Nazi Europe, they had no real collective motive to throw away their life in the old country and briskly start a new chapter in a new, distressful place. In their countries of origin, Arab Jews were a major element in the backbone of the local middle classes. They had no economic motivation to migrate suddenly to Zion and seek employment as labourers, as was the case with the early Yemenites and with today's migrant workers.

I know for a fact that Moroccan Jews do not exaggerate when they insist that they had no reason to leave their homeland except for the religious-Zionist excitement raised by the Israeli *Aliya* delegates. During the Middle East Business Peace Conference of 1994 – the only time I went to Morocco – the city of Casablanca was packed with foreigners. But the locals – taxi drivers, waiters, but also academics and high public officials – surprised us with an emotional upsurge each time we identified as Israeli. People called me "sister." More than once I was literally hugged, and total strangers would say, "But you are one of us!" just because they assumed, mistakenly, that I was a Moroccan Jew, a member of a well-liked, well-respected community that one day simply disappeared en masse and deserted their home to support other lost brothers in another land.

It does not take an over-rich imagination to describe how stunned were the small artisans and shopkeepers of Marrakech, Algiers, Baghdad, and Cairo upon discovering that the veteran residents of the new country, who called upon them to help build the Third Temple, actually considered them all a kind of proletariat intended for hard, unsophisticated physical labour. The Ashkenazi administrators, many of them with memories of how they spent at least a few months during their youth doing road work and draining marshlands in Palestine with their romantic youth communes, could not – or pretended they could not – understand the problem. It was a mystery to them why the new "primitive" immigrants were not excited to go out and do exhausting jobs in return for minimum wages to support their very large families. Or why new tiny two-bedroom flats in housing estates so liked by young Israeli couples were such a source of misery when eight or ten children, as well as an old grandparent, had to fit in. Immigrant families who were so housed should have actually considered themselves lucky, compared to the many thousands who dwelled for years in the *Maabara* (transitional camp) tarpaulin shacks. The only alternatives were the forsaken new remote development towns that offered a dubious future in the production line of a government-sponsored textile industry.

"I used to do staircases. We had a hard time at home," my home help sums up her own youth in the Maabara of Lod (*Lydda*). She often corrects my accounts and gives me useful tips about housekeeping, which makes me think how far she could have reached had she attended school regularly instead of being forced to go supplementing the family income – or if her local school had not been a miserable excuse for an educational institution, nothing to compare with the standards of my own beloved Educational Home for Children of Workers in the north of Tel Aviv, only about eleven miles away.

* * *

There is nothing surprising in the fact that during the 1950s, veteran Israelis, mostly of Ashkenazi origins, exploited their many advantages of capital control, language capabilities, technological know-how, and the whole institutionalized economy to improve their own positions at the expense of the weaker segments of the population.

Still, the Israeli Ethnic Demon (*hashed haadati*, a concept constantly referred to) cannot be fully understood if you do not see it against the background mechanisms of rejection and segregation created and perfected by the Jewish Halacha.

If you grow up in a system that trains you from day one to be wary of any contaminating contact with anybody who does not look, talk, or pray like you, a very deep mental revolution will be required for you to get over the feeling of revulsion inspired by the presence of a large group of foreigners who are ethnically and culturally very different from yourself. The mechanisms that preserved this attitude worked for Jewish communities everywhere around the globe, making sure Jews all over the Arab world as well as in Europe should avoid assimilation for generations. Segregation between the communities worked both ways. In certain periods, Ashkenazi Jews were the ones considered economically and culturally inferior. In Jerusalem of the nineteenth century,

Sephardic Jews of a certain stature did all they could to stop their daughters from seeing the penniless "Muscovites."

In the Jewish population of young Israel, the alienation felt by secular Ashkenazi toward the Arab Jews was soon rationalized by "technological and cultural" factors. The annoying myth concerning oriental Jews' "cultural inferiority" was fast created and flourished among the refugees from Europe and veteran Israelis who identified with them and naturally gave them an advantage in the struggle for the scarce resources in the new land, almost fully centrally controlled.

"While Zionism was nurturing its European dream model, it was forced to absorb so many Jews who came from Arab countries," historian Tom Segev once explained.[5] On another occasion Segev correctly elaborated this concept of a failed European dream:

The Zionist movement was born in Europe and the Jewish State it intended to create was supposed to belong to the European civilization. Some of the state's founding fathers dreamt of creating a "new man" who will replace the "old Jew," but although they wanted to skip two thousand years of Diaspora and associate the "new man" with the Bible heroes – his image was supposed to be rooted in European culture. Until after the Holocaust, the Zionist movement did not include Arab Jews in its vision, not beyond a mere anthropological interest. European Jews were supposed to be the main potential for populating the State of Israel. As they had been exterminated, Zionism discovered the Jews of the Arab countries. It did so with mixed feelings of alienation, reluctance and apprehension. The Jews of the Arab lands were needed as helping hands for labour and war. They were brought over so soon, before there was any infrastructure for their absorption, also due to the impact of the holocaust.

The documentation that was exposed over the years proves a policy deliberately intended to erase the ethnic identity of immigrants from both Arab and European countries. There is also documentation to prove a deliberate policy of discrimination against Jews from Arab countries. Some of the immigrants'

[5] *Ha'aretz* , November 4, 2001.

suffering originated in objective difficulties and innocent mistakes; some of it was unnecessary and was driven by ill will.[6]

Europe remained the cultural adopted homeland of the privileged Israeli elite. The dreamed-up "European" self-invented image of the *Ahusals* is in fact pathetic enough. For a start it has its roots in the same European ideology that nurtured the "new man" in its pure, Aryan model; the same model that aspired to ethnically clean Europe of all oriental, dubious, noisy, and obviously uncivilized elements, among which first and foremost were the Ashkenazi Jews.

Ashkenaz is (old) Hebrew for Germany. There is ample evidence that the top social tier of German Jews – well educated, quite assimilated – considered the masses of the Yiddish-speaking Polish Jews and their descendants who started to crowd the German cities in the early years of the last century as an embarrassing inconvenience. They unanimously identified them as *Ostjuden* and often described them as shameful "human dust": when Hebrew classic writer Yossef Haim Brenner wanted to express his disgust with the Arabs of Palestine – to him they seemed to be unhygienic, loud, argumentative petty traders, living in degenerating density (not to mention their sexual habits, which he considered scandalous) – he chose to name them disdainfully "The Poles of the Orient."

In the 1980s Austrian Jewish journalist Peter Sichrovsky published an interesting book documenting Jewish children who grew up in post–World War II Germany and Austria. Most of the interviewees reported deep cultural inferiority complexes because they grew up in warm, noisy, informal families that they felt did not measure up to the families of their well-ironed, perfectly mannered Christian friends.[7] (It should be noted that Sichrovsky, himself one of these Jewish Ashkenazi children, chose a remarkable way to try and get over his own feelings of inadequacies: he eventually joined Jorg Heider, the leader of Austria's extreme right-wing political party, and for years was his second-in-command and token Jew).

---

6 *Ha'aretz* , September 20, 2002.

7 Peter Sechrovsky and Jean Steinberg, *Fremde in Eigenes Land/ Strangers in Their Own Land: Young Jews in Germany and Austria Today* (Penguin Books, 1987).

Just like persecuted individuals, persecuted groups often adopt the behavioural patterns of those who reject them. At least part of the patronizing and disdainful attitude Jews of Eastern Europe developed toward Mizrahi Jews may be explained by the bitterness and injured pride of those who had become refugees due to their ethnic origins.

The phenomenon of being a refugee is essential to understanding the Israeli formative experience in the early years of the state. The lucky ones among the Jewish refugees from Europe made their way to Palestine before the outbreak of the Second World War, with the ground already burning under their feet. These people had been torn from their natural habitat, saved by the skin of their teeth. They had to give up homes and all other assets, and were deprived even of their mother tongue. They looked up with envious admiration to the Israeli-born Jews, seemingly so carefree and uncomplicated, a desired model for emulation. Many of the ex-refugees carry to this very day, or passed to their children, the scars of the indifference or disdainful attitude of the self-assured *sabra* natives. Quite a few repeatedly blamed the Israeli Jewish population and its leaders for not doing enough to save the European Jews from the Nazi horrors.[8]

Culturally, the children of the *shtetl* of Poland did not have a real advantage over the children of the Moroccan *Malach*. Many of the refugees from burning Europe had carried serious social and cultural setbacks with them, as inflicted by the Jewish Orthodoxy on their original communities. This did not stop Ashkenazis and their descendants of up to a fourth generation on insisting to this day on the concept that was fixed in the fifties: that the Arab Jews were not manoeuvred into the bottom of the Israeli class system as a result of an institutional policy, but "naturally" ended there as a result of their inherent inferiority. Everybody my age had a chance to listen to the supposedly winning argument in this debate: "Don't you know that at the

---

[8] Tom Segev quotes from David Ben-Gurion's memoirs: "If I knew that it was possible to save all the children in Germany by transporting them to England, but only half of them by transporting them to Palestine, I would choose the second." (*One Palestine, Complete: Jews and Arabs Under the British Mandate*, Metropolitan Books, New York, 2000).

time they arrived in Israel they were not even familiar with flushing toilets!"

So the connoisseurs of toilet flushing faired so much better, based on cultural superiority. Fortunately, Shakespeare, Mozart, and the genius Rabbi of Vilna were not evaluated for this particular skill, or they would all have failed to be considered cultured.

As late as 2003, the state's public attorney's office produced a stunningly racist report to justify the segregation of Ethiopian children in the state religious school system. According to this document, the children belonged to a "segment of the population" that "traditionally underachieves over many years." The Ministry of Education confirmed that the dear old flush toilet test was still relevant in the new millennium. Its senior officials explained the budget allocation discrimination against Bedouin pupils (most of them children of men serving in the Israeli armed forces) with the explanation that they are "unaccustomed to toilets with running water."[9] Private religious schools continue to openly defy court orders to stop discriminations against religious girls of Sephardic origins. Officials pretend they are helpless against Ashkenazi community cohesion on this issue.

* * *

As far as the state was concerned, the national mission of the fifties and sixties was most successfully accomplished. Newsreels of the period document the endless tent and shack camps as an amazing achievement. The Jews who arrived from North Africa, from Yemen and from Iraq, together with a large group of Romanian Jews, managed to double the Israeli Jewish population. A Jewish majority within the Green Line state borders seemed secure.

The mass immigration had achieved its main goal: to erase the risk that the Arab Palestinian inhabitants of Israel would gain a demographic advantage and so eventually erase the Jewish nature of the state using the democratic process. At the same time, the mass immigration tripled the number of native Arabic speakers in the land.

---

[9] Orith Schochat, *Ha'aretz* , August 17, 2001.

Within less than twenty years, concerned *Ahusals* were confronted with a new "Demographic Problem": too many Arab Jews, who were decisively attracted to political movements that cherished nationalistic ideology, with little regard for democratic liberal principles. Perhaps because deep down in the collective subconscious, they realized that Israeli democracy, with all its nuances, was not for Arabs.

18

SILK GOWNS, BLACK PANTHERS

What is in it for the Oriental Jews with this Peace that everybody tries so hard to force down their throats? Nothing! As a matter of fact, they only stand to lose... they will lose the Palestinian butt they so well kicked, on which they have constructed their own national identity.

Sámi Shalom Chetrit in "Peace, Justice, and Oriental Account Keeping," published in *On the Other Hand*, Centre for Alternative Information, January 2003

When refusing to share the world with other people, let us not be too surprised to wake up and find that Others do not wish to share the world with us.

Advocate Assaf Weitzan, Hotline for Migrant Workers, *Ha'aretz* July 28, 2013

The ground floor of the large Arab home where my grandmother lived was originally used for storage and as stables. It was deserted and sealed by the time my father was still a young child. A dirt pile around it allowed access directly to the first floor. The front door led into a communal patio for all the rented rooms of the families who lived on that floor, as well as the small kitchen cabinets, the communal toilets, and the shower. You had to wear wooden clogs to take a shower. The toilet was a hole in the floor and the sharp smell, I later discovered, was Lysol.

This urban residential style that had separate rooms for cooking, sleeping, and washing must have been typical of other cities in the Middle East, at least according to descriptions in novels by Sami Michael and Nagib Mahfouz. On the patio men and women hopped around in clogs or carried steaming aluminium cooking pots from the family's kitchen corner into the living room that also functioned as a dining room and a bedroom area at night. Savta Miriam's two large, high-ceilinged rooms connected together with a wide doorway was the most spacious apartment in the yard. All other families had one room only. It also had the great advantage of having the kitchen just next door. Savta's children owed their high standard of living to their mother's alertness. Once she heard that this rare dwelling had been evacuated by former tenants, she used all her personal charm and diplomacy to beat out other residents of the Yemenite Vineyard who were equally desperate to get hold of this comfortable property. The family moved there after its fourth surviving child was born. Before that they all lived in a flimsy wooden hut on the other side of the street.

As he was considered a serious and reliable boy, my father was saddled with the task of walking to Jaffa every three months in order to deliver the rent due to the Arab landlord. It once happened that his mother could not make up the full amount, and she briefed him to try and convince the landlord that the missing money would be paid in the next quarter. My father arrived at the old squire's home with trembling feet but was reassured by a generous response. "He said to me, 'Never mind; pay nothing this time. Give Mrs. Miriam her money back; I know she will pay when better times will come soon, with God's will. Give her my warm regards and tell her not to worry.'"

The landlord's generosity – or perhaps his good business sense that told him good tenants should be treated kindly – did not stand to his credit when the war broke out. In 1948 he was evicted with all his family from Jaffa, to become another Palestinian refugee, like most of the city's Arabs. From then on, the rent was collected by the employees of the Custodian for Missing Person's Properties. My father told me that Savta deeply disliked the "custodians," who were rude to her and threatened to evict her when once again she was short of cash and requested a delay in paying her rent. The fact that the Arabs were no longer there did not necessarily improve things for poor Jews.

Around 1960 Savta's children, most of them well into their thirties, initiated a revolutionary conversion in her rooms and lifestyle. A lavatory and a shower were installed in her old kitchen next to the ancient metal sink that for years she also used for washing herself and her hair. The kitchen door to the patio was blocked, and instead a connecting door was created through the bedroom door. One of the large bedrooms was divided and half of it became a kitchen area. Savta Miriam was almost sixty years old when she could start enjoying, for the first time in her life, the comforts of her own private bathroom and a cooking area that could compare with every kitchen in the North of Tel Aviv. I was ten at the time and could very well appreciate the dramatic improvement of Savta's standard of living, particularly because such changes did not happen for any of the other neighbours in the inner yard, who continued to use external kitchens and communal toilets well into their dotage.

Savta Miriam was very devoted. During her very rare visits to us, she politely declined any refreshments and would not even drink water from our non-kosher glasses. By the time my father's first-ever car was bought, in 1967, we made an effort when visiting her on Saturdays and on holidays to park the car as far away from her windows as possible. She was, however, remarkably forgiving about the fact that most of her family dropped religion altogether. "All Israel are Just," she would piously quote and shrug. She often reminded her frustrated neighbours that the first golden rule of life is to avoid interfering with one's children. "You must let them crack their own heads as they go their own way. It is the only way they learn."

On Friday nights one of her sons or sons-in-law always came to see her for the Sabbath sanctification, and by Saturday evenings, they came again for the distinction of the holy Sabbath and the beginning of the working week, using the spices and perfumed herbs she patiently cultivated in tin cans. Many years later I discovered that her Arabic-sounding herbs also had fancy Italian names like basil, oregano, and thyme.

My grandmother never passed on to me her wisdom in the medicinal qualities of spices, and I did not acquire her expertise in grinding the *hawaij mixture* with the heavy granite *maschag* stone. But I surely respect her devotion to irrational beliefs. My own adult life has always involved mineral rocks, astrological indications, clairvoyants, shooting stars, and readers of palms and coffee cups, as well as ancient rituals of all origins and sorts. I always felt protected under the benevolent influence of her blessings, authoritatively recited on my behalf: "May the Lord grant the desire of your heart, health, and joy," she would solemnly repeat at the end of all my visits with her, as I kissed her hand or the top of her head. Contrary to what one got used to in Ashkenazi families, she was very careful never to bring her mouth close to the faces of younger people, so that they should not be affected, she explained, by the bad breath of old age.

A failed cataract operation caused the loss of her eyesight when she was about seventy years old. For many years she continued to live alone in spite of her almost total blindness. She lived well into her eighties, but in her last years, her pride was bitterly upset by the need to be cared for on a daily basis. She had to be moved to Ofakim in the south where my aunt Zippora lived, but as her condition deteriorated, she had to be hospitalized in a geriatric ward near Gedera and died there several years later, lonely, confused, and depressed. Just like my other grandmother, Chaya, she spoke passionately about her hatred of being old. "What a cursed life," she regularly muttered, and I never dared to ask whether she meant the disabilities of old age or the fact that looking back, all her years were spent between the kitchen, the washing, the cleaning, and the sufferings of others as well as her own.

The Custodians got fed up with the old house eventually. Each time a tenant left or died, their room was sealed with concrete to avoid squatters. One day bulldozers arrived to demolish the building and to flatten the small hill made of the bungled stables underneath. It broke my heart when the plot became another parking lot for the market's shoppers. *Ha'Ir*, the city newspaper, reported that city hall broke its promise to the neighbours to make the place into a small public park.[1] I wonder if the landlord's children ever passed by.

* * *

---

[1] Shaul Bibi's column "State of the Kerem [vineyard]" – *Ha'Ir*, 1995.

In the early 1950s, David Ben-Gurion famously expressed the patronizing hope that "one day" the IDF would have a Yemenite Chief of Staff. Indeed, what higher vocation would the Jewish state ever have to bestow? In that period quite a few Yemenites already discovered that the fast track up the social ladder was elsewhere. They were certainly very prominent at the top echelons of Tel Aviv's underworld. According to a series of articles in *Ha'aretz*, 1973-1974, by journalist Ran Kislev, the "Eleven Most Wanted List" that surprised and dismayed the country in the 1970s contained an absolute majority of our landsmen who were the chief barons of illegal gambling, drug trafficking, and loan sharking. Some of them were my father's classmates and childhood playmates.

None of this spoiled the beloved image of the Yemenites as a particularly fine, modest, and delicate ethnic group with a gift of expressing great joy by tin drumming. For years the dark-skinned proletariat enjoyed unanimous public acclaim for being such a "useful" minority. I often found myself receiving compliments over the "natural nobility," industriousness, and humility of my people, the Filipino and the Thais of Israel's past. Being "undemanding" was particularly highly appreciated.

The truth is that Yemenite Jews were equipped with a realistic understanding of their position in the tough immigrants' society of the early Jewish settlement, as well as deep respect for private property and perfect sympathy to the self-segregating passion that comes with Jewish tradition. They produced some very astute businesspeople and successful entrepreneurs, scientists, artists, and writers, as well as some infamous murderers (Yigal Amir, Daniel Akov, Tovia Oshri, and Rachamim Gumadi, to name a few) and some charismatic eccentrics (Uzzi Meshulam and Yeshua ben Shoshan). The almost-forgotten stories of author Mordechai Tabib, born in this country in 1910, beautifully sketch the poverty-stricken, intrigue-infested communities that the Yemenites created at the fringes of the early Israeli settlements. Tabib, just like singer Shoshana Damary and choreographer Sara Levi Tanai, who founded the great INBAL ethnic ballet group, harnessed his considerable talent as a writer to the service of the optimistic Labor Party spirit of the state's early years. A staunch faith in the "melting pot" ideology was a basic ingredient in this spirit.

There is very little in common between the immigration of the Yemenite Jews to Palestine in the first quarter of the twentieth century and the mass transfer experienced by hundreds of thousands of newcomers from North Africa, Iraq, Yemen, and other Arab countries some decades later. The participants of the later unprecedented relocation effort landed in a social and economic catastrophe.

* * *

This is all history now. Many decades have passed, and the second, third, and even fourth generations of Arab Jews have mostly integrated into the Israeli mainstream. Still, there are some unresolved elements in their collective identity. While it becomes almost fashionable to connect to the Arab cultural components of this identity, the need to be distinguished from the Palestinian Arabs who live next to us both in Israel and in the occupied territories is stronger than ever.

In the problematic national myth and reality, Arabs must first and foremost be portrayed as the cruel, uncompromising enemies of the very existence of the Jewish state. In fact, the very obvious presence of nonviolent Arabs who have any other goal in life than punishing Jews would be vehemently denied, with some panic, by every nationally proud Israeli.

It did not take too long for the Jews who originated in Arab countries to realize that they were being rejected by the leading Ashkenazi ethnic group mainly because they were so similar to the other Arabs.

The solution to this embarrassing fact of life was to forcefully stress those ingredients of their cultural heritage that could differentiate them from the other Arabs and exonerate them from any suspicion that they were anything but non-Arabs. Jewish Orthodoxy was able to supply and deliver these elements in abundance.

Embracing religion did not happen overnight and did not occur naturally. The transformation of the Arab Jews into ultra-Orthodox Israelis was accelerated by dramatic events following the Six Day War. Our Israel had suddenly found itself in control of the lives of almost two million non-Jews.

The occupation and its implications did not register overnight. It was an ongoing process over many years, with continuous and tremendous brainwashing that deeply affected all the segments of the Jewish Israeli population. The process caught the Arab Jews at a touchy period of building a new class consciousness. It had some socioeconomic aspects that the Israeli Labor movement conveniently chose to overlook.

* * *

One could expect that over the years, the group of depressed masses of Jews with Arab origins should eventually produce natural leaders and educated elite who would be attracted by revolutionary ideas. Indeed, an authentic protest movement over social and ethnic deprivation reached a critical mass in the seventies, following the model – and even adopting the name – of the American Black Panthers. There seemed logic to the adoption of radical social theory by a group that was so obviously discriminated against within Israeli society.

For a moment it seemed that with the backing of the deprived masses, the revolutionary segment should have been able to force the privileged segments of society, the veteran Ashkenazi, to bring down some ethnic and social barriers in order to reach a new social equilibrium.

In the rapidly changing Israel, the radicalization process of the young Mizrahi was short-lived. The poor and the deprived unsurprisingly preferred the more exciting version of protest along nationalistic, religious, and right-wing patterns. Politics of hatred and exclusion offer a tempting compensation to the dispossessed, humiliated masses.

The Six Day War enlarged the territory controlled by the State of Israel fourfold and doubled the population under its rule. Concurrently the social and economic status of all the Arab Jews shot up overnight. They were suddenly delivered from their lowly position at the bottom of the Israeli class system. This bottom had been filled with new Arabs, who were even poorer and even more deprived, and they were not even Jewish.

The war was followed by unprecedented economic growth.

Hundreds of thousands of Palestinians from the territories that Israel had taken over as a result of the Six Day War started scrambling into the neighbouring Jewish Eldorado to offer their labour and skills for ridiculously low prices. The Israeli labour reservoir post-1967 was increased by a very large, new, cheap group of workers who set the economy moving in top gear for over twenty years.

The Jewish state was now comfortably maintained by countless guest workers who rose early in the small hours of the morning to make the trip from their towns and villages across the Green Line in order to start a long, rewarding working day in Israel. Restaurants, hotels, building sites, textile plants, and the farming industry prospered. The garbage was always taken out on time.

The traditional call for "Hebrew Labour" sounded now anachronistic and obsolete. There was no unemployment and no lack of jobs for Jews. The Israelis were convinced that with the occupation strategy, there was no "Demographic Risk" anymore.

The socialist secular Israeli Labor Party continued to run the political scene for ten years following the Six Day War. It did not even occur to a single Labor leader that the new, devoted labourers from Judea, Samaria, and the Gaza Strip should be given access to the Hebrew "Melting Pot." This was not because they spoke Arabic, or because they were poor or different culturally, or too dark skinned for the ruling classes in Tel Aviv and in Jerusalem. After all, this also characterized most of the Yemenites, the Moroccans, and the Iraqis in the shack camps that still decorated the cities' fringes. The Palestinians actually learned Hebrew very fast, many of them were well paid, and their standard of living rose accordingly; some of them had skins as fair as any Israeli Jew, and quite a few had academic qualifications or academic ambitions. But they were not of the Jewish religion, which meant they did not belong in the Jewish Israeli nation. There was no way that even a single one of them could make his or her way into the society that took their services for granted.[2]

---

[2] A few dozens, in refugee camps in Gaza or the West Bank, were fortunate to have mothers who were born Jewish and followed Muslim husbands before 1948; all their children were hurriedly equipped with proper Israeli ID cards.

These were our good Israeli years. Between the socialist Tzavta Club and the Mann Auditorium concert hall, the seventies and the eighties flourished. Tel Aviv became the nonstop city we all cherish, Jerusalem sprawled uncontrollably over the hills around it, and generous grants were produced for every nationalistic whim.

It is not a coincidence that the Israeli religious experience became the axis around which the occupying state now revolved.

The two principles that enabled Israel to clip the coupons of the occupation without seemingly paying the price were based, first and foremost, on a religious apartheid. In a reprehensible joint venture with the Jewish Agency, the idea of settlements exclusively for Jews within the occupied territories was conceived. And in a blunt defiance of Israeli labour laws – which in those years were quite progressive – Palestinian workers could be hired in Israel, and even reside next to their jobs temporarily, without the necessary social privileges and certainly without any civic rights.

These two principles perfectly facilitated the large venture of the settlements movement. Israelis attribute its success to the devotion and zealotry of the Gush Emunim movement, but in fact, in these peculiar towns, villages, and estates, where a non-Jew may never dwell, there is hardly a wall not erected by Arab Palestinian labourers, or not paid for by the Jewish state and the Jewish Agency.

Within the Jewish society of Israel, social and political developments fermented that would, in the long run, tighten the grip religion has on Israeli political theory and practice, while increasing its destructive potential. The Arab Jews set themselves the task of becoming a major engine of this dynamic process. They eventually learned how to make their voice heard and how to operate efficiently their considerable electoral power. Circumstances made them do this under the auspices of the Jewish Orthodoxy, as well as for Orthodoxy's sake.

* * *

In the lands of the Maghreb, religion was an important feature of Jewish life. It did not, however, have a monopoly of all areas of living in the traditional Orthodox Ashkenazi style, and there was no tight community control based on the yeshiva institutions.

Israelis of Middle Eastern origin had their first political experience at the Israeli Labor Party (*Mapai*). Ben-Gurion's political organ ran the country for its first twenty-nine years and enlisted Mizrahi voters with a systematic bureaucracy of privileges and favours. Its patronizing attitude was perfectly displayed in Ephraim Kishon's seminal film *Salach Shabathi*. Having fathomed the rejection by the veteran Mapai establishment, the oriental Jews became avid consumers of the glorious tradition cultivated by Menachem Begin's *Herut* (Liberty) Party that had an ideology modelled on the politics of the frustrated Polish middle classes of the early twentieth century. Herut, later merged into the Likud, made a cosy home for immigrants who came to Israel with the mentality of self-assured middle classes, only to experience a painful and massive drop into the proletariat.

The Likud afforded pride and patriotism. But the longed-for merger into the establishment did not materialize. Up at the top of the right-wing party that took power in 1977 thanks to the massive electoral vote of Arab Jews, it was too crowded. The Ashkenazi veterans of the revisionist Beitar movement, their children and their associates continued to hold the leadership.

Toward the end of the seventies, it became clear that Mizrahi Jews had to get their political act together if ethnic discrimination was to be halted. Aharon Abuchatzeira made a start at the potential direction, but his *Tami* (Movement for Israeli Tradition) Party was trailing badly, trudging due to the personal problems of its leader.

It was only with the energetic, smart leadership of Chief Sephardic Rabbi Ovadia Yossef and the young Rabbi Aryeh Deri that Israeli Mizrahi Jews managed a sectarian political power base that succeeded in badly shaking the Ashkenazi elite. Deri and Ovadia created a wonderfully simple winning formula. Under slogans calling for a return to religion and to the old faith, the long-suffering masses could regain their lost honour with the defiant claim that they are actually better Jews than all the Israeli "left-wingers" and more loyal nationals than the mainstream right-wingers. The road was opened to the fantastic success of a political movement that had invented a Sephardic-Orthodox identity that had never existed before and their followers appreciated this. The funeral of ex–Chief Rabbi Yosef, in October 2013, was attended by an unprecedented 800,000 mourners.

Independent observers were right to consider the Mizrahi revenge against the Ashkenazi establishment bizarre, bordering on the absurd. Having been looked down on for so long by mainstream secular Israelis, they hit them with a reverse mode. With the Mizrahi dressed up in the uniform of black suits and old-fashioned black hats they copied from their brethren in the Yiddish speaking *shuls*, it is hard for the uninitiated to distinguish between the new ultra-Orthodox from Morocco, Iran, Iraq, and Yemen and the veteran *haredi*m of Bnei Brak and Jerusalem who originated in Hungary, Poland, and Lithuania. Rabbi Aryeh Deri, choosing a silk evening coat as his attire for his eldest daughter's wedding in the Jerusalem Congress Centre in June 2001, had fixed the image of the new Mizrahi-ultra-Orthodox Jew. Never mind that he came to this event directly from jail.

Every one of Zionism's inner contradictions is on display by the Shas party and the movement for Sephardic ultra-Orthodoxy. It is actually the most appropriate representation of today's confused Israeli state. It is a political party that managed concurrently to adopt the Zionist idea in its most extreme patriotic version while loathing the group (of secular Ashkenazi) that executed this idea; to join forces with the ultra-Orthodox, anti-Zionist, Ashkenazi Jewish community while constantly complaining and rebelling against their continuous exclusion and discrimination against Sephardic Jews; to build up the rhetoric of Love of Israel and Making Inner Peace to new heights while exercising relentless religious coercion and constant calls for excommunication; to be mortally wounded by any hint of ethnic disdain or slur while at the same time articulating blunt insults and hate language against secular people, Ashkenazi, left-wingers and Arabs that are well within the definition of criminal racial incitement.

* * *

The New Jew created by the revivalists of Sephardic tradition imported a novel character into our region. Shas has proved how easy it should be to integrate into the rabbinical yeshiva world of Eastern Europe major components of the Muslim culture, which was never really estranged from the principles of Orthodox Judaism. With some positive imaginative effort, one might detect a potential – unrealized so far – for a new kind of Israeli interethnic, interdisciplinary mediation.

Islam, very much like Judaism, considers itself a religion of charity and mercy but is entrenched in a staunch masculine hierarchy. Both religions force a very strict modesty code on women, dictating dress instructions that should neutralize the sexual provocation they are supposed to embody. In both religions women may not be actively involved in public prayer or in any other form of worship except within the home environment, while serving husbands and other family members. Mosques are men-only areas, while the synagogues have special alcoves to keep women concealed.

There is no real mental distance between the much-maligned *burka* and the *hijab* that women in Muslim countries are supposed to wear and the traditional Jewish view that not only the sight of a woman's hair amounts to pubic public exposure,[3] but even the sound of a singing woman's voice is a "pubic" immodesty. Attempts by *haredi* women to preserve some of their femininity with the use of wigs is constantly under attack by self-appointed rabbinical authorities who insist heads should be shaved on the wedding night and covered only by scarves for the rest of the wife's life. In an ultra-Orthodox school, a ten-year-old girl might be penalized for improper behaviour if while raising her hand to say something in the class, her sleeve should slip back to expose her elbow. A new Jewish "Taliban Women"[4] group has adopted the idea of covering one's face with a shawl.

Both Jewish and Muslim communities attach major importance to the public chopping of the male organ in the patriarchal circumcision ceremony, emphasizing paternal authority. Fasting

---

[3] "Hair of a woman is pubic; Voice of a woman is pubic" – very common phrases based on Jewish Halacha (Talmud, tractate *Brachot*, 24). See also in chapter 24.

[4] This is a common pejorative nickname to a group of ultra-Orthodox women otherwise known as the "Shawl Women."

and other kinds of food deprivation, as well as the strict keeping to kosher commodities and slaughtering animals only under religious license are instrumental in forcing community control over Jews and over Muslims alike. In fact, in European countries that try to enforce more humane methods of slaughtering, or to ban baby circumcisions, Jewish and Muslim religious authorities join forces to object.

Both religions nicely reward the believers in happy family and community celebrations on a regular basis. Both encourage all members of the community, not just the priests, to advertise their *frumness* by traditional attire the year round. Mutual influences have been obvious for quite some time. In Arab communities, fashion-conscious Muslim women can be seen wearing head covers that were originally used by the Shas matrons. The wild Jewish hill mobsters of Judea and Samaria have adopted the large white lacy caps favoured by the Muslim Dervish, and sometimes their *galabia* gowns as well.

The eccentric, fanatic settlers of the hills show an enormous interest in goat herding, following the Bedouin model, and in aping the olive harvesting of the *fellahin*. Unfortunately, they harvest other people's olives. In the mosques the sheikhs have learned to build up a political power base that starts with affordable nursery schools following the successful *Source* kindergarten network strategy invented by Shas. When it comes to the high priority given to fantastically high birth rates, while efficiently making use of the crumbling Israeli welfare system, the patterns of behaviour are remarkably similar in the very religious Muslim population and the ultra-Orthodox Jewish sector. Both segments of the population produce also great numbers of violent and very frustrated school dropout youth.

Israeli secular society constantly complains of being outflanked on both sides with very large groups of citizens – Jews as well as Arabs – whose standard of living and lifestyle approaches third-world standards, putting pressure on the more affluent segments of this unequal society. The deprived, poor, ignorant, and helpless offspring of multi-child families make easy prey for hate professionals. Still, the so-threatened secular Israelis show remarkable tolerance with most caprices of their Jewish fanatics while blaming the secular Palestinians for not setting out to eradicate Muslim extremists.

* * *

As the years went by, even the bustling port city of Ashdod became more and more Orthodox. Whole communities of poor *haredi* came to settle in the town's eastern housing estates during the 1980s. At the same time, the emergence of the political Sephardic-*haredi* movement deeply marked the veteran North African Ashdodians. Kabala wise men, clairvoyants, and self-appointed holy rabbis made good business in the densely populated quarters. *Haredi* state-sponsored educational institutions for all ages as well as state-supported yeshiva high schools with dormitories became ever more popular as they eased the pressure on the households' bedrooms.

In the early 1990s, my parents, already retired, sold their pretty Ashdod flat and moved back to Tel Aviv. Veteran Israelis no longer felt comfortable in the new atmosphere. It seemed that Saturday's traffic across the city's junctions was about to be banned as the religious communities demanded Sabbath roadblocks based on the Bnei Brak and Jerusalem model.

But the constantly changing Israel was already going through a novel demographic shake-up. This time the rise of the Orthodoxy in Ashdod was reversed, and its Jewish-North African flavour much diluted.

A major torrent of a new kind of immigrants had swamped the city in the nineties, altering its character altogether. The mother tongue of these immigrants was Russian. Unlike my maternal grandmother and grandfather, who emigrated from Russia in the 1920s, the newcomers made no effort to shake off their Russian identity. To the great chagrin of the religious establishment, many of them are not even Jewish.

19

RUSSIANS ON THE MOVE

If indeed Russians who are not Jewish forge their certificates and even learn Yiddish clandestinely, this is the great victory for Zionism. Who would have believed in November 1917, when the Balfour Declaration was issued and the Bolshevik Revolution was on its way – that in less than one hundred years the Jewish State should be so attractive to non-Jewish Russians too.

Former Communications Minister Amnon Rubinstein, "And still they come," ***Ha'aretz,*** **June 17, 2001**

Children of the third millennium are very familiar with the image of the magic broomstick used by witches for flying. They have all read *Harry Potter* and seen the movies. In May 1988, such a broomstick – a thick cane with a bunch of dark straw tied at its end – was for me a vision out of ancient fairy tales, best illustrated in Walt Disney's "Sorcerer's Apprentice."

I was therefore quite enchanted to discover a real, life-size version of the said sweeping aid held by a tall Russian woman who seemed to be about ready to use it on a Moscow street corner. Within seconds of gaping at this apparition, I was even more surprised to discover that it was multiplied at every junction of the city. People holding large broomsticks seemed somehow to be using them, presumably for sweeping a small area of road or pavement. Sleepy Moscow was fully lit by the early spring dawn. Having just landed in Moscow by direct flight from Washington, I was traveling in a battered Lada taxi toward a hotel next to the Red Square, and the silent army of street cleaners gave me a first glimpse into the economy of the dying communist regime. The pretence of supplying every person's needs while working to the best of his or her ability created this spectre of municipal employees equipped with fairy-tale sprigs, a perfect sample of many millions of preposterously superfluous jobs. One year before the Iron Curtain eventually collapsed, the Union of Soviet Socialist Republics was as pathetically intriguing as it was odd.

American President Ronald Reagan called the rival superpower "an Empire of Evil," but his assistants knew well that its rotting structure was on the verge of falling apart. The West panicked because a nuclear war seemed inevitable, due to the enormous arsenal of weapons of mass destruction that both superpowers had assembled. Soviet leader Mikhail Gorbachev considered disarmament a high priority. The Americans promised trade concessions and economic support as part of a package deal. In return they pressured the Soviets to make concessions in matters of human rights. Very soon the Americans discovered that in the propaganda war, the issue of Soviet Jews was winning them many media points, and as a result, this became a major item on the agenda for the summit meetings that the leaders of the superpowers held. There must have been a noble motive for prioritizing human rights, but it was also clear that the Soviet regime would no longer have the power to silence dissidents; its days were numbered.

Ma'ariv dispatched me to join the hordes of journalists who scrambled around each of the Reagan-Gorbachev summit meetings. As a rule, correspondents on such occasions would hardly get a glimpse of the world leaders shaking hands, receive well-rehearsed versions of what went on in the hermetically sealed conference rooms from the public relations officers of both sides, and hope to gather some extra copy at the fringes of the massively orchestrated production. More than once we heard ourselves pompously reporting home events as seen on CNN screens that broadcast the live "pool" report to the whole world anyway, adding our own extra "feature" flavour that was mainly based on interviews with other frustrated members or the three-thousand-plus press core, and with some luck, a low-ranking official.

Fortunately for Israeli reporters, we had the theme of Soviet Jews as a major item, and this produced a lot of original copy. The first Reagan-Gorbatchev summit in Geneva, in November 1985, had charismatic Avital Sharansky as its chief media star.

Her husband Anatoly Sharansky (Nathan), who later became an Israeli government minister, was at the time a prisoner in Siberia. At the Reykjavik Summit a year later, the field was packed with amateur Sovietologists, mostly Russian Jews who now lived in the West, with mysterious jobs as media KGB connoisseurs. The friendly prime minister of Iceland was available for Israeli journalists in his modest residence. He gave an exclusive interview and expressed his full support to the "Let My People Go" slogan that summed up most of the Israeli foreign policy issues, fully endorsed by the United States.

The pressure worked. The Evil Empire opened up to issue hundreds of thousands of exit visas. But then the Jewish exodus from the USSR took an embarrassing turn. Tens of thousands of Jews with authorized exit documents simply refused to travel to Israel. The land they had set their hearts on was the United States of America, and they were not going to settle for a Middle Eastern substitute. The US government was not too keen. Thousands of Jewish refugees with families, children, and all their belongings were therefore stuck in Europe for many months. At first they lived in transfer camps near Vienna, and then a very large camp was built for them in the Italian coastal town of Ladipol .Soviet Jews made it clear that they were prepared to wait as many years as it took until it was their turn to receive proper green cards. Only very few agreed to follow the path to the Jewish state that truly desired them as new citizens.

The Israeli government and the Jewish Zionist establishment in the United States would not resign themselves to the failure of the plan to fortify the Jewish state with Soviet Jews. Israel needed the Soviets to combat the "demographic menace" of our being such a small people within an ocean of Arabs.

The right-wing government and its ministers, spearheaded by the minister of commerce and industry, Ariel Sharon, wanted the millions of Soviet Jews to settle in the occupied territories of the West Bank and the Gaza Strip. These expectations made a good excuse to keep the territories under Israeli occupation. On the Left, growing weaker with every election, some Israelis believed that reinforcements from Russia and its satellite states were needed to combat quite another "demographic menace" from within the Jewish population. I had found this out during my work as *Ma'ariv*'s correspondent in Washington a few months before my trip to Moscow.

* * *

In the United States' system of government, the position of the attorney general is considered one of the most powerful and is normally entrusted to a close confidant of the president. In the Ronald Reagan administration, the US attorney general was an intimate of the president, a pleasant fellow named Edwin Meese. In the last period of Reagan's second term, Meese got involved in some serious accusations over corruption and bribery allegations. One of these affairs had a strong Israeli angle.

The sociable Meese had as one of his own confidants a corrupt Jewish lawyer named Robert E. Wallach. Wallach was found guilty in connection with the Wedtech scandal that involved government funds and a high-tech company that had invested money in several countries abroad, including Israel. Wallach was also a friend of Israel's then prime minister, Shimon Peres.

Wallach had managed to enlist the support of his friend Meese for an ambitious project to build an oil pipeline from Iraq to Aqaba in Jordan. This plan was pushed by one of his clients, a Swiss Jewish millionaire named Bruce Rapport. Bruce Rapport was also a good friend of Shimon Peres. The pipeline project was supposed to make many millions for its backers. The public attorney who was appointed to investigate the affairs believed that certain sums of money that mysteriously padded the attorney general's private bank account were actually an "advance" for his good will in supporting the pipeline entrepreneurs.

The enterprise needed – and received – a promise by Prime Minister Shimon Peres that Israel would not attack the Iraqi pipe after its completion. The promise was perfectly legitimate: it made a lot of sense for Israel to cooperate with the keeping of peace in the area. The scandal only erupted over a well-documented claim that in return for Peres's support, the pipeline entrepreneurs had promised financial remuneration for both the Israeli government and the Israeli Labor Party.

The story exuded the unpleasant odour that Washington was too familiar with from the days of the illegal arms sales to Iran. The new scandal, just like the Iran-Contra affair that dominated the mid-eighties, was made of the unholy mix of senior administration officials, contacts in affluent Arab countries, and fast Israeli dealers with good Mossad connections. Big money was aimed for. The royalties for Israel alone were estimated at a yearly $65 million to $70 million for ten years.

The *New York Times*, which blew the story open, considered these "royalties" bribery for a foreign government. Fury was expressed over Meese's involvement in such an attempt to make illegal payments, which is completely against US regulations. Peres's men unsurprisingly denied the allegations altogether. The only incriminating evidence against the Israeli ex–prime minister was his handwritten note to Meese, which read, "I have asked my friends Bruce [Rapport] and Bob [Wallach] to bring the whole story to your attention. I rely on your best judgment as to how it should be dealt with." Two weeks after this note was written, the lawyer Wallach submitted a detailed memorandum with his good friend Meese at the service of his good client Rapport, summarizing his version of the understandings with his good friend Shimon Peres.

As Meese's political adversaries were hoping that the Israeli press would make a big fuss if an uncensored copy of the Wallach Memorandum was to be published, one of them offered me a copy of the original document to be published as an exclusive *Ma'ariv* "scoop."

"You will find something there that will be far more embarrassing to Shimon Peres than funds for his party," the source promised.

Damaging Shimon Peres was the last thing I was interested in. I have always considered Peres the only reasonable politician in the National Unity Government, certainly in everything concerning the Israeli-Palestinian conflict. But new revelations are what journalists live for, and the Wallach Memorandum was quite fascinating.

It was impressive to realize what an expert on internal Israeli party politics Mr. Wallach turned out to be. He was actually briefing his friend the US attorney general about the Israeli

Labor Party's desire to generate a mass immigration into Israel of Ashkenazi Jews, to balance the growing influence of Sephardic Arab Jews, who at that time were so unfortunately displaying a unanimous political appetite for the anti-Labor forces.

This is how the document of September 1985, marked "Private and confidential – for your eyes only," read:

It is necessary to supply Israel with a growing number of Ashkenazi Jews (from the USSR) to balance the flow of Oriental Sephardic Jews who have a natural affinity and liaison with Likud. From the point of view of American interests, the advantage is obvious.

Taking into account the enormous interethnic tensions that characterized Israel during the 1980s, this paragraph was real dynamite – indeed, even more explosive than the indications, already published a few months earlier, that the pipeline's entrepreneurs intended to bribe Israeli politicians. Or so I thought.

My editors in *Ma'ariv* did not see it this way. For them the direct quote from Wallach reading "part of the money will go to the Labor Party" seemed more important and became the headline,[5] although this information was not new. The sectarian remark that I thought should make the title was pushed to the end of the story and barely mentioned in a subtitle, never to be repeated or discussed. It was credible enough but did not seem to surprise or upset anybody, certainly not in the media. The Israeli right and left wing were at that time united in the conviction that the strong right-wing tendency of the Israeli electorate was directly related to the Middle Eastern origins of half the Israeli Jewish citizens. I, for one, thought that the Wallach Memorandum gave a new and suspicious angle to the Israeli passion for Soviet Jews.

* * *

Ethnic conspiracy or not, the Jews of the Soviet Union continued to play a major role in the global arena. The Reagan-Gorbachev Moscow Summit Meeting in May 1988 was about to become another exciting scene in the grand political show.

---

[5] *Ma'ariv,* February 22, 1988.

The colleagues in *Ma'ariv* gave me some useful telephone numbers for Moscow, and as soon as I arrived in my room at the Hotel Intourist, I made a call to the refusenik Yuly Kosharovski. This turned out to be a very lucky move, as Kosharovski invited me on the spot to a clandestine meeting of dissidents with the deputy to American Secretary of State Richard Shifter, an energetic Jewish politician who held the human rights portfolio in the State Department.

I immediately grabbed a taxi and arrived just in time at the Moscow suburb, about half an hour's drive from the centre. About thirty men and women crammed into the tiny flat of another dissident by the name of Sergey Makropchian, expecting the American senior official. I was completely taken with the sense of anxiety and isolation, deep inside the big bad sick Russian Bear. Shifter showed up punctually, and a lively conversation started. According to the reports that had been translated for Shifter by the participants, two activists who were supposed to join the meeting had been arrested as they boarded the train in Leningrad. This was going to be a great exclusive story for the next day's paper.

When the meeting ended, Shifter and his assistants sailed back into the city in the embassy's large limousine. The activists all went their separate ways. Only after walking on my own a few blocks away from Makropchian's flat did I realize that my expectation of finding a cab on the main street that would take me back to the Intourist was completely unfounded. I continued walking, realizing I was now completely lost, with no idea where I was or how to find the place I had left earlier. For another period that seemed like eternity, I wandered over some deserted, barely paved roads, hoping to find directions to a bus stop from which I could travel to the nearest subway station. The sky was still very bright on the white Moscow night, but it was very late, and I reckoned it would take me hours to find my way back to Red Square. The chance that my story would not make the Tel Aviv deadline was distressing. This was the pre–cellular phone era, and there was no way to make overseas calls from public phones in Moscow, as one did in the United States in those days. Away from anything and anybody familiar, I felt panic on the rise. Mercifully and unexpectedly I was eventually picked up by the driver of a passing Lada who presented himself as a cab driver.

Two days after this very secret assembly, the Reagan-Gorbachev meeting was in full flow, and the dissidents no longer played hide-and-seek. The participants of the "clandestine" meeting in the suburb flat all presented themselves at the American Embassy in the heart of Moscow for a very public audience with the American President Ronald Reagan. Upon exiting the embassy, they stood in Red Square and gave interviews to every television channel in the world, including Israeli TV, without any fear or worry. Their exit visas from the Soviet homeland were as good as issued. Big Brother seemed exhausted and had given up this lost battle.

* * *

It was not at all difficult to understand why the Jews were so eager to be released from this sad country. In the three days I wandered around Moscow, I saw many surprising and interesting things, but from the outset, I discovered that the most challenging task for a foreigner was to find something to eat. There were places that served food, even rare delicacies beautifully prepared, and ridiculously cheap, but these places opened and shut at very mysterious hours. If you did not have contacts and inside information, you could not guess they even existed. Some simply refused to serve you if you did not have the right certificate or for any other excuse. Twice I went to sleep on an empty stomach, not being able to get as much as a sandwich in the hotel bar, although I had a wallet packed with local and foreign cash. Alcohol, by contrast, was abundantly available. In the evenings the area around the Intourist was packed with men in deep stupor. Cheap vodka seemed to flow from every tap in town.

There was a heavy heat wave over Russia that week, but no air conditioning anywhere. Sweaty journalists and photographers tried in vain to buy simple T-shirts to replace their suffocating suits, but the clothes shops were half-empty warehouses offering only the most impossible items made of appalling synthetic materials. However, good tickets to the Bolshoi Ballet Theatre and to Moscow's famous circus were easily available for nominal prices.

* * *

I was pleased to leave this difficult city by the end of the summit discussions. There were two days left before my flight home, and I had planned in advance to use these days for a "roots-searching trip" to Odessa, where both my maternal grandfather and grandmother came from. Organizing such a trip for a single foreign journalist required an enormous amount of red tape, but I adamantly filled every form and kept visiting the tourism desk in the Intourist until a positive answer came, and I was allowed to purchase a package that included a flight ticket and two nights at the best official hotel.

The plane was a worryingly shaky Tupolev, and some of the fellow travellers seemed as though they had just landed in a time machine out of sixteenth-century Mongolia. Two of them had to be told that it was not a good idea to start cooking on their small primus stove in the aisle. The "best hotel in town" offered tatty rooms with youth-hostel-style showers. But the old centre of Odessa was a pleasant urban area with very little traffic. The large, unkempt gardens around the big blocks reminded me of fifties Tel Aviv. I did not find any relatives in the city, but I gained a new and interesting perspective on the "Let My People Go" theme.

Ulitza Pushkinskaya, which was the street Savta Chaya's family lived on, turned out to be the main street. I walked it up and down; took photographs of the famous staircase at its end going down to the Black Sea, eternalized in Eisenstein's *Battleship Potemkin*; and even discovered a Mr. Tchesnin in the telephone book. The mandatory guide I had to have for one day according to the tourism office regulations was horrified when I asked her to call him and ask if he happened to be related to my grandmother, and refused to assist me in this matter. I gave up. She introduced me instead to the Isaac Babel Museum and instructed me on Odessa's Jewish history, which also happened to be the city's criminal history. Apparently all of the local mafia bosses at the end of the nineteenth century kept a kosher diet.

Once freed of the guide, I went out to find a present-day "Jewish Angle" on Odessa. The activists I met in Moscow had given me the address of a local Jewish contact. He and some of his friends had no problem meeting with me.

They seemed to be living in a curious harmony with the Communist regime, spoke very openly about everything, and did not seem to worry about anything. They also did not seem wanting for material needs. The dollar in those days was considered a much-desired currency in Russia, and as I needed local roubles, I assumed my hosts would be pleased to change money for the official, much-underrated rate. To my surprise the man shrugged and said that if I needed money, he could simply give me as many roubles as I wanted; he had no use for US dollars, and there was not much to buy for roubles either.

His observations on the political situation in his country turned out in retrospect to be more accurate than what the greatest Sovietologists in the West were predicting at the time.

"Once communism is terminated here, everything will fall apart," he promised. "Nothing – no democracy, no free economy. Hooligans will take over the state, and it will be total chaos."

He was patronizing and condescending to the "Israelskaya" journalist who asked silly questions. It was clear that he considered me the representative of a particularly backward Middle Eastern state. His friends and family informed me that they had no intention of ever going to settle in the Jewish homeland that they considered a war-ridden, dangerous, and inferior place. Many people in Odessa wanted to emigrate from Russia, but they would rather have spent the rest of their days in Ladipoli than join the Zionist state.

We communicated in Yiddish – all the elderly in the small group spoke it fluently, and I could understand them very well through my knowledge of Hebrew and German. My German grammar irritated them as it sounded like very bad Yiddish, but they had no problem comprehending what I was after. They all thought I was funny to try and locate relatives named "Yuthem," and just like the guide, they vehemently refused to contact Mr. Tchesnin of Pushkinskaya Street for me. I was beginning to understand that it was unacceptable for anybody to be approached by total strangers on personal matters. At that stage of my trip, I was getting less keen to confront Russians I did not know and to ask if by any chance they had a Jewish grandfather.

On my second evening in Odessa, I returned to the hotel exhausted from the day's rambling. The heat wave in the Ukraine was even crueller than in Moscow. I sadly decided to give dinner a miss once again. Food was sold in the hotel bar, but it was too packed with unpleasantly inebriated men. I was looking forward to the end of my forty Odessa hours, but I was in for yet another surprise. The Jewish activist with whom I had spent my morning had just called the hotel and asked to meet me again. Upon arriving he informed me that another good friend of his, who was already in possession of an exit visa and was about to leave the Soviet Union for good, was very interested to talk to me. He had something important to say.

My impression was that something had changed in my favour. My local contact was friendlier than in the morning and was more forthcoming with information. Bubbling with curiosity and hoping to get a good story, I set out with him in his ancient Lada. We were heading somewhere into the suburban housing estates. Upon arriving we climbed some staircases over families of neighbours who were using the landings as balconies in the suffocating heat, all front doors wide open and displaying very poorly furnished flats. The small flat we entered was empty of furniture. The young family that expected us – a couple with one small child – had already finished packing all their belongings for their emigration. Everything they owned was packed in suitcases and parcels. Like everything else in the Soviet regime, the exit document arrived slowly and incoherently. The fact that you had an exit permit did not mean that you had the permission to purchase travel tickets, or had any idea when you might be allowed to use the tickets once you had them in your possession. The final papers, they explained to me, could arrive within one hour, and by then if you did not make a move at once, you might lose your chance to travel. On the other hand, it might take weeks before the documents arrived.

The young husband, wearing only a white cotton vest on his enormous, muscular body, looked a typical Russian *Muzhik*. It was explained to me that both he and his Jewish wife had lost their jobs as soon as they submitted their exit request. They were keen to leave but still had no idea when their dream was going to come true. Their immediate destination was Ladipoli, the standby camp for the American Green Card.

At last I understood how I suddenly turned out to be a desired guest. It was my visiting card with the Israeli *Ma'ariv* logo that I left with my new pals at the end of the morning meeting. Having carefully scrutinized it, they discovered that the card introduced me by the haughty title "US Bureau Chief, Washington, DC." Well, these words worked magic in Odessa. I was no longer a nagging Israeli woman but a personality with a printed card, a superior job, and an address in the land of endless opportunities. I actually lived in its capital. Their conclusion was that I was prominent enough to pull strings for comrades who would be landing in America.

The Muzhik spoke to me fervently in Russian, and the go-between Jewish friend explained. "Look here," he said. "The guy is telling you that he was born here, in Odessa. All his life he has lived here by the sea; this is what he is used to. Now we all know that most Jews waiting in Ladipoli and in Vienna end up in New York. New York, as we all know, is a very noisy, crowded place. This does not suit my friend at all. He needs wide-open spaces, nice views. San Francisco is much more suitable for his needs. The climate there is very good, and it is also by the sea. There is a large port in San Francisco, and my friend is used to working in a port. He has worked all his life in the port of Odessa; he is really a good hand. You must help him, please, that he and his family should be sent to San Francisco, not to New York."

I was speechless.

Then I started to apologize humbly. "Ich bin nur ein Journalistine," I mumbled, paraphrasing the confused actor screaming in Ishtevan Sabbo's *Mephisto*: "Ich bin nur ein Schauspieler!"

I confessed that I did not really have any useful contacts with the immigration authorities of the United States. With a certain Zionist zeal, I pointed out that Tel Aviv and Haifa are seaside cities too, and there is a large modern port in Ashdod.

It was a dialogue of the deaf. The comrades would not take a negative answer from Mrs. Bureau Chief. Nobody was foolish enough to believe that with such an important-sounding title, and having just been covering the Reagan-Gorbachev Summit, this woman could not make things move in the "Washington, DC" so clearly printed on her red-and-white card. If I had no liaisons with these important agents in high places, what had I come to Odessa for in the first place? I was either an impostor or most horridly unkind.

"Just talk to them; you can explain," the interpreter urged me following the torrent of excited words that came from the beach-loving young man. "You are from Washington, you are the Bureau Chief, and there must be some jobs in San Francisco. This man works really hard; he is very good in the port. He knows all about working on ships."

It was getting late; my flight back to Moscow was early the next morning. I wrote down the name of the family who would rather live in San Francisco instead of New York and said that if I should have a chance, I would do whatever I could to fulfil their wish.

Early in the morning, it appeared that Saba and Savta's native town was to put me through yet another minor trauma. The lady at the tourism desk who was supposed to arrange my transfer to the airport informed me point-blank that unfortunately I was not to fly to Moscow for another two days, as the flight was full, and there was nothing the next day either. This meant that I was to miss my flight back to Washington that was due the next morning. For a moment I was knocked dumb with a severe shock, but as soon as I came back to my senses, I produced an enormous angry outburst worthy of a Bureau Chief, dropping subtle menacing hints about my good contacts within the highest echelons. It was amazing how efficiently this worked. Miraculously a seat was found for me on board the Tupolev to Moscow, well overburdened with very large families from the less developed regions of the crumbling empire in their exotic attire. A feeling of great relief was with me throughout the long flight back to capitalism.

* * *

It took about eighteen months for whatever removed the anti-Israeli fixation of the Russian Jews to take effect. By the end of 1989, at the very point that the Communist regime had ceased to exist, the emigrants had become amenable to the Zionist option, and Israel gained the desired supply of immigrants from the former USSR.

In sharp contrast to the expectations of advocate Robert E. Wallach and his important Israeli friends, the purely Ashkenazi Russian speakers did not produce the longed-for turnover for the Israeli political scene. Quite the contrary. The majority of the well-educated and hardworking people from Russia and its satellite republics who had landed in Israel displayed unmistakable distaste to anything that sounded "left wing." Just like the immigrants from the Arab countries, these newcomers had developed a political frame of mind fervently supporting the occupation and passionately hating the "Arabs." In heavy Russian accents, they recite the worn-out mantras about our "rights over the country." Just like those who came from Morocco, from Yemen, and from Iraq, many of these new immigrants observe the supposedly "degenerated" well-established bourgeois left-wing veteran Israelis with deep mistrust, harshly criticizing their defeatist disposition vis-à-vis "the enemy."

Most of these new Israelis and their charismatic leaders fully uphold the ideology that generated their heavily subsidized immigration into the country and the Israeli consensus over the need to preserve a "Jewish majority" in the Jewish state. It is the ideology that insists on the eternalizing of positive discrimination in favour of the Jews, at the expense of the non-Jewish inhabitants of the land.

Never mind that so many of them have nothing to do with Judaism, except sometimes having a grandmother who married a Jew many years ago and forgot about it until it was discovered to be a key to a better socioeconomic future for her all-Russian or Moldavian grandchildren.

At the roadblocks that make their lives miserable in the occupied territories, our Palestinian cousins often come across Russian-speaking Israeli soldiers who find it hard to follow their fluent Hebrew. Christians among these Palestinians held up on the roads may find a lot in common with these new Israelis, visibly moved about being stationed in places like Bethlehem, especially when Christmas approaches.

The Israeli potential for absurdities is unfathomable. During seventy years of communism, most Jews in the USSR had no interest in the strict ban on marrying outside their communities, and almost all of them had chosen non-Jewish spouses. The Israeli Law of Return magnanimously includes anybody who is next of kin to a Jew up to three generations removed (in a creepy resemblance to the Nuremberg Racial Laws in 1930s Germany).

As a result, a majority of the immigrants from the former Soviet Union who arrived in Israel in the last few years to become instant citizens do not meet the religious criteria laid down in the Halacha. A report by Shachar Ilan in *Ha'aretz* of May 13, 2005 revealed that "about 70 percent of the Law of Return immigrants to Israel who are under 40 years old in the last several years are not Jewish." These people are pleased to become vociferously nationalist Israelis, but most of them rightly refuse – or are unable – to go through the process of an Orthodox conversion.

This makes their nationality quite problematic, as Israel does not recognize Israeli nationality, and only Jewish nationals are entitled to all the privileges. It is a source of embarrassment and inconvenience. Pressure on the rabbis to be a little more "flexible" with conversion procedures in favour of our new brethren proves ineffective. These men and women were born Christian Russian Orthodox or Catholics. What if they are nice people, hardworking, and well educated, all prepared to send their children to fight and possibly get killed for the Jewish right over the Promised Land? Too bad – the religious establishment is not at all interested.

The Israeli Army, a mighty state-within-a-state, promptly started its own "Conversion Courts," but they are mostly for willing young male soldiers. One evening I enjoyed watching a televised political debate that had the representative of the secular *Shinui* (Change) political party harshly criticizing the unsympathetic attitude of the rabbis to the conversion aspirations of new immigrants. The representative of religious politics happened to be the Minister Rabbi Shlomo Benizri, a prominent Sephardic-Orthodox leader, (until he, too, was indicted for corruption and served a jail sentence in 2009). The rabbinical eminence was not put out by the eloquence of the enlightened intellectual.

"If we need to start acting on fast track conversions – why start with Russians?" he wondered aloud, unimpressed. "Why not start with the Arabs of the land, the Palestinians? They were here first, and they are actually our cousins."

Of course there was no answer to this most logical attitude. His adversary did not even consider pondering the rhetorical question, although it summed up so nicely all the confusion, the sadness, and the twists of our existence as a society. In the 1950s and '60s, the State of Israel had made a tremendous effort to drag masses of Arabs into its territory because they were Jews. In the 1990s and in the first years of the new millennium, it exercised a mass import of non-Jews because they were not Arabs.

Part VI – Cousins

Question: Should one not consider the Israel-Lebanon War as another move in what you described in your *March of Follies*?

Barbara Tuchman: In the case of the Lebanon War I see no reason to speak of an act which is contrary to the national interest. The fact is that the PLO was exiled from Lebanon, and it has been getting weaker and weaker ever since. It is less influential in the international arena, which is an achievement for the Israelis.

Historian Barbara Tuchman to the author, on the occasion of the publication of the Hebrew translation of her best seller *The March of Follies, Ma'ariv,* September 5, 1986

20

SWEET AND THORNY

The Sharon Government turns the occupied territories into one large prison. Its own citizens become jailers who need to put down an inmate mutiny on a daily basis. This is not what Zionism was expected to do.

Professor Zeev Sternhell,
Ha'aretz, March 8, 2002

The beach was the only air-conditioned area we knew in the steamy Tel Aviv summer months. On the way home from Gordon Beach, up the steep alleys of the *Machlul* shanty neighbourhood, later to be buried under the monstrous *Atarim* seaside mall, we were already half-fainting after many hours under the sun – baking oneself and one's children in the midday sun was in those days considered to work wonders for your health. The shout "*Sabras! Sabras!*" was a tempting call for a refreshing delicacy. Tanned skinny boys offered the cool fruit that were lying on broken ice blocks inside rusty oil tins.

We would observe their bare fingers holding the frightfully thorny skin of the sweet cactus fruit with fascinated awe. They would skilfully make three deep cuts and offer the fresh deep yellow, reddening flesh on the tip of the knife for our pleasure, for one or two *groush*. Every child knew that it was strictly forbidden even to touch a prickly pear without thick rubber gloves. But the young sabra peddlers, mostly children of nine to eleven years old, did not seem bothered – perhaps because they were so different from us. They were Arabs.

Sabras – Arab for prickly pears – was actually the term of endearment coined for our kind of youngsters, Israeli-born Jews. It implied that although we were bad-mannered thugs, our hearts were pure; we were terribly thorny on the outside, but sweet and soft within, just like the fruit of the common local cacti, mainly to be found sprawling over the ruins of deserted Arab villages.

Fouzi El Asmar was one of the Arab boys who figured out at an early stage of his life that prickly pears had solid economic potential. He would arrive by bus from Lod (Lydda), carrying a large tin full of sabras picked next to his home and sell them at a good profit to the children of Tel Aviv, by the corner of Nachmani and Yehuda Halevi Streets. He was completely besotted – so he related in his autobiographical book that was written in Hebrew and published in Tel Aviv in 1975 – with the freedom Jewish kids enjoyed, and especially with the liberties exercised by the girls. Contacts with the majority ethnic group had many faces. "More than once I was offended by insults that referred to my being Arab, and I always asked myself what had made the person who insulted me my better, and should I put up with all this because I am Arab. But each time I was hurting I also told myself that after all, there are also Jews who treat me well,"[1] El Asmar summed up his first experiences as a member of a minority group in the Jewish state.

I met Fouzi many years after he had been exiled from Israel. He was already a highly respected member of the Palestinian press core in the United States when I arrived there in 1986. A large, solidly built man, he was generous with smiles and sharp with observations.

Israeli and Palestinian journalists often share the same beat in the American capital, and they find themselves spending much time together. Working the mazes of the news production industry around the Administration, we scrambled around the same State Department and White House briefings, and crowded the same learned lectures by the many experts on the Middle East in the research institutes and think tanks. Together we stuck around the large delegations that swarm into Washington, DC, each time a

---

1 Fouzi El Asmar, *To Be an Arab in Israel*, published by Professor Israel Shahak, 1975

major Israeli or Arab politician got into town. We often compared notes from on- and off-the-record briefings, designed mainly to boost the visitors' image back home. We had mutual professional interests in good copy, and exchanging information was very useful. Often, the cooperation yielded truly friendly relations. We shared the experience of being foreigners speaking English with heavy Mediterranean accents in this buttoned-up, oversophisticated city. We would never really live up to its smart, coded standards that included celery and carrot sticks with mayonnaise dips for cocktails, bad brownish water for coffee, and very cool manners, against our own stormy, uncontrolled Middle Eastern temperament.

Fouzi liked to entertain. Large quantities of barbecued meats, salads, and hummus with pine nuts were fed to the guests, who engaged in lively Hebrew discussions with the host. The pale white- and pink-flowered oleander bushes, justly unpopular in the Washington area, were a conspicuous statement of nostalgia for the homeland in the immaculate garden of his all-American house in a suburb of the capital. Before he gave me a copy of his book, I was not even aware of the long administrative detention followed by an even longer house arrest inexplicably imposed on Fouzi, then an Israeli journalist, in the early seventies. The only Israeli publication that actually followed – and protested against – such scandals, was *Haolam Hazeh,* which my parents considered inappropriate reading. This weekly magazine, published and edited by Uri Avnery, specialized in exposing political as well as sex and other scandals. For many years it was almost the only source of news that the government tried to muzzle.

To Be an Arab in Israel, a memoir Fouzi wrote during his house arrest, clearly maps the road that pushed hundreds and thousands of Israeli-born, Hebrew-speaking Arabs, who never aimed at anything except making a decent living, to join the Palestinian organizations that hoped to shake the Jewish state.

Fair and square, with not as much as a whiff of self-pity, *To Be an Arab in Israel* documents the enormous efforts and energies that the State of Israel via its different agencies had been investing over the years in alienating and excluding one single talented, non-Jewish Israeli individual, blocking any chance that he should become an integral part of Israeli society.

Like many of the Arab intellectuals of Israel and in Palestine of the early years, Fouzi was a child of a Christian family. Christian Arabs had always been a minority in Palestine. With little or no interest in nationalistic ideas from the outset, they thrived during the British mandate. Fouzi was born in Haifa and grew up in Lydda. His father worked for the railway authority; his mother was a poet and a publicist. The middle-class family owned land and cultivated its contacts with both Muslims and Jews. Fouzi's father had a particular liaison with the Jewish Marxist-Socialist Mapam party. In the 1940s, Mapam endorsed the option of Jewish-Arab coexistence in Palestine.

It would be hard to explain rationally the attitude taken by the Israeli Jews to the Israeli Arabs, who had no wish but to try and make a good, useful life for themselves next to the Jews, and with them after the 1948 war. The stance was fully in line with the religious rules that had been inserted, almost subconsciously, into the Israeli national consensus from day one.

The autobiographical story evokes a picture of an easy adaptation, almost a desire for integration. Coexistence in a mixed society always suited educated minorities. The boy Fouzi went, as all his family did, through the traumatic experience of Lod's takeover by the Israeli forces, the Nakba that drove out thousands of neighbours, and the tough years of the military rule over the town. He grew up to be a survivor and learned to cope with big and small injuries to his pride, his livelihood, and the family's property, but his disposition remained healthy and optimistic. He had always been searching for solutions to problems rather than dwelling on past wrongs. He merely strove to find a way to get on with a life that would match his abilities.

At school he had studied Hebrew and learned Hebrew literature, then completed his studies in bookkeeping and approached the job market. He was surprised and worried to discover that most doors were closed to him and to his peers. In the socialist, fully nationalized Israeli economy of the 1950s, jobs were controlled by public institutions – the government, the Histadrut Workers' Union, or other national organizations. Non-Jews had no access to these jobs. The Israeli Electricity Corporation and the largest bank (Leumi) made clear that Arabs could not even apply for positions. An attempt to study in Israel's Technological College (the Technion) exposed the fact that Arabs were not allowed to study electrical engineering or mechanics. They were permitted to apply for construction engineering only.

There was no ethnic or cultural difference between Fouzi El Asmar and young people with names like Masud, Samir, or Jamille with Arabic for their mother tongue who in those years arrived in Israel as immigrants. Fouzi, if anything, was better adapted to life in the fast-developing Israel. Coming from a well-established, supportive home, his education and qualifications were better than those of most new immigrants. He was fluent in Hebrew, which most of the newcomers were not. His upbringing was more European compared not only to most Arab Jews but also to many eastern Europeans. He was a perfect member of the bourgeoisie, the middle class that is supposed to make the backbone of any democratic society.

But the Zionist narrative was already a captive of the uncompromising Jewish codes that consider any liaison with non-Jews an existential menace. The socialist Left, seemingly so unreligious, was fully governed by these attitudes. Fouzi's first encounter with Jewish paranoia took place in the holy of holiest heart of the Zionist Left: the kibbutz. Many years before the kibbutzim started importing volunteers from Europe, the need for friendly, cheap working hands was already there. A family friend who was a Mapam member arranged positions as live-in workers for Fouzi and another Arab friend, both high school graduates, in Na'an, a kibbutz not too far from Lod:

The secretariat of the kibbutz knew very well that we were Arabs and that we had been sent by the Party. Still, the first foreman we worked with in the vegetable plot delicately explained that it would be better if we chose Hebrew names. I was named Moshe, my friend became Baruch. The explanation was that it was better not to identify us as non-Jews as some kibbutz members lost sons or family members in the War of Independence.[2]

---

[2] *To Be an Arab in Israel*, p, 39. (Quotes translated from Hebrew by author)

Impersonating Jews was not too difficult. The two youngsters' heavy Arab accents were not different from that of new immigrants from Arab countries. Their cover story was that they arrived on their own from Egypt, having left their families behind. Fouzi had only to worry about meeting Jews from his presumed native land who might be curious about the neighbourhood he used to live in. His friend, having lived in Cairo for several years in his childhood, did not have anything to worry about at all. Both had to be careful about using the communal showers. Both were Christians and uncircumcised.

Still, Fouzi had nothing but good memories from his days in the kibbutz. Especially pleasant was his acquaintance with a young female member who took a personal interest in him and did not fail to guess his real identity before inviting him to his first-ever sexual experience. He lived in the kibbutz a whole year and admits in his book that his time there had deeply and positively shaped his views. Women's liberation and the need for social equality were new and attractive concepts.

Social equality had its limits. Had Fouzi tried to join the kibbutz, he would have discovered that none of these revolutionary communes accepted Arab members. Jewish female members who fell in love with Arabs and wished to marry them were asked to leave. This was the case even in the single communist Israeli kibbutz, Yad Hanna. I heard from a veteran comrade of Yad Hanna about at least two cases of Arab men who tried to join their Jewish partners, but both were rejected. "It seemed too complicated," was the explanation.[3] Still MAKI, the Israeli Communist Party, was the only political home where Arabs could feel comfortable enough. Mapam in the meantime was swept with Zionist zeal and deserted the binational ideology.

Israel of the 1950s and '60s was perhaps a cohesive, supporting community that valiantly upheld its noble values, but that was mainly the case if one was a Jew, preferably not a Jew with Arab upbringing. It certainly had elements of a western democracy with strong socialist principles that lasted until enough wealth

---

[3] Memories of Yad Hanna I heard from Pnina Feiler during a women's conference in Nazareth, September 2002.

was collected by the powerful, and then it made ready to move to a more traditional class hierarchy. In the meantime, both the legal system and the national consensus solidly shaped the State of Israel from day one as a modern democracy for members of one religion only.

Discrimination on a racial, communal, or religious basis was at that period the norm in other places around the globe, just emerging from a long legacy of colonial habits. The US Constitution did little to stop discrimination against blacks; "natives" had inferior status in most colonies of the so-called enlightened European states; South Africa was fortifying the apartheid policy with little notice or objection from the rest of the world. Jews were openly discriminated against in most western societies. Racism, anti-Semitism, and xenophobia are still rife all over the world, and many people from third-world countries still find Israeli society quite accommodating, when compared to some of the alternatives. But as the new millennium progresses, Israel is now almost unique in allowing its legal system to openly and officially preserve discrimination based on community and religion.

* * *

For a guy so robust, vivacious, and hardworking, with a gift for writing poetry and for making friends, 1960's Tel Aviv was a natural, happy habitat. Fouzi El Asmar was an optimist. He published his verse and gained modest fame with the Arab reading public. At the same time, he contributed articles and opinion pieces for the Hebrew press. For a while he was employed as an editor and correspondent for the Arabic language weekly *Al Fajer* (The Dawn) that was owned by Mapam. Upon being invited to join a group of Arab intellectuals who started the *Al Ard* (The Land) group, he willingly accepted. The group, he noticed, was politically incoherent to start with. Nationalists, left-wingers, and centre positions of the Arab Israeli public were all represented. Eventually a joint platform was agreed upon. It included – the year was 1963 – a demand for the establishment of a Palestinian state next to the State of Israel.

Jewish public opinion was automatically shocked and appalled. A wall-to-wall panic made it easy to declare *Al Ard* an outlawed organization. There was a limit to what Israeli-style western democracy could take.

It was the end of the cosy job with *Al Fajer*. The Party gave Fouzi an ultimatum: Join Mapam ("For Socialism, Zionism, and the Fraternity of all Nations") or be fired. As he was unable to call himself a Zionist, he had to find other means of making a living. He chose to embark on private enterprise and started his own small publishing house for books in Arabic, including his own translations from foreign languages.

But at that time, he was already marked by the vigilant Israeli security services, who managed to turn his business career into a nightmare. Time and again his office was raided with false allegations. The books he had been printing were confiscated, and he was left with large financial losses. He was blamed for distributing "subversive" materials when he sold to Israeli Arabs *The Philosophy of the Revolution* by Gamal Abd-Al Nasser, then the president of Egypt. A Hebrew translation of the book, published by the Israeli Defence Ministry's own *Maarachot* publishing house, was available in all bookstores in Israel. On other occasions he was instructed to alter verses or even illustrations that annoyed the secret service. While the demand for his merchandise was healthy enough, Fouzi went bankrupt quite soon, with most of his confiscated production stored at the secret service's depots. Eventually the poet-entrepreneur found himself begging for work as a day labourer in a factory for plastic utensils.

Amazingly, Fouzi remained a believer in Israeli democracy. With astounding resourcefulness, he wrote a short letter describing his predicament and asking for support, then duplicated it 120 times and sent it to all the members of the Israeli Knesset in Jerusalem. The one member of Knesset who actually reacted was the late Dr. Eliezer Rimalt, of the right-wing General Zionists Party (later merged into the Likud). Something told him that the way this young Arab was being treated was actually scandalous.

Fouzi was invited to meet Rimalt and present his case. The politician used his own contacts to check on the story and came to the conclusion that an honest, well-meaning citizen was badly wronged by the system. He was actually so impressed with Fouzi and his parents that he and his wife became family friends with the El Asmars, showing political and human common sense that has since been seriously absent in his followers' circles. Dr. Rimalt volunteered to find Fouzi a dream job as an employee of a large public construction company, Shikun U-Binuy. And if this was not enough, he even stood firmly on the side of the El Asmars when the State's National Bureau for Land started to confiscate their privately owned land. It is surprising indeed to discover from Fouzi's memoir that the bureau executive he had to struggle with was no other than the late Reuven Aloni. Aloni's wife, Shulamit, later to become the pioneer of human rights and civil liberties in Israel, was at that time still a member of the young generation of the ruling Mapai Labor party.

* * *

Then came the Six Day War. The colossal earthquake that shook and changed everything and everyone in the country also thrashed and damaged much of the delicate tissue of early Jewish-Arab affinities that had just started developing. To Fouzi El Asmar's dismay, a considerable majority of left-wing Israelis had been swept along with the messianic euphoria that overtook Israel following the war and the Israeli takeover of more Arab land. He was deeply hurt as some Israeli human rights icons – he names them in his book, starting with Amos Keinan, through Uri Avnery, all the way to Moshe Sneh – chose to keep silent about blatant breaches of human rights in the newly occupied territories. Mass transfers of citizens, harsh collective penalties, and the destruction of villages were ignored, Fouzi claims, even by those otherwise true champions of liberty and justice.

Arab intellectuals were deeply bitter and depressed after the war. Fouzi at that time had a Jewish girlfriend named Yossefa, and he chose to describe her reactions with sincere empathy:

She too had her moments of total bliss with the joy over the victory, the general enthusiasm over a state three times enlarged, the open roads and the possibilities to travel and see new places. But soon enough she realized how terrible the events had been.

As soon as the initial shock reaction was over, she understood that not only did Israel's achievements come with horrible bloodshed for both sides, but also that Israel was taking a road that was not about to bring peace, but on the contrary would cause further bloodshed for many years to come, increase the hostile rift between Jews and Arabs and further minimize the chance for peace. Although she was a young Jewish woman, educated in Israel and thrilled with the fact that she could now reach Anatot and Beit El, to see with her own eyes the Tomb of Rachel, the Temple Mount, the Machpela [Sepulchers of the Patriarchs in Hebron] and the Western Wall, it was time to do some serious soul searching.[4]

Yossefa was part of a tiny group of Jewish Israelis who could fully identify with their Arab comrades, but to no avail. In the summer of 1968, Fouzi was arrested by the secret service. He was convinced this was nothing but a mistake. After a few days, the excuse was presented to him. A letter was found in the pocket of a Palestinian who had infiltrated into Israel from Jordan. The letter recommended that contact should be made with "Poet Fouzi El Asmar, by the railway station in Lydda." There was no proof that Fouzi had any idea that somebody was trying to get in touch with him, let alone that he consented to such a meeting, but for the investigators this made no difference. From the very first stages of his interrogation, Fouzi received "friendly" advice to agree to leave the country. He refused, and was kept for eight months in administrative detention, an infamous practice, left over from the British mandate, which does not require trial or proof of guilt, still widely used by the Israeli occupation regime. When he was released, he was confined to Lod and barred from Tel Aviv, ten miles up the road, which had been the focus of his life for so many years. He had spent the confinement writing the book that his friend, the late Professor Israel Shahak, published. A few years later, El Asmar already was part of the growing Palestinian Diaspora. Israel had left him with no other choice.[5]

---

[4] *To Be an Arab in Israel* p. 145.

[5] Fouzi El Asmar died in Washington, DC, on September 19, 2013, three weeks after the death of his wife Maria, mother of his only daughter Lila. His coffin was flown to the funeral in his native Lydda/Lod.

* * *

I have met a number of Hebrew-speaking Palestinians abroad, all ex-Israeli citizens. Every single one of them had a tale about some deep disappointment following contact made with the apparently modern, democratic, open-minded Israel; meetings with enlightened liberal Israelis had always ended with the exposure of unbridgeable rifts.

"The Palestinians," to quote the liberal *Ha'aretz*'s chief political commentator, Yoel Marcus, "are the source of it all. Their violence created a situation of no partner to talk to; they are the ones who are exclusively responsible for the Likud ascent to power and the Sharon ascent to divinity." Just like Marcus, many Israeli peace seekers are very sad and unhappy about what they are convinced is "the Palestinian clear preference for the terror option."

Two years before I met Fouzi, I interviewed another Palestinian in exile, who deeply influenced my own perspectives. Sabri Jiryis was a senior official of the PLO who had been running the public relations section of this organization in Beirut and presently ran the cultural section of the organization in Cyprus. He too was one of the founders of *Al Ard* and was forced to leave Israel in the late sixties. His book "The Arabs in Israel", published in 1966 (and translated into English ten years later) is the first ever detailed work about the way the Israeli regime had been treating Arab citizens.

I met Jiryis during a conference that was organized in 1985 by a well-meaning West German institution. Israelis and PLO representatives were invited to stay in a modest hotel in Saint Augustine, a suburban town on the eastern bank of the River Rhine opposite the capital, Bonn. As both groups refused to participate in a joint event, the conference officially had two separate parts: first a Palestinian two-day discussion, then an Israeli one. The Palestinians were invited to stay for the Israeli conference, and some of the Israelis came earlier and listened to the Palestinian discussions. The idea was to try to find common denominators that would make a peace process possible. It was hoped that the guests from the Middle East might be inspired by the experience of the European hosts. Only forty years earlier, blood had been flooding the killing fields near Saint Augustine, which now was famous mainly for its large shopping centres.

In Israel the government was in a rotation agreement between Labor's Shimon Peres and Likud's Yitzhak Shamir. The presence of Ora Namir, a member of Knesset from the Labour Party, next to the special emissaries of Yasser Arafat, was a breakthrough for Israeli thinking and a refreshing challenge to the norms gradually forced by the Israeli right wing. The Knesset was already working on the law that declared all contacts with PLO members illegal and it was finally passed by the Knesset in August 1986.

I was at that time correspondent for *Ma'ariv* in Bonn, and my aim was to get an interview with Ahmad Dajani, who at that time was considered the number two for Yasser Arafat. Dajani, a big man with silver hair, was rumoured to have some new insights. His speech in the first part of the conference was impressive enough, but when I approached him, he turned me down with male chauvinist chivalry and eventually left the conference early in order not to be seen in public with the Israelis. Jiryis, a Hebrew-speaking lawyer born in the Christian village of Fassuta in the Galilee, was pointed out to me as the Palestinian who the PLO members decided in advance might grant the first interview of a senior PLO official to an Israeli daily. Thirteen years earlier, in 1971, three Fassuta residents were sentenced to long prison terms because they were suspected to have been in contact with Sabri Jiryis. Israeli authorities claimed that he had tried to enlist them for terror activities.

Jiryis turned out to be a man in a brown suit who carried bitter memories of Israel and of the Israelis. He had lost his wife, the mother of his two children, when a car bomb destroyed the PLO headquarters in Beirut. The terror act was attributed to the Christian Phalangists. For Jiryis, Israel, which supported the Phalangists, carried most of the responsibility.

His politics in the PLO marked him as one of the "doves" committed to the Territories-for-Peace formula. He was not overwhelmingly friendly to start with, making it clear that he was all too familiar with the patronizing attitudes of left-liberal Israelis. I managed to break the ice by pulling out my ethnic ticket and identified myself as a Yemenite on my father's side. It was a trump card that never failed. In fact, I was also quite charmed.

Sabri had a gentlemanly comportment and a sarcastic sense of humour. Like most Middle Easterners – Israeli and Arabs alike – he had no qualms about touching on the most personal matters with total strangers. During dinner at the hotel, he stunned my husband and me when he scolded us for not being parents yet. "There is nothing more important than children in this world," he lectured us, totally ignoring the fact that whatever children we might bring to this world would supposedly be the enemies of his own kids.

Jiryis had good answers to most of my Israeli worries. The right of return, the fate of Jerusalem – he, as well as some of the Palestinian speakers at the conference, inspired the confidence that with genuine good will and some creativity, no problem is ever unsolved. For us Israelis, the major obstacle seemed to be the PLO basic covenant that included a commitment to the destruction of the State of Israel. The European, the Americans, and even the Egyptians demanded that the Palestinians give up the offending paragraphs of their covenant. Jiryis shrugged and put things in perspective: "What can we do? We, too, have our Likud." He managed to convince me that his colleagues in the moderate section of the PLO were making a sincere effort to alter the covenant (this did happen two years later).[6] They proved their interest in a compromise solution by the very fact that they stayed for the Israeli part of the Saint Augustine conference, openly defying the PLO extremists.

Jiryis wore a poker face when I pointed out to him how discredited and mistrusted Yasser Arafat was. During the eighties Arafat was hated throughout the Arab world. "This is the leadership we have; this is what we should all be working with," he cut me short.

When we finally sat down to the interview, I started by asking him whether it would not be correct to call him a terrorist. After

---

[6] It took me almost fifteen years to realize that the PLO's original call for one secular democratic state – officially retracted to please Israel and the United States in 1987 – will in fact become the only vision worth campaigning for.

all, he did belong to an organization that for years had been openly planning and executing violent attacks on civilians. His answer was "I do not see any difference between a terrorist leaving a bomb in a Jewish area, and a pilot who drops bombs, indiscriminately, over urban areas and refugee camps full of civilians."

As he was himself a victim of a terror attack in which he lost his wife, his words carried some weight. For me he personified a Palestinian "Peace Now" movement that must one day be ready to shake off the past and work for a better future for both peoples.

Ma'ariv was in no hurry to publish my copy. The editor of the weekend magazine, Zvi Lavi, was actually quite keen to print a controversial first interview with a PLO official, but was vetoed by the chief editor, the late Shmuel Schnitzer. The interview was shelved. I called from Bonn to protest. Schnitzer was an outstanding journalist. During the evacuation of the town of Yamit in 1982, he gained international acclaim by leading the chief editors' demonstration near the Gaza Strip, to protest the sealing off of the area by then–Defence Minister Ariel Sharon. Sharon chose to bulldoze the town houses to rubble so that Palestinians and homeless Egyptians would not move in, but he did not wish to have this act on camera. Schnitzer was a staunch right-winger, but I had never before encountered him allowing his politics to take the better of his support for the freedom of information.

He knew me well enough as a so-called raving leftie, but regularly published the few opinion pieces I produced, and in fact it was his idea to offer me the job of chief correspondent in Europe, against the vehement opposition of some senior colleagues in the newspaper. But when I called to argue my case for my rare interview with the PLO official, he was adamant. "During the Second World War the British media never published interviews with Nazi leaders, and there is no reason why *Ma'ariv* should be open to airing the views of Israel's enemies," he said, dismissing my complaint and informing me resolutely that his decision was final. It was the first time I had heard this senseless line of argument, recited ad nauseam to these very days by Israeli right-wingers each time moderate Palestinians are quoted in the Hebrew media. There was no room for further arguing. The interview with the "sabra" of Fassuta was put away.

Not for good. About five months after the Saint Augustine conference, Shnitzer retired, and Ido Dissentshik became the new chief. Ido was a first-class professional, a graduate of the Columbia School of Journalism, and he was happy to resurrect the piece from the archives. He called me from Tel Aviv to tell me about it. Naturally I was very pleased. "I must tell you that I had to make a small change while editing it," Ido told me. "One has to take into account the readers' feelings; they would find it difficult anyway."

A copy of the magazine landed with me about a week after the publication, and I found out what the "small change" was. My question to Jiryis, "Should you not be considered a terrorist?" was replaced with the announcement "I told him that as far as I was concerned he was a terrorist, and this is how he will be presented to the readers."

I thought I would blow up with rage and frustration. Far away from home, completely dependent on the monthly salary to sustain us in Bonn, I was simply not in a position to do the "right thing" and proudly hand in my resignation because my piece had been so seriously distorted. Pride had to be swallowed. I did not even call the chief editor to register my complaint. The story had been edited and printed; in Tel Aviv nobody would even know what I was going on about. A retraction was inconceivable.

Years later, when people used to ask me with great surprise, "But how could you give up journalism, give up the freedom to express yourself independently?" I used to say that freedom of expression is a relative business.

While the interview was being prepared for publication, I called Sabri Jiryis in Cyprus happily to tell him that it was about to come out and also to ask him for more photos, as the magazine editor had requested. He nervously answered that things had changed since the spring and he would rather not have this story published at all. Following the publication, I was not able to get him on the phone anymore. I wrote to him, but he did not reply. Apparently, freedom of expression was a relative business for the head of the PLO cultural section too.

* * *

The Israeli Peace Camp constantly courts Palestinian leaders who should "accept a peaceful solution." Such a solution, seen from a left-liberal Zionist perspective, must "of course" include the renouncing of all Palestinian claims on the land from which they had been driven away, all in the name of the "necessary" Jewish demographic and cultural supremacy.

Such Palestinians actually presented themselves. They embraced the "Two States Solution" discourse and wished for an end to violence. But it never took them too long to realize how empty this vision had always been. "Islam" has nothing to do with the reality of non-Jews in Israel. In fact, Christian Arabs were faster than most of their Muslim compatriots to figure out the problem with Zionism.

Time and again Palestinians are requested to declare, recognize, and accept "the Jewish state." Right-wing governments – and we have had nothing but right-wing governments for years on end – present this as a "minimal" precondition even for peace negotiations to start earnestly. But Palestinians – whether under occupation or Israeli citizens, Hebrew speakers, or even members of the Israeli Army – eventually understand that "Jewish state" is not merely a cultural or ethnic phenomenon, based on a large group of an immigrant population anxious about its unique character. It is in fact an institutionalized system that legitimizes the denial of civic and property rights to non-Jews. It is hard for non-Jews to sustain such a system over a long period of time.

Equally, it is hard to imagine a self-respecting Arab capable of wholeheartedly endorsing the present Israel, with some of its best legal minds constantly at work on further racist legislation discriminating in favour of "those who are eligible by the Law of Return and their descendants." The 18th Knesset, dispersed October 2012, dedicated hundreds of hours to such legislation; some clearly racist laws were passed with the coalition's majority. The 19th Knesset, sworn in on February 5, 2013, and the 20th Knesset, sworn in on March 31, 2015, eagerly pushed forward the rest of this legislation and most of it became law.

It is yet harder to fathom Israeli liberals who are truly appalled by the spirit of their fellow nationals; who are prepared to demonstrate, protest, and sign petitions against the land grabbing, the separation fence, the check-point harassments, the looting of the olives, the destruction of homes, the thousands of arrests, the mistreatment of minors in military prisons, and the brutal treatment of the civil population by the Israeli Army – but they do all that to protect their own fantasy of a would-be proper, "democratic Jewish state." It never occurs to them that by making our religion the law of the land, we renounce any claim to proper democracy.

21

LOVE-SICK IN BALTIMORE

Every child comes with the message that
God is not yet discouraged of man.

Rabindranath Tagore

God obviously cannot stand humans.
The proof: He kills them all the time,
everywhere, by every possible method.

Anonymous

The capital of the United States of America is in a particularly unusual climate zone. An Israeli landing there for the first time in July or August might be amazed by the steaming heat, worse than anything one was used to in summertime Tel Aviv. In the winter one could easily be stuck in a bad snowstorm, and in between, even hurricanes occur. In the leafy, comfortable suburbs of Washington, DC, the wild presence of the subtropical forest that once covered the area is still very much in evidence. Red squirrels and cardinal birds survived by making the thick vegetation of the large private gardens their new habitats. In the spring the city is awash with a stunning celebration of pink and white beauty as magnolia, azalea, and cherry go into full blossom.

Once in every seventeen years, nature runs a particularly unusual show. With well-predicted accuracy, billions of seemingly disgusting creepy-crawlies emerge from the well-kept lawns and start moving slowly over yards and streets toward the many large, old trees. Having completed their sluggish ascent to the treetops, they start pumping air into their wings and become adult cicadas. Now they can start to constantly fly around, making a nonstop buzzing noise that lingers over the area from dawn to sunset every day for about six weeks. Residents, particularly newcomers who have not encountered the cicada invasion before, react with differing degrees of panic and disgust to the noise, the frightening insect clouds flying around, and the mess left by the thousands that end up crushed on the ground before reaching the trees, leaving behind sticky, horrible goo.

Unlike its biblical North African relative, the locust, who sometimes visits the land of Israel, the seventeen-year cicada does no harm and does not eat any vegetation. The life of the two-inch-long adult insect, which has five red eyes, is dedicated to mating and proliferating. By the end of this period, billions of new eggs are left on the trees. The tiny larvae will come discreetly out of the nests by the autumn and crawl back to the lawns. They feast on the tree roots before becoming cocoons that will hibernate for the next seventeen years, when it will be time to start the new generation.

For the many Washingtonians making a living by producing texts for the written as well as the broadcast media, the seventeen-year-cicada show of 1987 was a reliable source of inspiration for fine philosophical musing over life – its mysterious meaning and its eternal cycle. The firm hold cicadas had over the city's grounds, as well as their bustling, short apparition, evoked metaphorical comparisons with the short duration of many professional careers in this town, and the toughness of political cycles in a democracy that can send its best men and women packing every four years.

It was too bad that journalists were not sent to DC to report on flora, fauna, and the weather. There is never a dull moment for Israelis, with the nonstop political action in this town, so critical to our own life back home in the Middle East. The mid 1980s occasionally supplied some powerful drama, as did the Jonathan Pollard affair, the Iran-Contra scandal, and some juicy VIP intrigues that created the cocktails of money, sex, and corruption much favoured by the media.

Still, the most moving story I found myself working on during three years on the job in the United States had no American political relevance whatsoever. It was the story of two young people who had met in the Israeli town of Petach Tikva, and found themselves struggling with the most fundamental problems of

Jewish Israeli society, fighting for an unborn baby. It was a simple story about courting, mating, and starting a new generation.

* * *

A long-distance telephone call came one morning from a woman who said she was the spokesperson of the Israeli Human Rights Association. She asked me to help a young labourer from Gaza who approached the association with a story that sounded grim and almost unreal. The man, who lived in Tel Aviv and had a job there, claimed that his Jewish fiancée, who was pregnant, had been kidnapped and taken out of the country against her will so that their baby would be adopted by a Jewish family in the United States – apparently for a handsome fee. Zaki – this was the guy's name – insisted that his girlfriend, Nurit, was being kept forcefully with an ultra-Orthodox Israeli family somewhere in the United States and that she was employed as a house cleaner until she gave birth. He thought the association was the right body that could provide him with legal help and support him in his effort to claim back his unborn child.

Advocate Shira Dunevitz, then legal adviser for the association, checked the story and realized that even if the association could manage to get the Israeli legal system moving in favour of Zaki, his case was as good as lost. Litigation on such a complicated matter needed many months; the birth of the baby – and its immediate disappearance into the American Jewish Orthodox community – was a matter of weeks, perhaps only days. Dunevitz thought this was a classic case where only the media could help. I said I would be happy to hear more directly from the persons involved.

Within minutes, Zaki called me from his Tel Aviv flat for a first, very detailed conversation. He told me that he had met Nurit a year earlier. They both took the same bus to work every morning from Kiriat Ono to Petach Tikva, both in the Tel Aviv area. Nurit was eighteen, a daughter of a traditional, multichild family from Persia, who had just graduated from a religious high school. Zaki lived with a number of his friends from Gaza in a small flat near the Carmel market in Tel Aviv. These were the days before the first Palestinian *Intifada*. Palestinian labourers, always available in large numbers for minimum wages, still held the backbone of the Israeli economy.

On the bus, the two noticed each other, exchanged looks for a few weeks, and then started to chat regularly. Nurit initially believed that Zaki was a Sephardi Jew, and he did not bother to correct her. Only after they started dating did he reveal to her that he was an Arab. The young woman was startled, but she was already in love. The interethnic romance grew ever more serious, and the two took the bus to Netanya to consult a famous clairvoyant over their predicament. The woman checked her tarot cards, read marks of their coffee cups, and prepared astrological charts, then announced that they were made for each other and that their great love would survive all adversities. They chose to believe every word. When it turned out that Nurit was pregnant, they decided to marry on the spot. As Nurit came from an observing family, their idea was that Zaki should convert to Judaism and join the family. As simple as that.

At a relatively advanced stage of the pregnancy, Nurit confessed the situation to her parents and asked them to help her and Zaki approach the necessary rabbis who could make the conjugal situation respectable. To her great distress, she immediately found herself the centre of an enormous scandal. An experienced, highly efficient bureaucracy of religious officials was in motion to remove the Arab man from the life of the Jewish girl. The family – angry, upset, and very worried about its own reputation – presented the confused Nurit with an ultimatum. She was not allowed to meet Zaki ever again or even talk to him over the phone. She had to agree to consider this option. A twenty-four hour a day vigil was put over her, but she still found ways to communicate with the man she loved. Rabbis and rabbis' wives were constantly brainwashing, threatening her with grim earthly as well as heavenly consequences for her horrible sin. Within days she found herself being dragged, sobbing, onto the steps of an El Al plane. Her first-ever passport had been issued by a hasty procedure.

A *haredi* middleman escorted her to New York. She stayed with a local family for a few days, while the adoption deal was being closed. They then moved her to another *haredi* family in another city to pass the time until she was due. The family home served as a day-care nursery, and the pregnant girl was kept busy cooking and cleaning.

This was no fun at all. As a daughter of an oriental Jewish family, graduate of the religious state system, Nurit had not the slightest basic knowledge of either English or Yiddish – the language the toddlers were educated in.

A New Yorker middleman-interpreter was on the phone whenever the family wished to communicate something to the young Israeli, or when she herself needed something. The girl had not the faintest idea where she was. With no English at all, she was not capable of crossing the street to ask for help. Her flight ticket and her passport were kept by the landlord.

Language barriers were not the only hedges between her and her hosts. The pious couple spared no gestures to make clear their negative feelings toward her. She was a sinful girl who got into trouble with an Arab; as far as they were concerned, they were doing her a huge favour. Luckily for her – so the New York middleman never stopped reminding her – the Jewish baby she was carrying was a valuable asset, as Jewish communities were always short of Jewish babies for adoption.

The one privilege Nurit did have was an open phone line to Israel. She would have gone mad without somebody to talk Hebrew to. The family who was expecting to get the baby was affluent, Nurit was told, and they were paying for the phone bill. Nurit soon realized that she was not the first Israeli single girl who had been exported to the United States to have a baby out of wedlock for the benefit of childless American Jews. A well-oiled system was in motion to take care of these cases.[1]

Nurit's hosts were not bothered therefore about the girl making lengthy long-distance conversations every night to her mother, her sisters, and some close bosom friends. They could not imagine that the chief interlocutor for the tear-flooded talks was Zaki. When he first heard from her, the young man, who at the time was making frantic efforts to find intermediaries to appease Nurit's family, was stunned to discover she was already

[1] In November 1989, a network of smugglers that specialized in bringing Jewish pregnant women was exposed in the United States (*Ma'ariv*, November 22, 1989).

out of the country, in another part of the world. Zaki told me on our first telephone conversation that Nurit kept telling him that she bitterly regretted her momentary agreement to sign a waiver allowing her baby to be adopted. She also claimed that she was constantly begging the middleman in their daily telephone talks to let her go back home to Israel, but to no avail. According to Zaki, she never stopped sobbing, begging him to save her and bring her back to Israel with their child. He felt helpless and humiliated, a man who could do nothing to keep his woman safe and was about to lose his own baby.

In the few telephone calls I had with him, Zaki sounded like a highly intelligent, articulate, sensitive, and responsible young man. For years he had been living among Jews, he told me. He adored Israeli democracy, he said in perfect Hebrew, and his great ambition was to become Israeli and get further ahead in Israeli society.

Oded Granot, then foreign editor of *Ma'ariv*, was surprised when I informed him that I intended to take time researching a story that sounded more suitable for a woman's magazine or a soap opera. The timing was indeed inconvenient. It was a Thursday morning, and the Israeli press corps in Washington had just been invited to a rare meeting with Secretary of State George Shultz. We were to be briefed on another well-engineered but empty strategic initiative dreamed up by the administration in order to pacify Arab public opinion without really upsetting Israel. Dealing with the problems of the distraught lovers had to be put off until after the paper in Tel Aviv was put to bed at midnight, 5:00 p.m. eastern time.

To start with, nobody knew where Nurit actually was. A single clue was the telephone number in the house where she had been kept. Zaki cleverly instructed his girlfriend to say that she needed the number, seemingly to make it possible for her sister to call her. Zaki innocently and boldly decided to try and talk directly to the landlord, but the phone was put down on him. At that moment the lovers' secret was revealed, and Nurit's employers became suspicious of all her telephone calls. When Zaki approached the Israeli Human Rights Association, they easily identified the area code as Baltimore, one hour's drive from Washington, which was probably the main reason they chose to speak to me.

My own first move was equally unsophisticated – silly, in retrospect: I called the number Zaki gave me and asked to speak to Nurit, identifying myself as an Israeli journalist. The phone immediately went dead and was unavailable from then on. Somebody was under pressure. So was Zaki. We all assumed that the next move would be a transfer of Nurit to another location, which would be impossible to identify as we would not even have the telephone number.

I started a marathon of telephone consultations with everyone I knew in town – journalists, lawyers, politicians – trying to find out who could help. It turned out to be quite complicated. As I never got to speak to the girl myself, I was unable to legally prove that she even existed. A legal adviser from the American Human Rights Association eventually gave my story some consideration and then gave me his verdict on Friday morning. The only possible way to get to Nurit, he said, was to launch a criminal complaint with the police in Zaki's name. He was, after all, the only person who could claim from first-hand knowledge that Nurit was being held in the United States against her will.

I had serious reservations. Taking this course meant that I was to turn myself into a part of the story rather than merely research and report it, as befits a journalist. On the other hand, this was a seriously unusual situation. Zaki's pleading over the telephone, Nurit's presumed misery, the unborn child's future, and the potential for a really good story quickly got me off the fence.

I phoned 911. The local Washington police would have nothing to do with a Baltimore case, they told me. I got the number for Baltimore and was informed that if I needed police attention, I should present myself personally at the precinct.

My then-husband volunteered to join me and to take photos. We left immediately. From the moment we stepped into the police station in Baltimore, we were at the mercy of the American law enforcement system. The experience was unforgettable.

The precinct police put us through a thorough cross-examination. We were asked to give detailed information about ourselves and whatever contact we had with Zaki, the person on whose behalf we wished to launch a complaint concerning involuntary confinement of a third person. Long forms were meticulously filled in, our ID papers were looked at, and after we finished answering all the questions, we were asked to wait. Twenty minutes later we were back in the interview room. Police detectives in plain clothes, members of the special investigation unit, started their own questioning. They asked the same questions and filled in more forms. At the end of this session, there was still no sign of anybody offering to take any steps that might help Nurit. Disappointed, we were asked to continue waiting. Within half an hour, another law enforcement team arrived to hear our story. This time they were federal agents.

The FBI was interrogating us! It was not the most relaxing experience, but at least we were being taken seriously. Again and again the same questions were repeated, probably to make sure we were not making things up.

The fact that our complaint concerned a native of a foreign country, who had not even been seen on US soil, made things complicated. I was unable to tell them when Nurit had arrived in America, or what kind of visa had enabled her entry. The investigators kept their thoughts to themselves, and sometimes I was not sure they believed my story. From their point of view, my tale was based on hearsay from an Arab man in Israel whom I did not even know personally. The subject was highly sensitive and politically loaded. My own involvement seemed dubious. Being a journalist made me a potential troublemaker and raised a large question mark about my motivation. If my story was true, the federal detectives were supposed to raid the private home of an Orthodox Jewish American family who resided in a Baltimore suburb. The potential for an outcry, in case no evidence for my allegations should be found during the raid, was off-putting. I also had to admit that it was very likely that even if the girl had been kept in this home, by now she might already have been removed elsewhere.

I was crestfallen. After three hours in the precinct, I realized that the law keepers would do anything to avoid getting involved in such a messy business. They told us they were calling a general consultation with higher officials and sent us for a long break at a nearby diner. When we came back, we discovered that the cops, the detectives, and the federals had come up with a creative solution.

They summoned the representative of yet another powerful body: the Immigration Authority.

In retrospect I understood that the police did wish to help, but they were reluctant to enter into a situation that would force them to indict the hosts involved. It might have been difficult to prove that Nurit had been kidnapped or that she was being held against her will. The other side could always claim that the girl flew to the United States willingly and even signed adoption papers. She could have been confused and perhaps manipulated, but she was not a minor and was responsible for her own actions. Dragging the normally law-abiding, respected community of the ultra-Orthodox Jews of Baltimore into a criminal affair was certain to become a media event.

The law enforcement agencies' decision was to abandon and ignore the complaint that concerned illegal confinement. They decided instead to focus on Nurit herself as a suspected culprit, having apparently violated US immigration laws. It is forbidden – we were told – for a pregnant woman to arrive purposely in the United States to have her baby born on American soil and be accorded US citizenship.

So now we had a brown-suit member of the Immigration Authority interrogate us all over again. For the fourth time, we went through the exhausting questioning: who were we, what were we doing in the United States and how did we arrive there, why did we come to the police station, and what was known to us about the persons of Nurit and Zaki? Forms were filled in, and then compared to the previous versions to make sure we were not making things up. Only this time, by the end of the interview, the system was put in motion with a stunning efficiency. Armed with an authority that turned out to be far wider than that of the policemen or the detectives, the immigration man called the local telephone company, which immediately supplied the address of the house from which Nurit's telephone calls were made. The local policemen got up to their feet smiling. The place was two blocks away from their precinct.

We set out in an impressive convoy: an official squad car with flashing lights for the uniformed local police; a grey saloon car with a single, turned-off, blue light on top for the special unit's detectives; an unmarked green Chevrolet for the FBI; and a brown Buick for the man in the brown suit. It was almost twilight, about half past three on a grey December afternoon. The four cars neatly parked in a very quiet neighbourhood, next to piles of old snow, opposite the house we were headed for.

The uniformed policemen crossed the street and opened the gate; the rest of the party followed. We walked through a large frozen garden with many leafless trees and then stood still behind the cops, who politely knocked on the door. For a few minutes, we were kept waiting, but at last the door opened, and a large woman wearing a head scarf frowned at the police, explaining that with the Sabbath due very soon, this visit was highly inconvenient. The uniformed men explained the purpose of their call, and the landlady point-blank denied any knowledge of a young woman who would fit the police's description. She was then asked to allow the house to be searched, and for the first time, she lost some of her composure and asked permission to make a phone call first.

We all waited patiently in the freezing air, my husband and I blending in with the small crowd on the landing. The woman returned to say that she would agree to a quick inspection of her two-story home, on condition that the party would be out before the Sabbath. We all squeezed into her hall. Only the uniformed men toured the rooms and went up to the second floor. They discovered nothing except a large number of potties, which confirmed that this indeed was a day-care nursery. The smell of soiled nappies was everywhere.

"She isn't here anymore," I whispered with enormous disappointment. The whole thing had been in vain, or so it seemed. Presumably the telephone calls in the last two days put Nurit's keepers on guard, and the girl had already been moved elsewhere.

To my surprise, one of the FBI men turned to me and shook his head. "She's here all right," he said quietly, volunteering an observation based on vast experience.

The lady with the head scarf was now asked to produce the key to the lock on her basement door. She made a show of not finding it, but eventually handed it to the policemen. As soon as the lock was off and the door wide open, there was no more need to go down to the dark bottom. A sobbing noise could clearly be heard, and up the steep staircase a small girl stumbled. She had very curly dark hair and looked even younger than eighteen, with a very large belly and a red, tear-swollen face.

The landlady did not let her say a word to anyone, but thrust into her hand the telephone that had been off the hook all this time, gesticulating that she must first speak with somebody who was on the line.

The girl dutifully obeyed and continued weeping loudly into the mouthpiece. I could hear her say, "Yes, yes, all right" in Hebrew to whoever was briefing her on the other side. When she put the phone down, the law enforcement men tried to talk to her, but they immediately realized that she could not understand a single word they said. They had to ask me to interpret.

Her eyes lit as soon as she heard me speak Hebrew. "Zaki sent you!?" she immediately exclaimed. I thought she seemed transformed. "Is he waiting outside?" She asked with great longing. I realized she was convinced that her fiancé had come personally all the way from Tel Aviv to claim her, but I had to explain that the policemen wished to speak to her at the station. Would she agree to join us?

The girl looked miserable. I translated the short exchange to the police, and the woman with the bonnet who listened attentively turned to Nurit with a horrified expression. "You want to go by car on the Shabbos!?" she scolded and continued to interfere in the conversation with a mixture of English and Yiddish. The girl seemed lost in fear. She hesitated. Was she going to give in and say, as the landlady demanded, that she did not require any help and wished us all to go away?

The policemen, who noticed her clear distress, told the landlady she must let me speak to the girl in private.

We went into the dining room and closed the door behind us. "Where is Zaki?" was all the girl wanted to know. When she understood that he was still in Israel, waiting for her safe return, and that she would have to fly back all the way on her own, she burst into tears again.

"What can I do?" she sobbed. "It is bad here, but I have no choice. You see, I am pregnant!"

"There is nothing wrong with being pregnant," I said, dismissing that point with a shrug. "There, I am pregnant too; so what?" I was indeed in my sixth month, clearly showing.

"But Zaki... He is not Jewish!" the girl choked miserably, as if she was revealing an enormous dark secret that broke her heart.

"So what?" I shot back impatiently and pointed at the man holding a camera standing next to me. "See, this is my husband; he is no Jew either."

These simple words had a very far-reaching impact. Nurit's hesitation seemed to have evaporated within a split second, as if the intimidation campaign she had been subjected to for months had suddenly cleared into thin air. With visible assertiveness she agreed at once to leave the house and join the police for a drive to the station. She ignored the landlady, and when the telephone was once more stuck in her hand with the Hebrew-speaking go-between presumably on the line, she just said, "*Beseder*" (ok), several times and seemed to be giving no second thought to what had been said to her. To this day I am convinced that she would not have escaped that place so light-heartedly had she not, by pure chance, bumped into an Israeli woman who had married a goy and seemed to have survived. Undoubtedly my spontaneous reply had made me step well beyond mere investigative journalism into a deep involvement – almost too deep – in the life of my protagonist.

"You will go by car? On the Sabbath?" The landlady again scolded, but Nurit had already turned her back to the house and marched with us toward the convoy that parked on the other side of the road. The girl shrugged and did not even bother to reply. If anything, the occurrence of the Sabbath had given her full protection from any further interference from the side of the devout hosts and their partners, who were prevented from following us or starting to pull strings and activate lawyers.

At the police precinct, my husband and I were informed that our presence there was no longer desired. An official professional interpreter was called to interrogate Nurit in Hebrew so that her version could be registered without any suspected interference from me. I later learned that she was allowed to make a telephone call to her Zaki in Tel Aviv, who was then also asked to have his testimony registered.

It took well over two hours. Only at seven in the evening of this really long day were we invited back from the diner, where we had spent our time drinking tea and speculating. The law enforcement gentlemen were apparently satisfied that Nurit was only too pleased to avoid breaking US immigration laws, and she really did not purposefully wish to have her baby born on American soil and then claim US citizenship for it. She truly wanted to go back to Israel and have the child where his father was waiting for them both. The only problem was to find her a place to stay before she could be transported away. According to the normal regulation, she should have been kept in custody until a suitable flight to Israel would be available and organized. All the parties involved were clearly relieved that we agreed to keep her in our house and also to see to it personally that she caught the first plane to Tel Aviv. I signed some papers, and she was all mine.

A squad car carried us both back to the Orthodox family's home to collect Nurit's few clothes and her flight ticket. The landlady's face darkened when she noticed me. "This woman will not set foot in my house!" she insisted angrily. Unkindly I thought that it was more than just the lost peace of the Sabbath that upset her – that a considerable financial loss was obviously suffered with the failure of the adoption project.

I waited in the frozen garden until Nurit finished packing her small suitcase. When she eventually left the house escorted by a policeman, the pious nursery teacher stood out on her landing and cursed us both very loudly, from the bottom of her heart. "I shall be praying to the Lord that your airplane will blow up in midair!" she screamed, surprisingly ignoring the strict ban on shouting and cursing during the Holy Sabbath.

* * *

Ma'ariv had an interesting front-page headline with my story in the news section on Sunday, with other media following up with credit to our newspaper. I was very disappointed to be refused space for a longer feature for the weekend political supplement and had to argue and beg before a space was found for a feature at the back page of the less political Friday magazine. Without enthusiasm, the editors agreed to send a photographer and a correspondent to meet Nurit, as she had landed in Israel a few days later.

Zaki, in the meantime, was warmly courted by the other media and by the weekend, *Ma'ariv*'s arch competitor, *Yediot Aharonot*, carried four full pages covering the story of Romeo and Juliet from Petach Tikva. My chief editor was furious with me for "allowing" Zaki to be interviewed by someone else rather than insist he protect our exclusive rights on his story which *Ma'ariv* did not wish to carry anyway.

Ma'ariv was not the only media outlet taking a disparaging view of the love story of an Arab man and a Jewish woman. A friend who worked for Washington's *Jewish Week* thought his readers would be highly interested in a tale of an Israeli girl being kept clandestinely in neighbouring Baltimore's ultra-Orthodox Jewish community. But by the time we both finished working on a suitable version, the editors told him that there was "no space" for this particular subject.

* * *

The four days Nurit spent in our home were eye opening and mildly amusing. We set out to shop at the super kosher supermarkets so that she could be comfortable eating from disposable plates and crockery. She was an expert on kosher regulations, and it was funny to hear her solemnly explain that her baby was so highly desired by ultra-Orthodox adoptive families because he or she was to be born of a woman who had always been nourished on kosher food only. When I eventually took her to the airport and we spent some time in the cafeteria, she was dumbfounded to spot a bacon-and-cheese sandwich on public display.

She was a sweet and clever young person, but her ignorance over subjects that I considered basic never ceased to amaze me. Still, she was very much aware that there had been big gaps in her education and felt particularly bitter about not having learned any English, as opposed to Zaki, whose English was adequate for a high-school graduate. Her observations about the dynamics of the system she came from were surprisingly accurate. "At school they purposely never let ultra-Orthodox girls matriculate," she sadly explained. "They do not wish that we should learn too much and get away from religion. Actually, we wasted most of the twelve years there." I could not agree more.

* * *

Zaki and Nurit called me from their flat in Tel Aviv two weeks after the birth of their first daughter. Confinement was easy but the circumstances quite dramatic, they told me. The couple had been visiting Zaki's parents in Gaza when labour started, and they immediately walked together to the Shifa hospital in the city. The first *Intifada* had just started. In the maternity ward Nurit was treated well, but she was made to understand that it was not a good idea for an Israeli woman to stay on next to the other patients. "Can you imagine this?" Zaki told me, half-amused. "Two hours after the baby was out, we picked her up and walked back home in the complete darkness; we were literally shaking with fear."

They contacted me again in the autumn. I was back in Israel, having finished my term in Washington, with my own baby girl. They had moved to another city next to Tel Aviv, and I understood that they were quietly blending in with the Jewish neighbourhood, maybe even with new names. Zaki's marriage to an Israeli citizen was supposed to yield him a blue Israeli identification card, a document and a meal ticket much longed for by thousands of Palestinian Arabs. I very much wanted to meet them, but things did not work out for a while, with my new job and Nurit already expecting her second baby. When two months later I called the telephone number they had left with me, they were no longer at that address, and they never got in touch again. I do hope they live happily ever after, as the fortune teller from Netanya had predicted.

* * *

The only really unusual element in Nurit and Zaki's marriage is the fact that it is still such a rare situation in Israel today. Mixed marriages between different ethnic and religious groups are a widespread phenomenon throughout the rest of the world.

"Natural" apartheid, exercised by ethnic and cultural groups to preserve their unique characters as separate communities, normally gives way and begins to be diluted after one or two generations of living within the conditions of an urban modern society.

My own parents, after all, were considered a "mixed marriage" when I was growing up. The ethnic-cultural gap between my two grandmothers had been far greater than the gap between the parents of Zaki and Nurit: middle-class Palestinians living in Gaza, on the one hand, and traditional Persian-born Jews, immigrants in an Israeli town, on the other hand.

In the much-confused Israeli reality, the natural dynamics of mixed marriages and assimilated society are being efficiently blocked by a religious bureaucracy well anchored in the state's laws. The idea that a Jew would marry an Arab is unanimously condemned. In the very fringes of society, such matches do take place, often creating serious drama and often ending with bitter tears. Interethnic marriages between Jews, in the meantime, have become normative and even yield a positive image dividend – as long as one is not a member of one of the ultra-Orthodox Jewish communities.

Most secular Jewish Israelis, historically the majority of the population – a society that considers itself liberated, modern, and free – cannot even imagine a situation of one of their daughters, or a sister, marrying an Arab or even dating one. I know at least one such mixed couple who ended up in great misery. Both of their beautiful daughters, going to school in a small Israeli town, grew up in a semiconspiratorial reality in which their father's identity was supposed – for a while – to be considered a shameful secret.

Before the state was started, such mixed marriages were more common. In the Arab refugee community that was created as a result of the Israeli War of Independence, there were quite a few women who were born Jewish. After the 1967 War and following the Lebanon War of 1982, the press occasionally had revelations about Israelis, parents and siblings, who had set out to bring back some of these "lost souls." The children and the grandchildren of these women were quick to claim Israeli identity cards according to the Law of Return and blended in very well with the population of the Arab Israeli villages. Their relatives could only watch them with envy. For all other refugees, descendants' talk about the Right of Return continue to be considered the ultimate Israeli nightmare.

Arab society, traditionally considering women as a man's property, have no problem at all accepting foreign women, Jewish or others. Jewish attitude to wives is equally proprietorial, but has no tolerance for crossing ethnic borders. In the early 1980s, Rabbi Meir Kahane, a charismatic American Jew, managed to start an Israeli political party. The main item on this party's platform was a commitment to legislate against mixed marriages. According to this proposed "law", an almost perfect copy of Nazi *rassenschande* legislation, any non-Jew having intercourse with a Jewish woman would have been jailed.

By the time Kahane started promoting this legislative idea, I had already been married to a non-Jew. It was uncomfortable to think that, were the rabbi to have his way, my husband would become vulnerable to criminal proceedings were he ever to set foot in Israel. In 1984 Kahane was elected to the eleventh Knesset. His kind of teaching was eventually outlawed, and he himself was murdered in the United States. But his legacy is very much alive and even thriving in today's national religious circles. "Kahane is Alive" graffiti are a common sight all over the country. The LEHAVA racist NGO presents its mission as "preventing assimilation" and "saving" Jewish girls from contact with Arab men. Acting openly and publicly with Ku Klux Klan-like ideology, its activists have direct access to military units. according to a *Ha'aretz* report in January 2016. In July 2015 two LEHAVA activists were sentenced to two years in prison for the arson of an Arab-Jewish elementary school in Jerusalem. When the trial ended they declared that "it was worth it".

In reality there must be hundreds and maybe thousands of Arabs, many of them with a very good education, whose first introduction to the limitations of Hebrew nationalism came with a broken heart over a first love for a Jewish girl. Tira-born writer Sayed Kashua has evoked such an experience very well in his first Hebrew novel, *Dancing Arabs*.[2] In the canonized Hebrew literature, on the other hand, love between Jews and Arabs is usually described as a traumatic, sometimes catastrophic, complicated event, rife with sinister existential depths. In early 2016 *Borderlife*, a prize-winning novel by author Dorit Rabinyan was officially removed from the matriculation syllabus of secular Israeli schools because it described a love affair between an Israeli Jewish woman and a Palestinian Muslim. The fact that the two, who meet in New York, eventually decide to give up their politically incorrect love and NOT live happily ever after, did not save the book from the ethnic purists (but the scandal turned it to an overnight bestseller).

The almost total lack of any family contacts between non-Jewish Arabs and Jews surely symbolizes a quintessential element of Jewish Israeli pathology.

There is nothing like inter-ethnic marriages to activate social dynamics. The very desire of a young Arab man to marry a Jewish woman consists of a powerful social-political statement. At least some of the Arab men showing an interest in Jewish women belong to the educated, articulate section of society, who mostly appreciate the independent and equal status of Jewish women and are ready to cope with the demand for equal rights.

In the opposite direction, there is hardly any action at all. Jewish men have little or no motivation to risk courting women who belong to the weakest and poorest section of Israeli citizens. The pressure on Arab women in their own society makes most of them unable even to consider a man who would not be acceptable to the family. It is a particularly harmful magic circle. Interethnic marriages are one good option for all women trying to escape a depressing patriarchal system. For Arab Israeli women, this option of social mobility is closed, no matter how pretty, clever, or affluent they are. An Arab Israeli woman who chooses the life of a liberated woman risks losing her chance of finding a partner and starting a family. A good friend who had a long and

---

[2] An English translation by M. Shlesinger was published by Grove Press Books, 2004. Kashua has since become a most beloved Israeli-Arab persona, *Dancing Arabs* was made into a film with director Eran Riklis (2014).

serious relationship with a remarkable Palestinian Israeli woman explained to me that they both recoiled at the reality that defines as outcasts the children of such a match. Muslims accept into the community only children of Muslim fathers; Jews do not accept children of a non-Jewish mother.

* * *

Progressive Jewish communities around the world have long realized that mixed marriages are the norm wherever social dynamics and ethnic mobility is aspired to. Reform and Conservative Judaism make great efforts to attract non-Jewish partners of their youngsters and make them part of their own communities rather than lose sons and daughters of Jews in favour of the local churches. Israeli rabbis and politicians are well entrenched in their furious ban on conversions made by these overseas communities.

Jewish American sociologists reveal that the highest rate of assimilation in the US Jewish communities applies to the ex-Israelis: 72 percent of them marry non-Jews. Theodore Herzl, who was pro-assimilation, would have approved.

Even a particularly low rate of mixed marriages over the course of more than a hundred years of Zionism would have necessarily created in Israel a meaningful mixed Arab-Jewish population, strongly committed by family connections to both adversarial national groups, desperate to make coexistence an option. But Israel chose to be the one spot in the whole world where Jews may not choose non-Jews as partners. Israelis have every reason to sound confident when they knowingly predict that "never" will there be an end to the armed struggle in this part of the world.

22

BACK TO THE WATER CISTERNS

If man could find a state in which he felt that though idle he was fulfilling his duty, he would have found one of the conditions of man's primitive blessedness. And such a state of obligatory and irreproachable idleness is the lot of a whole class – the military. The chief attraction of military service has consisted and will consist of this compulsory and irreproachable idleness.

Lev Tolstoy,
War and Peace[1]

I have no idea why I was decorated. I merely wanted to get back home in one piece.

Yoram Tehar Lev,
"Ammunition Hill," 1967

We feel the biggest special interest group is the military. It's so big, with more than 150,000 people feeding off the system [...] Possibly the reason an interest group that huge can exist is that it's a hermetically sealed entity, unmeasurable and tied to the ethos of the establishment of the Jewish state.

Guy Rolnik,
Ha'aretz , July 29, 2013

Two weeks after the last day of the Six Day War, we set out to tour the occupied West Bank. My parents had been the proud owners of their first-ever family car, purchased earlier that year. The money to buy it came from savings originally earmarked for the purchase of an apartment, but they had given this up because to own one's home had turned out to be unaffordable

---

[1] Book two, part four, translation by Louise and Aylmer Maude (Oxford University Press) p. 519.

for them, even during the recession of 1966, which brought house prices down considerably. Our 1300 Countessa was a Japanese-Israeli product put together in Nazareth by an entrepreneur called Ephraim Illin. It was offered at a reasonable price due to heavy government subsidizing, but Illin went spectacularly bankrupt anyway a few years later.

Israelis might have been proud about winning the war, but nobody was as proud as my father as the Countessa effortlessly overtook a long line of broken-down cars, all with boiling radiators, on the steep hill between Ramallah and Taybeh. The majority of Israeli drivers in those days had to make do with scrap.

It is hard for a contemporary person to even imagine that June 1967 Saturday trip. More than anything it seemed like a journey into a large and hospitable oriental bazaar. Along the roads, and at the outskirts of every town and village, stalls were laid out heavy with merchandise. Locals eager to do business were offering souvenirs, fruit, and imported brand products that at that time were unavailable in Israel. My parents were particularly pleased to discover the small blue tins of *Nivea* Cream and *La vache qui rit*'s triangular melted cheese that they remembered from their childhood in Palestine under the British mandate. The merchants were well informed about the value of Israeli *lira* that they gladly accepted, and we were enchanted with the low prices.

A few days before setting out to go on that trip, we were moved by the speech of Chief of Staff Yitzhak Rabin, who came to open the Spievak club for handicapped IDF veteran soldiers in Ramat Gan. He was speaking for everybody present in this small gathering when he said this last war had been forced on us. If only the neighbouring Arab countries had agreed to accept Israel and to let it exist next to them, all would have been so different. In the meantime, it was our fate to become enlightened occupiers. Rabin's famous Mount Scopus Speech, a week later, was along much the same lines.[2]

Now, together with a crowd of other enlightened occupiers who also happened to own vehicles, we scrambled to cast an eye over

---

[2] On June 28, 1967.

a pretty spring and small waterfall and then rushed off to more shopping at the kasbah in Nablus. It was the first and last time in my life in this particular quarter, which soon became the IDF's most problematic nightmare in the occupied territories. The Countessa carried us further down into the heat of the Jordan Valley all the way into Jericho, lush and lazy with small open-water canals that ran along its streets cooling the open-garden restaurants.

Never before had I consumed a vegetable salad so minutely chopped or so well-seasoned. The restaurant owners could not believe their luck with so many hungry Israelis landing on them all at once. Some of the tourists were Hebrew-speaking Israeli Arabs, proudly displaying their advantageous economic and civil status over the locals as part of the occupying state entity. My father entered into a long conversation with the men sitting at an adjacent table, then came back to report that the single Israeli Arab men were particularly pleased with the low cost of Palestinian brides, as bride-price inside the green line had been skyrocketing for some time.

By late afternoon we went up to Jerusalem. Bulldozers had already flattened the neighbourhood next to the Wailing Wall, and the Old City was now open for tourism. Traffic police directed us to a very large improvised parking lot next to the Nablus Gate, in the area that had previously been no-man's-land. As we marched toward the city's wall, I remembered that I left my purse in the car. My parents, my brother, and my boyfriend waited by the shops at the gate. The sun had just set, and the evening sky was very bright. Traipsing over the rough surface on high heels was tricky, but the green sandals I was wearing were a perfect match to the dress I chose for this trip – a flowery sleeveless mini that went very well with my favourite plastic Mary Quant imitation earrings.

I must have radiated more than some smugness as I locked the car door, keys pleasantly sounding in my palm. Two youngsters, about my age, sitting on a low stone wall next to the parking cars had muttered some words that sounded insulting and hateful and were directed toward me. I felt the blood draining from my veins. I did not know what annoyed them more – my bare arms and legs, my father's pretty car, or the obvious liaison between me and the heavy army excavators that had destroyed so many homes in their city over the past week. Trapped in enemy territory, I was truly scared.

I pulled myself together to raise a brave Zionist head against the adversarial elements and managed a respectable retreat, moving as fast as I could from the car park toward the thick tourist crowd and joining, unscathed, all the people I loved most in the world. Late at night we returned home loaded with boxes of sweet baklawa cakes, melted French cheese, cold creams, and colourful scarves. I was also carrying a first notion about how unpleasant being an occupier might turn out to be.

* * *

My father and I were convinced that nothing would make Savta Miriam happier than seeing the holy sites that had just been liberated, and we very soon arranged another trip round the new territories, this time with Savta and my Aunt Mazal.

Our first stop, at the Wailing Wall, was not a success. Savta reacted with disbelief to the sight of the wall at the end of a huge empty plot, divided piously between men and women as a kind of enormous field synagogue. It did not look anything like the impressive stone wall she remembered from the rare visits she had made to Jerusalem with her devout family before 1948. She insisted that my father was mistaken and kept asking where the narrow Wall Alley was. Her face darkened as we broke the news to her that the dense Arab neighbourhood next to the wall had been removed, its residents politely asked to vacate the premises and find new homes before the whole quarter had been ground to dust.

The Tomb of Rachel, on the road to Bethlehem, was packed with women lighting candles in a small sooty chamber. Savta acquiesced as we asked her to do the same. She duly lit the candle we bought for her and closed her eyes for a short, silent prayer, showing no emotion. We continued directly to Hebron. To my great surprise, the Cave of Machpelah, tomb of the nation's patriarchs, turned out to be a very large mosque in the centre of the town.

Savta tried to identify the stairs going up that had once been a source of great longing. Jews were only allowed up to the seventh step, she told us, explaining what we already knew. Newspapers were packed with memoirs of past humiliations. Full of victorious glee, we led her to the top of the staircase and from there into the large, carpeted halls. Signs in Hebrew already announced the names of the patriarchs and the matriarchs, whose skeletons are preserved, according to ancient Muslim tradition, inside the wood and stone sarcophagus in each room. Worshippers were kneeling on the carpets in typical Muslim style. It was very hot and stuffy inside. Savta was tired. She was not inclined to say any prayers. With some disappointment we had to conclude that she was not going through the deep religious experience we were so hoping to create for her.

Leaving Hebron, we stopped by the Pools of King Solomon on the way home. *Fellahin* wives, hair tucked under colourful cloth, scrambled to sell us the fruit of the large orchards – peaches and prunes bigger and nicer than the ones usually sold in the markets of Tel Aviv. My grandmother, in her white Yemenite scarf, looked as if she belonged in there and was warmly received. Soon my family was engaged in lively conversation of which I was the only one who could not understand anything except the welcoming "*Tefaddlu*." The large ancient pools exuded blessed coolness, and we easily found a comfortable spot in the thick shade of the fruit trees for a picnic that we would remember fondly for many years to come.

* * *

So Sorry, We Won! was the title of a popular album by national cartoonist Dosh (Kriel Gardosh) and the national satire writer Ephraim Kishon. Behind the blatant arrogance was a true complex. During the three weeks that preceded the Six Day War, we lived through a collective traumatic experience of genuine existential fear. The Hebrew-language radio station of the United Arab Republic, "Thunder Voice," was broadcasting belligerent messages that we used to listen to in a mixture of anxiety and ridicule. The anchorman speaking incorrect Hebrew with a strong Arabic accent called on Israel to "put on its black dress" for the day of reckoning and assured attacks on "all fronts" (which also meant bosoms). Our laughs were somewhat nervous.

It is possible, as learned commentators analyzed in the years that followed, that the Egyptian head of state, Gamal Abdel Nasser, demanding that UN observers vacate the Sinai and the Gaza Strip, meant only to gain some political propaganda advantage using empty rhetoric. But he was taken seriously, at least by those unaware of the Israeli war machine's capabilities. The international press was writing about our faith with some compassion. People who had relatives abroad were quietly disappearing with their children. Fauzi El Asmar describes in his memoirs an Iraqi Jew he was acquainted with who suddenly remembered to inform him that he felt far more Arab than Israeli and asked for his protection following the forecast Arab victory.

The official National Calmer was General Chaim Herzog, Irish born to a rabbinical family, who introduced an Anglo-Saxon spirit into his daily radio briefings. True to the model of Londoners during the Blitz, Herzog told his listeners that the best way to cope with the enemy would be to "carry on the daily life routine as usual," which would prove our national resilience. Dutifully following this recommended mode of conduct, school continued as usual, and we never stopped working toward our matriculation exams that were due to start in the second week of June. Worrying about the future was no excuse for idleness. After school hours we were recruited for community service. With paint cans and brushes, we were dispatched to road junctions to put blue camouflage paint over car headlights, preparing for the blackouts. We also received sticky tape to help shop owners create tape grids on their shop windows, anticipating air bombing.

Back home we covered the windows, as instructed, with black, hard, thick paper, the same as we did ten years earlier before the Sinai campaign. Standing on a ladder in our kitchen, I was trying to imagine what would happen to us in this flat if and when Egyptian armoured cars should storm the nearby Dizengoff Street, as the Thunder Voice constantly promised. Would hateful, destruction-crazed Arab soldiers climb the steps all the way up to the third floor? I planned to use the advantage of living above street level to bravely defend our home until the very last minute. Maybe heavy items should be prepared, so they could be dropped on their heads? Perhaps boiling oil should be used?

The war eventually started, with air-raid sirens early in the morning of June 5th. We went down to the entrance of the house, where a sandbag wall was supposed to have protected us, but it was not yet complete. One of the neighbours hysterically screamed that we might all die because we had no sandbag protection. She held the men who lived in the house – except her own husband – responsible for exposing the women and children to the perils of immediate violent death. Ugly accusations were also pointed at my father, who as an employee of Israel Aircraft Industry was always absent in those days, working from seven in the morning till midnight every day for the war effort.

Near eight in the morning, the all-clear siren sounded, and I headed off to catch bus number 4 to school, to continue regular life routines and affirm national resilience. There were more alarms during this morning, and in the protected area in the first floor, above the gymnastics space of Municipal High School E, some pupils organized a sing-along. The new hit "Jerusalem of Gold" mused over "The dry water cisterns and the empty market place." I had a scheduled university entry exam for that day. When the all-clear siren sounded, I insisted on setting off to the exam. I took number 4 to Ben-Gurion Avenue and walked down to Reines to catch number 25. In the almost empty bus, the radio vigorously sounded, "We shall build our homeland"; the words "Thirsty for liberty and independence, let us march to free our people" never sounded more appropriate. It was too bad not to have any role in the liberating of the nation. Continuing the regular routine, as General Herzog had instructed, was becoming problematic as very few would-be students showed up for the exam.

Around noon the newspapers put out special editions with enormous headlines reporting the success of the Israeli Air Force as well as armoured divisions on the ground. There was no mention of Israeli casualties, and horror rumours were aggressively distributed everywhere. "Knowledgeable sources" claimed that a whole battalion of paratroopers who were sent out to parachute over the Golan Heights had all been shot dead from the ground while still hanging up in the air.

We were bereaved and anxious. The boys in my class expected to be called up into early service any moment, to make up for the fallen soldiers. When the war came to an end six days later, the reported number of the dead reached over six hundred. Photos of the fallen soldiers were printed in the newspapers and we spent many hours examining their young faces. Most of them were just the right age to attract girls like me. Our male classmates were frustrated over having missed the chance to participate in the fighting, just because they were born one year too late. The first matriculation exam took place according to the preset time table on June 11th, the day the war officially ended.

The draft was not brought forward, but the boys of our class were to have plenty of other opportunities to kill, get killed and get maimed. In the years that followed, Gil Segal, a tall, good-looking kid who was the subject of my (and most of the other girls') secret romantic interests from the third grade until the eighth, was the first casualty. It was forbidden to report the circumstances of his death or even discuss it but everybody knew that Gil, having been accepted into the most coveted combat unit of the Marine Commando, lost his life during a training course with explosives together with two other soldiers. Over his fresh grave, the charismatic young Rabbi Israel Meir Lau – later to become Chief Ashkenazi Rabbi – made a moving speech. It was very important for him to convince Gil's mother, almost fainting with grief and tears, that her son's death was just as meaningful as if he had "fallen in action" for the sake of the country. Nobody in those days could conceive that the case actually required an investigation, and perhaps the terrible sloppiness that had caused the needless death of three fine young men did not help the country at all. Had the mourning Mrs. Segal tried to insist that the responsible officers in command be court-martialled for their neglect – as bereaved parents would today – she would have been immediately committed for insanity.

The Arab countries called a summit conference in Khartoum and declared that there would be no peace with Israel, no negotiations, and no recognition for the Jewish state. Our government heaved a sigh of relief and declared that there is "nobody to talk to" about returning the new precious territories. The Arab states – commentators explained – are all captive to corrupt governments who nurture the popular hostility to Israel as a way of securing their grip over the depressed, ignorant masses. There was no way we could imagine an Israeli government that occasionally initiates a military escalation for purely internal political needs.

The Egyptian Army continued to shell the IDF's positions along the Suez Canal. From time to time, the front pages of the newspapers were covered with black squares around photos of the fallen from our class age group and of the younger ones who followed. The soldiers coming back into town from the front line for short breaks celebrated in disco parties and refused to speak about casualties. Yechiel Zik from our class lost a leg.

Along the Suez Canal, big, deep fortified strongholds were built. The fortification system was named the Bar Lev Line after the Chief of Staff who was fond of horse riding. It was an impressive engineering project that had given work and livelihood to many families of Palestinians from the Gaza Strip and from Rafah and turned some well-connected Israeli entrepreneurs into millionaires overnight. Tel Aviv admired a new fleet of large luxurious American cars. The owners of the cars were builders who were busy transferring tractors and bulldozers into the Sinai Peninsula. They had to use air-conditioned vehicles while supervising the works. Senior army officers were not left behind; they, too, were visible in the city being driven in khaki-coloured American saloon cars or having them parked on the pavements while dining in the new steak houses, often in the company of the new entrepreneurs.

In August 1970 Palestinian resistance – we called it terror – finally reached our Gretz Street home. An enormous explosion at two in the morning made us all jump up to the windows in panic. The sky was a red flame, and people in their pyjamas ran down the stairs into the street. A car bomb had gone off at the junction of Keren Kayemet Avenue (later to become Ben-Gurion Avenue) and Dizengoff. In the morning it appeared that miraculously the damage consisted mainly of broken glass. Melted, deformed, metal shrapnel landed on our roof, and I collected some for souvenirs as I went up on the roof to hang out the washing to dry. I thought they came directly from the young boys who hated me at the Nablus Gate in Jerusalem, three years earlier.

* * *

In September of that year, I started my military service. During the initial training in the recruit's base 12 for female soldiers, we heard the news of the sudden death of Gamal Abdel Nasser. Maybe peace was a possibility after all, one expert speculated over the radio. The Palestine Liberation Organization that had been established six years earlier had during that month managed to hijack four jet airliners. All were blown up, empty, in a Jordanian airport. Later reports came of massacres of Palestinians by the Royal Jordanian Army, as the guerrilla organizations became a real threat to King Hussein's rule. From now on this would be remembered as Black September.

As I had graduated from university before military service, I was posted to an Intelligence unit in the Army Headquarters in Tel Aviv. Fortunately for me, at this exact time, a young press officer with academic credentials had decided to get married, which meant a coveted position in the Army Press Liaison Office, then part of the Intelligence Force, unexpectedly became vacant. Normally service in this prestigious unit, housed next to the Sokolov House of the Journalists' Association, was reserved for the daughters of people with excellent contacts in the highest echelons. By pure chance I suddenly found myself part of the thrilling, extremely privileged world of the military media industry.

The IDF Spokesperson's Unit was a source of pride and admiration. The international press praised the integrity and the sincerity of its reports and normally did not doubt its official statements. My boss was Reuben Leviathan, a civilian journalist. Generations of young people had acquired their first lessons in journalism and public relations next to him. He knew all there was to know about the delicate ways in which the media and the government work together.

Our job was to assist journalists interested in feature articles and photographic stories, to initiate positive coverage for army units which deserved to be reported about, and from time to time to organize tours of zones worthy of attention for the military correspondents, the news editors, and sometimes even the venerable Committee of the Chief Editors.

Military aircraft and helicopters were at the disposal of our unit as we escorted the important journalists up to the Golan Heights or into Sinai, at that time a cordoned-off military zone. I could personally witness the impressive dimensions of the Bar Lev Fortification Line and figure out how so much money could be made for the people involved in building it.

We had special relations with the military censorship personnel who were housed one floor below us in the Government Press Liaison's Office in Itamar Ben Avi Street. The censors had no authority to cross out negative or critical remarks about the army's behaviour or even to correct factual mistakes. The Army Spokesperson's Unit received a copy of every problematic article, and we were often asked to exercise our contacts and plead with journalists to moderate unfavourable copy.

Our sources of information were the Chief of Staff's headquarters and the Intelligence Command. When the military were into cutting slack for themselves, the Military Spokesperson was part of the deal. I particularly recall an episode in the days of the manhunt of Palestinian guerrillas in the Jordan Valley. In some cases, Israel suffered casualties and heroic myths were created and cultivated. In the winter of 1971, the Central Command had started registering an impressive increase in the numbers of "captures of terrorists infiltrating into the Valley over the Jordanian border." Until then, a typical "terrorist unit" contained two or four fighters. Now we were releasing laconic spokespersons' communiqués proudly counting thirteen or even twenty-one "terrorists captured in action by an IDF unit." An innocent reader had to deduce that this was reporting a very successful battle, particularly as the communiqué ended with the calming heroic boilerplate "our forces suffered no casualties."

The truth was that following Black September, the Royal Jordanian Army's policy toward armed Palestinians had been even more violent than that of the IDF. Defeated PLO troopers had fled for dear life out of Jordanian territory and given themselves up to the first Israeli soldier they encountered under the usually correct assumption that Israelis did not shoot prisoners of war.

Chatting with a military correspondent who knew exactly what was happening in the valley, I expressed my discomfort at the peculiar drafting of IDF spokesmen's releases. The next day the censor sent for our attention a prepublished copy of an opinion piece by the very same writer, who called the IDF communiqué "a kind of deception." Embarrassingly, my boss, Reuben, charged me this time with the job of pleading with the journalist to give up this disrespectful phrase. The chief of the Central Command, General Rechavam Zeevi (nicknamed Gandhi), would have been furious if such doubts were to be aired in public.

In those heydays of Israeli militaristic megalomania, General Zeevi had imported into the country lion cubs from Africa, which were positioned in a cage next to his fortress in Ramallah. Drafted soldiers were trained to feed the lions and clean their excrement for the glory of the Central Command. A cheeky young journalist named Nahum Barnea dared to report in the ruling Labor Party's official periodical "Ott, about an ostentatious party in the garden of an IDF general where conscripts were used as waiters. Sokolov House was up in arms; our officers considered the report a disgrace. Barnea did not identify the hosting general, and naturally it was assumed to have been Gandhi. In fact, this party actually took place in the Southern Command, in the garden of General Arik Sharon, who was about to become a farmer.

In 1972 Sharon purchased a very large farm in the Negev, using an interest-free loan that was granted by a wealthy American-Israeli admirer. I found this surprising. During recruitment courses we had been made to memorize the rule of the Military Code that strictly banned anybody in uniform from receiving payments, favours, gifts, and rewards from citizens, especially from abroad. I realized that in the army, like in many other places, there must be different rules for generals and for recruits.

* * *

I ended my army service in May of 1972. In the spring of 1973, I was called for my first reserve duty. The IDF was about to exercise an unusually large military manoeuvre that was coded *Targil Kardom* ("Hatchet Exercise"). Our role in the army spokesperson's unit was to follow the manoeuvre with press releases that described how an act of aggression by Israel's enemies was being aborted. I was introduced to expressions like "Crossing the Canal" and understood what an "Armoured-Bridge-Tank" was for. We stayed up all night to coordinate the news from the front and get it ready in time for the newspapers' deadlines in early morning. The manoeuvre was a great success.

The enemy alone failed to read the message of this success. Or maybe it did carefully analyse the feature stories of canal crossing and instant victory that I was privileged to help compose. When war actually started, in October of the same year, it took a different course.

* * *

Through the open door of the packed Nachman Hall in Sokolov House, we could hear the chief of staff, General David Elazar, brief the international press corps using the words "We shall break their bones." He did not say what was going to happen to our bones. Far south, in the Sinai Desert, the killing was in full swing.

The grand system of fortifications that made for successful VIP excursions, so perfect a location for photo opportunities, had become a death trap. Two thousand six hundred young Israeli men had been mown down within a few days. Tens of thousands of survivors, some with serious handicaps, still live those days in their nightmares. I often hear men from my age group describing themselves as shell-shocked. My friend Eli Barnea, then only twenty years old, managed to put down in writing his chilling memoirs from this war twenty-five years later. He still refuses to publish these memoirs, mainly because he does not wish to cause any more grief to the parents of his dead mates. "Everything I had believed in was crumbling around me," he wrote, laconically summing up the third day of fighting:

One hour earlier I still believed that I was serving in the best army in the world, a victorious military machine storming towards Cairo. Now I realized that beyond the horizon a kind of an enormous slaughterhouse existed. On the one side of the road healthy soldiers drive into it, on the other side human parts are being brought back. And here I am, locked at the bottom of a tank, moving straight ahead towards this place.[3]

No such defeatist reporting passed the Army Press Liaison's office, where we were all busy supplying well-edited stories by a pool of drafted military correspondents to all the newspapers. Some of Israel's best writers and authors were sent to the front escorted by press officers, and from a safe distance, they registered their deep impressions. It was our job to have the stories typed on stencil pads, print dozens of copies, and distribute them through the pigeonholes in the Government Press Office on the ground floor. There were no descriptions of carnage and horror, and no television cameras documented the killing fields. One writer offered a chilling description of infantry under an avalanche of what looked like "fully burning electrical poles," referring to hundreds of Frog and Scud missiles that landed on the forces that were commanded to hold their ground in the infamous battle of the "Chinese Farm." Artist Yigal Tumarkin came back one day to the office with contact sheets of hundreds of photos, all of them piles or close-ups of corpses. These were not for publication, but I am sure Tumarkin appreciated the unique opportunity to document real-time macabre aesthetics.

Tel Aviv during blackout was exciting and romantic. Foreign correspondents with generous expense accounts filled the bars around the hotels. The BBC (Bernie's Bottle Club) at the north end of Dizengoff was a favourite. Uniformed officers who were lucky enough to have backroom jobs, other lucky men who were not drafted, and occasionally someone who had been "there" and survived to report back, all showed insatiable thirst for entertainment. In Pe'er Cinema, Stanley Kubrick's *Clockwork Orange* was launched in Tel Aviv. The undrafted company of six young men who invited me to the matinée had no intention of reminding the army that they were available for combat. They all survived to build good careers. I was mainly offended because they found the blatant violence so attractive.

Even before the first cease-fire agreement was signed, several journalists had organized a fast publishing venture. The

---

[3] Quoted from the unpublished memoir.

entrepreneurial producer offered me a moonlighting job while still on reserve duty with the army: to interview soldiers who survived the battles. On the last day of the war, I went down with a bus full of foreign correspondents for a trip around the new positions of the IDF in the south. On the way we collected some eighteen-year-old yarmulke-wearing soldiers who were hitchhiking from Refidim (Be'er Gafgafa) to the west bank of the canal, which was actually in Africa. I sat with them on the steps of the bus and recorded their stories. They spoke with shining eyes about General Ariel Sharon, whom his admirers called "King of Israel." His adversaries bitterly condemned him for recklessly wasting human lives. Coming back, I drove to Tel Hashomer hospital and spoke to half-burnt soldiers from the Fourteenth Brigade who had been the first to be attacked on the first day of the war, then to a sanatorium in Netanya to meet some shell-shocked boys. My ex-boyfriend's younger brother supplied me with precise stories over the messy, disorientated urban combats in the city of Ismailia.

The texts that I supplied to the venture became part of the best seller *The Failure (HaMechdal)*, documenting the catastrophe of the Yom Kippur War. The cover was decorated with the aged, bereaved face of Prime Minister Golda Meir. None of the men who had actually been running the defence of the country would have been caught sobbing in such an incriminating manner. None of the men were such an easy target to blame the disaster on.

The Failure had become the symbol of that war and the impressive protest movement that rapidly grew in its wake. The movement focused on blaming the government for the horrors of the war. It was somewhat mystifying for me to watch the thousands of Israelis who had started a pilgrimage to Jerusalem to join the demonstrators in front of the Knesset, all united around the spontaneous outcries: "Why were the reserve forces not drafted early enough?" and "Why was the emergency military equipment storage in such shambles?"

These were legitimate questions, of course, but not the really relevant ones as far as I could understand. Only a handful of Israelis believed that Golda Meir and her defence minister, Moshe Dayan, should have been blamed first and foremost for letting the nation fool itself for six years with the idea that the Jewish state may and should run enormous territories under military occupation while completely ignoring the population living in them and all the neighbouring countries.

A small left-wing movement called for a meeting at the Cameri Theatre hall in Tel Aviv. Meir Pa'il and Yair Tzaban presented the line of questioning I was looking for. A young lieutenant colonel of the reserves named Ran Cohen, a *kibbutznik* I knew from university days, stood on the stage and screamed, "What are we doing in Africa anyway? What have we to be looking for in any occupied territory? We need to go back home!" The hall vibrated with applause. I was convinced a mass movement was starting with an agenda that made sense to everybody.

By the end of the meeting, the participants went out to a quiet march along Dizengoff Street. It was a cool Friday night. On Sunday, Cohen dutifully went back to his battalion in Africa. A few months later, an election campaign ended with Cohen and Pa'il's *Moked* party barely passing the threshold of votes needed to have one member in the house.

* * *

Working conditions at the *Ma'ariv* news desk had changed dramatically during the Yom Kippur War. Due to the fierce competition between the two lunchtime papers, previously put to bed at nine in the morning, we were now starting work at four in the morning; some of us came at three, so that at seven thirty, the updated paper would hit the streets and be sold to people going to work. Between putting the paper to bed and receiving a first copy from the printers, there was enough time to air political differences. Almost every morning some loud arguments took place.

I can remember being shocked and appalled after having edited a report from Hebron describing how the Rebbetzin Levinger, whose family had just moved into the old city illegally, emptied a bucket full of dirt on the head of the chief of the Central Command. His offence had been to ask her politely to move out of the house in which she was squatting.

"How come this woman is not being arrested?! Why should she not go to jail?!" I called angrily.

"It is people like you and your lefty traitors who should go to jail!" one of the editors, a man of my parents' generation, screamed back at me.

This was alarming and totally unfounded. Traitors? In the Zionist Left? I did not believe there were any Israelis who loved our country more than I did.

* * *

Over forty years later, Hebron's third generation of Jewish settlers is well-established and fully armed, controlling powerful positions in government. With the protection of the military it perfectly personifies the national disgrace. In the early summer of 2016 the appointment of ultra-right winger, Soviet born Avigdor (Evet) Lieberman as Minister of Defence, the ultimate war lord of this constantly belligerent military empire, was greeted with gasps of disbelief even by conservatives. Zvi Bar'el summed it up nicely in Ha'aretz (June 1, 2016): "Lieberman doesn't understand security. He is corrupt. He represents one sector. He is fascist and racist. [...] But such a minister is not only appropriate for such a government. It also fits the sentiment in the country like a glove. It's the price tag hanging on the neck of a society that cultivated this approach."

New heights in the harassing and molesting of the local population are constantly reached, under the auspices of the loyal army and fully financed by the taxpayers. The State of Israel and its military authorities invoke our laws mainly against the conscientious objectors who refuse to serve in the occupied territories and against the very few Israelis who join the Palestinian struggle against land theft, illegal arrests, house demolitions, the monstrous Separation Wall and checkpoints system. Left-wing activists who document the horrors of the occupation – most of them still believers in the Zionist project, hoping innocently to "correct its wrongs" – are defined as state enemies. Educators and media gurus make it clear to an ignorant, incited public that words like "human rights organizations" or "human rights activists" denote anti-Semitism: supporters of such ideas must be crushed.

23

NO ENGLISH TRANSLATION

The pro-American regimes in the Arab world, mainly Saudi Arabia and Egypt, are grand incubators for terror. They have a clandestine covenant with the Islamic clerics: the government allows religion to have a monopoly on education; the religion allows the government to have a monopoly on the corrupt management of state affairs.

Nahum Barnea,
"Everybody's Terror," Yedioth Acharonoth,
September 11, 2002

M*a'ariv* was at its best on November 20, 1977, with a large colourful headline across the front page in Hebrew and in Arabic that read, "Welcome, President Sadat." The landing of the Egyptian president at Lod Airport on the previous evening was an emotionally loaded event for most Israelis. Like everybody else, I was glued to my small black-and-white television screen, excited about something great happening that should decisively improve my chances, as well as everybody else's, of a better life.

Anwar Sadat's official state visit was to last four days. The country held its breath to see his tall figure at the door of his airplane. Until that very moment, speculations about the whole thing being a hoax never stopped. Commentators warned against overexcitement that might end in tears. The chief of staff of the day, whose enterprise had the most to lose if peace were suddenly to break out, went further than most and officially announced that the idea of the visit seemed like a dangerous deception scheme that the Egyptian government had been plotting. Now, as Sadat descended the stairs to the tarmac and started shaking hands with a long line of Israeli dignitaries on live TV, I was beside myself with joy. Four years after the terrible crumbling of the Israeli fortification line in the Sinai, the strange Egyptian who had made this happen was about to topple the main argument supporting the sincere Israeli creed that "The Whole World is Against Us," and no Arab would ever allow us to live in peace.

Thousands of journalists flooded the media centre that was erected in the Jerusalem Theatre. On Monday Sadat was due to make a speech in the Knesset, next to Israeli Prime Minister Menachem Begin. Naturally, Sadat's speech was to be in Arabic. Begin was going to answer in Hebrew. In the Knesset a simultaneous translation facility was being prepared for both languages during the event, and Israeli TV had exclusive rights to transmit the speeches all over the world.

Following radio reports throughout the day, I heard that the American networks were surprised and concerned that the organizers of the Knesset event did not see to it that an official English translation should be provided throughout the live broadcast. I thought this was simply wonderful. With a sudden euphoria, I instantly produced an article with the headline "No Translation into English." I mused, "The decision of the Egyptian President and the Israeli Prime Minister to make no use of the English language for the purpose of their first public exchange heralds a welcome trend of breaking free from the traditional patronizing of the West over the East." I submitted this 350-word opinion piece, the first I ever ventured, that Sunday afternoon, and to my surprise, the stern Shmuel Schnitzer accepted it for the next day's prestigious op-ed page of *Ma'ariv* that he was editing. "It is very pleasing," I wrote, "that the Israeli and Egyptian heads of state have finally given up the services of western go-betweens and would now, for the first time ever, engage in dialogue using their own Semitic tongues, so closely related." My thesis seemed (to me) simple and straightforward: the visit of Sadat and the recognition of Israel by the largest Arab state in the world brings Israel back into its true vocation, which is to become an integral part of the East. The neighbourly Middle Eastern unmitigated dialogue is a thousand times better than any foreign diplomats' meddling in "meetings where the negotiating parties are under the auspices of chairpersons and landlords... to whom one must constantly report and translate everything that has been felt, considered, and expressed in the eastern mode of speech into a third, completely foreign language."

I went further than that:

It is the belief in a National Liberation rightward and eastward that joins Menachem Begin and the Egyptian President; the similarities between their politics have long been noticed: the deep affinity with tradition and the high regard for the middle classes.

It was no coincidence, I also pointed out, that in Israel the chief antagonists to this visit were typical representatives of the Ashkenazi elite, people like Chief of Staff Motta Gur and the ex-Minister of Finance Yigal Hurvitz. I called them the "pseudo-Western generation that had created in this country... patterns completely alien to the spirit of the Middle East and equally estranged from the Hebrew tradition." I called them "groupies of the Anglo-Saxon school..., captives of the English-language thinking parameters, shaped by Teutonic origins, which restricts the power of imagination and forces a tendency for sterile, obsessive precision.

"One should remind them, and the rest of us," I enthusiastically pontificated, "that what might be suitable for Europe and for North America is not necessarily appropriate for the reality of lands with at least three hundred sunny days every year. We are, after all, in the Orient, which has always been the land of unlimited possibilities. A harness on one's imagination was never an appreciated gadget around here. Against all western predictions a Jewish state has been established here out of nothing, almost into glorious dimensions; and the Arabs have become the new masters of wealth within one decade – an achievement Americans had to work on for two hundred years."

So this was my "conception" many decades ago: Israel, attentively following the fine-tuning of Jewish-traditional-Middle-Eastern innuendo would be quick to discover how much she has in common with its neighbours. In the background was the ascent to power earlier in the year of the Israeli right wing, made possible by the protest vote of the oriental Jews who woke up to political awareness. It was surprising how within a few months, the Right – for the first time running the government since 1948, after the first-ever failure of the Labor Party in April 1977 – had made this astounding political breakthrough; the old Labor establishment, trapped in its fake European orientation, had failed to make any progress in its relations with the Arabs in almost thirty years.

Peace Now demonstration along the road to Jerusalem, April 1978, protesting at delays in the Israeli-Egyptian negotiations; author with *Ma'ariv's* secretary Sara Kashi (left). Photo: Shmuel Rachmani

It was indeed hard to imagine a leader moulded on Yitzhak Rabin or Shimon Peres talking to Sadat about religious convictions, using lines from the Koran or the Bible. Menachem Begin, the idol of the Arab Jews, was a natural when it came to tradition. I was celebrating a chance to score against everything I had learned to despise in the Ashkenazi-Secular Israel, which for years had been doing all it could to stay at arm's length from anything Arab or Middle Eastern, denying everything that I considered the true origins of Judaism and its historical heritage. It seemed that the winning combination of conservatism and oriental Israelis should shake the state away from the chains of traditional separatism dictated by the ancient Ashkenazi view of the world. I believed our state was walking safely toward a new era where we would be free of the terrible pain and horror of wars. Together with our Arab cousins, Israeli Jews could make the deserts of the Middle East blossom. Arab resources and Jewish professionalism should present an alternative to the western way of doing things rather than try to duplicate it.

My grand theory did not hold water by the time the newspaper with my article was printed on Monday morning. The Knesset and the Government Press Office in the meantime hurriedly got organized to supply an official English translation for the live broadcast of Sadat's and Begin's speeches. Not for one second had Hebrew and Arab speakers been left alone to solve their problems that (to me) seemed so simple.

Best remembered from the things Sadat and Begin said in that historic November was an English phrase that had been turned into the jingle of the late "Voice of Peace," Abby Nathan's piratical radio station. "No More War, No More Bloodshed," they both promised. The Egyptian president has since paid with his life for his vision and courage. Begin withered away agonizing over the next war that started in Lebanon five years later, apparently without his consent although he was the prime minister. The peace made with Egypt only helped Israel dig its heels into the uncompromising position on the occupation and rapidly promote the settlements' reality, nurturing religious animosities under the iron fist of the ever-inflated armed forces.

* * *

My reading of the political developments could not have been more wrong. The peace treaty with Egypt opened new horizons for Israeli Religious Nationalism. Sadat's initiative had neutralized the threat from the most powerful and dangerous enemy in the south. It allowed Israeli governments to start earnestly on realizing the fantasies of both the revisionist Herut Party – brainchild of Polish nationalist megalomania – and the messianic teaching of Rabbi Yehuda Hacohen Kook. Incomprehensibly enough, the supposedly left-wing Labor Party, led by would-be Nobel Peace Prize laureate Shimon Peres, turned out to be a willing and cooperating partner with most of these governments since 1977.

The elitist Gush Emunim ("Block of the Faithful") movement led the action with a clearly mapped-out strategy. One by one, new estates, communities, and neighbourhoods for Jews only were started in the heart of Palestinian populated areas. Billions in taxpayers' money was openly and officially funnelled into building roads, housing estates, public institutions, educational facilities, and leisure facilities for the new settlers. Jobs, affordable, quality, subsidized accommodation, and excellent welfare privileges were offered to them and made for a superior quality of life compared to life "inside the Green Line."

The Eretz Israel zealots soon started a mass marketing effort. The new settlements were offered to nonpolitical Israeli Jews, young and old, as the only option for affordable housing in the centre of Israel, at commuting distance from the big cities. The so-called Left did not register much protest.

The hard core of the settlement movement was almost exclusively made of the Gush's supporters, easily identified by their knitted yarmulkes. They are considered by themselves – but also by a majority of Israelis – as the new spearhead of modern Zionism. They had turned their backs on the traditional Jewish religious politics that advocated moderation in political involvement and patient attendance for the coming of the Messiah. Theirs was a mode of operation based in aggressive activism. They found their greatest supporters and admirers in the men in uniform: the non-kosher-eating, non-Sabbath-keeping, highly promiscuous professional officers of the IDF, the mightiest military machine in the Middle East, found a source of "spiritual values" to legitimize their well-paid brutality.

These were the Jewish groups that had shaped the image of the New Israel of the seventies and the eighties: a powerful occupation force, armed to the teeth. Ethnically, both the Gush and the top soldiers were Ashkenazi; ideologically they shared a highly male chauvinistic *Weltanschauung*, righteously supported by their women. Arab Jews were a negligible minority in the hard core of the settlers' movement in those days – not because they were not attracted by its macho messianic vision, but because most were not found worthy of joining the yeshiva schools of Gush Emunim and were unable to reach the top positions in the army. The socialist elitist Left, on the other hand, was very well represented both in the military and in the illegal (according to international law) settling of occupied land. For over twenty years, the socialist youth movements had been sending the cream of their graduating youth to "realize the vocation" in the romantic *Nachal* (Fighting

Pioneer Youth) settler communities in the occupied territories. Understandably, the "Working Youth" and the "Young Guards" youngsters discreetly gave up the convenient Arab *Kaffieh* head cloth, which in my days was an almost obligatory part of our attire in the blue-shirt youth movements.

Arab Jews, however, showed constantly growing support for this right wing, extremist Ashkenazi leadership. It was the perfect balm for their collective injured ego. The frustrated Peace Camp loudly complained of the "cultural differences" that so despairingly made peace politics impossible in democratic Israel. The more the so-called elitist Labor movement lamented the gap between its own highbrow members and the riff-raff, the more estranged from the Left Arab Jews had become. Their youngsters chose instead to further their identification with religious Jewish tradition, as the marking of their detachment from the rest of the Arabs as well as their disdain for the veteran elites.

Sephardic Israeli secular intellectuals, while often critical of the settlement movement, show great understanding of the right-wing political affinities of the Sephardic masses as an expression of their "roots" and their cultural authenticity. They also identify correctly the massive presence of Arab Jews in the settlements' population as another proof of their socioeconomic inferiority, imposed by years of Eastern European domination. It is too painful, I suppose, to clearly define what the deprived children of immigrants from Arab countries are really complaining about: their parents were summoned to support the Zionist enterprise but were not allowed to have an equal share in the distribution of the booty taken from the Arabs of the land.

* * *

The quest for the elusive "peace process" was set in motion by Sadat's historical visit and has been in full swing ever since. Americans and Europeans lavishly sponsor meetings, conferences, and negotiations in cool venues. The best hotels are available for the noble cause. All participants speak good English and seem to be having a very good time.

24

THE NAKED HAT

> Then something started jamming and cracking, things were going wrong and unravelling, the sweet dream is again drifting away, seemingly about to be smashed up and be blown to pieces. And the glow is no longer a light to the nations, not even bright enough for my own small home, no longer so small actually. But why?
>
> **Dan Shilon,**
> Israeli TV icon, *Ma'ariv*, May 5, 2003
> (a special edition for Israel's fifty-fifth Independence Day)

In the autumn of 1998, the consulting company I started three years earlier in our rented flat in a Tel Aviv suburb had already stabilized into an active little business. We moved to a large duplex on the same street, which was well suited for the needs of a live-in office employing two full-time account managers. When one of the women left for the United States, I started looking for a replacement, and a friend recommended a young woman, a first-class graduate of Bar Ilan University whose life's ambition was to work in public relations.

Hagit[1] made an excellent impression when she came for an interview. She was highly intelligent, energetic, and articulate. The round hat and long skirt indicated that she was a modern religious Orthodox married woman. This was no problem as far as I was concerned. Actually, the other account manager in the office also happened to be observant, with the only difference being that she chose not to cover her hair following her wedding.

It was clear that in my home, the kosher rules as well as the Sabbath regulations were not observed; my husband was not

[1] Name changed.

Jewish and denominational freedom had to be taken for granted. Both girls were perfectly OK with this arrangement. They used to bring their own packed lunch and used utensils that did not mix with ours, as they would have done in any office in town.

Hagit fit very well into our little enterprise. She proved industrious as well as creative. We were only women in the office most of the time, and during working hours, Hagit conveniently used to take off her head gear, showing her short blonde hair. She seemed transformed and much younger with the hat off – she was only twenty-two years old. We would smile at the haste with which she rushed to cover her head each time the doorbell rang, in case the visitor – a messenger, the postman, or a client – might turn out to be male. "Exposing a woman's hair is equivalent to exposing her private parts," as page 64 of the Babylonian Talmud's Sabbath tractate puts it.

Hagit put an abrupt end to the leisurely uncovered hair habit in January 1999, as my then-husband moved back permanently to Israel after two years of living and working abroad with occasional home leaves. His study was in the first floor of the duplex, but he could emerge unannounced into our second-floor office space at any time, thus potentially embarrassing Hagit by accidentally witnessing her hair, so offensive when displayed to members of the opposite gender. I was sorry about the inconvenience to our talented account manager and suggested to her that the man in the house should be trained to announce himself by giving an early notice each time he was about to approach, so that she might go on working safely with no hat on.

It pleased me that she came back after the weekend to tell me this was not necessary. Apparently she acquired a rabbinical ruling on the matter. The rabbi decreed it was quite all right to continue working with a bare head in our office. He also enlightened Hagit that she may regard the office as a home environment, which allows such liberties, since it was part of a family abode, and she was practically a member of the household. In such an intimate habitat, apparently, hair may be freely on display, as it is in one's own home. I was impressed with the wisdom of the spiritual leader who did not wish his flock to be pressured unnecessarily, and thought it was one of the advantages of the much-praised *Halacha*, always to aim at supplying smart solutions in order to alleviate even tiny human distresses (that admittedly were created by the strict Halacha ruling in the first place).

* * *

These were the hazy days of high-tech frenzy. The workload was enormous but gratifying. For the Passover holidays of that year, we chose yet another family trip to Sinai. It turned out to be an exceptional experience for five members of our small family: my mother and father, then well into their seventies, my ten-year-old daughter, and us, her parents.

For this particular trip, we acquired Egyptian visas that allowed us to enter the non-tourist-designated part of the peninsula. On the Taba border checkpoint, we made another bold decision. Rather than collect the rented car we intended to drive, as we had done on previous holidays, we accepted the offer of a local van driver who for the same price offered to chauffeur us around for five days.

We started the regular tracks: from Taba to the Nuweiba Tarabin beach oasis, then to the new town of Saint Catherine, where we checked into the (supposedly) five-star Plaza Hotel. Following the traditional nocturnal climb of the frozen Jabal Mousa to see the rising sun illuminating the desert (only my daughter and her father signed up for this pilgrimage) and the tour around the sixth-century church reputed to lie directly on the site of the Burning Bush, we crossed the Egyptian police checkpoint into the enormous Faran Oasis.

It seemed like a time machine transfer. The dirt road over the palm-clustered wadi, with scattered presence of Bedouins in traditional attire and no sign of western technology or comforts, was as exciting and challenging as my father and I remembered from our first backpacking trip to Sinai in 1969. Our present driver Mubarak, a native of Abu Zenima on the Suez Bay coast, was very familiar with the sites I was longing to revisit after all these years: the spectacular Ras Muhamad coral reserve, the fishermen port At-Tour, Hamam [hot springs] Sidna Mousa, and

Hamam Faraune. Even the thick black smoke above the Ras Soudar refineries made us heavy with nostalgia for our innocent old days as "enlightened occupiers."

The highlight of the trip this time was a journey to Serabit el Khadim, an obelisk-packed temple site next to the ancient turquoise mines of the pharaohs. Not even a dirt road exists to this place, and in order to get there through the dunes, we needed a long ride with a pickup truck that belonged to one of Mubarak's mates. A member of the local Bedouin tribe near Sarabit then accompanied us as a guide on the exhausting climb on the hills. The site was spectacular, well worth the enormous effort. Still, the most memorable adventure of the expedition took place the night before this trip, which we spent at Mubarak's own private home. Abu Zenima, the nearest settlement next to our destination is a Bedouin town with no tourist facilities, and we were grateful to accept our driver's generous offer of hospitality. Our evening in the guest rooms of his hut was an enormous privilege and a genuine eye opener.

We already knew that Aysha, Mubarak's wife, was fifteen years younger than her husband. She turned out to be an eighteen-year-old stunner, a head taller than her stout, dark husband. Mubarak considered Aysha's fair skin her most valuable aesthetic asset. "She is really white, and my youngest daughter Fatma is just as white," he told us with great pride, while openly expressing his disappointment with the dark complexion of his son Muhammad, a perfect impish copy of his dad.

The hut had an external reception room for male visitors, while women could be invited to the guest room inside, together with the lady of the house and the relatives. As we were special guests, we could all be asked into the more intimate and lucrative "women's chamber." The fair Aysha, who received us outside the hut properly enveloped in the traditional Hijab covering her hair, neck, and forehead, did not think twice about getting rid of it inside the yard, in front of two foreign male visitors. I registered that just like Hagit she made a clear distinction between modest public appearance and casual in-home rules.

The young woman charmed us all. As a real child of the desert, she did not receive any schooling and could not read or write, let alone speak foreign languages. But my father, for whom Arabic was a native language, enjoyed translating her lively conversation. Mubarak was a model husband when it came to providing for the family, getting fresh food, and helping in the kitchen. The trouble was that he never stopped chatting and bragging about his great dream and ambition to marry at least one more wife, to be kept in another Bedouin township. His older brother, he revealed enviously, already was married to three.

Aysha was not amused. "She says she will murder him if he takes on another woman," my father translated. Even if it was humorously spoken, there was an evident tension in the air.

"She has no right to stop me," Mubarak protested – he spoke perfect Hebrew and good English. "For us this is the norm. I am a well-established member of the community, and many Bedouin fathers will be delighted to have me as a son-in-law. They know any girl I marry will have a good home that I must build for her specially. They know I will always be a good provider. I can have any sixteen-, fifteen-, or maybe even fourteen-year-old girl and make her very happy, because I am well respected and hardworking, having my own van and earning good money."

Aysha repeated the death threats with tight lips, vowing that any woman stupid enough to marry her husband would find her death next to him.

Dinner was a heavenly kid roast cooked in rich soup. Our eating accessories included two aluminium spoons for the five guests. Meat and rice were to be rolled by the hands. We agreed not even to mention that there was plenty of plastic disposable cutlery in our picnic luggage, and went native, enjoying every bit.

To avoid the domestic argument, we turned our attention to the TV set. An Egyptian musical soap opera was on, the kind that was very popular in the 1970s on Israel's then-single channel. The improvised satellite dish produced an unstable screen that kept changing into snow, but we managed to stay glued to the drama, studded with much belly dancing and orchestrated singing. We did not need much translation. It was obvious that the elegant female protagonist was an opinionated, affluent, fortysomething urban lady who simultaneously ran the family and the business while deeply involved in a clandestine, sinful, and painful relationship.

I was hoping that the designer clothes with deep low cuts, the blonde-dyed hair, and the assertive manner of the TV singing diva were subtly informing Aysha about an option for a feminine existence that did not include dependence on a providing man who must be obeyed. Perhaps she will see to it that her daughters will not be forced to marry in return for food and a roof over their heads.

As an answer to this idle thinking, several children from the neighbourhood arrived to scrutinize the rare visitors. Mubarak's nine-year-old niece approached us with great confidence and tried her English vocabulary. It was heart-warming to realize that unlike her mother and her aunt, who grew up in tents in the middle of nowhere, this girl not only visited school regularly but was also first in her class in arithmetic. According to the proud Mubarak, the child was a prodigy destined to become an engineer. They did not yet have Internet in Abu Zneime in 1999, but it was expected to arrive soon. Cellular phones and other gadgets would soon follow. The technological revolution was well on its way, and we knew that this remote third-world corner was being transformed in front of our eyes.

* * *

The Abu Zenima little girls must be well on their way to progress now, courtesy of the former Egyptian government, which had worked out a detailed master plan for the development of the Sinai Peninsula. A visit to an Israeli Bedouin settlement a few years after this Sinai excursion made clear that on our side of the border, the prospects of little Bedouin girls were less promising. Many of them have parents who arrange marriages for them when they are only twelve years old. Thirteen-year-old mothers who are second and third wives to a bossy middle-aged man are a common phenomenon. The state turns a blind eye to this scandalous usurpation of young lives. What we do hear are complaints about the child benefits that the child-mothers are entitled to.

* * *

In early 2000, business around the high-tech and equity bubble peaked to unprecedented levels. I was no longer able to cope with the workload on my own. Luckily a senior financial journalist agreed to join me and become my business partner. My home office had to be deserted in favour of proper office space that we hired together in the Ramat Gan Diamond Exchange area.

A few weeks after the partnership was launched in its new premises, I noticed that Hagit no longer took her headgear off. One of her round hats was constantly perched on top of her, hiding her hair at all hours. I was surprised because the office doors were always closed, and as always there were very few outside visitors.

"What happened to the rabbinical waiver that allowed for your hair to be loose in the home environment?" I wondered (stupidly, as it turned out). "Udi has been with us for over a month, and he is the only man around this place. Is it not time that he, too, should be considered one of our little family?"

Hagit was hesitant for a moment, but then she gave me the candid answer, accompanied with an apologetic smile.

"Truth is, in your home I was able to take off my hat because your husband is a non-Jew. I did not feel comfortable explaining this before. As Udi is Jewish, I must always keep my hair covered in his presence."

Words failed me. Until then I had no idea that a Jewish woman need not worry about a non-Jew seeing her bare head, representing the idea that "exposing private parts" is permissible if the onlooker is a goy. It was a kind of enlightenment that accorded a new dimension to everything I knew so far about Israel and the nations. Personally I was deeply offended with this enormously rude attitude toward my husband. At the same time, Hagit's hat became for me a private symbol of the whole Jewish problem. We are forever astounded with the level of rejection others express toward us through – apparently – no fault of our own. We truly feel like innocent victims: Jews, after all, do not hate non-Jews, and most of us do not act in order to harm them. We simply see non-Jews as a different species of human beings. This however often evokes problematic reactions that are hard to foresee.

* * *

I cannot pretend to have been completely ignorant as to the strong feelings of alienation that Israeli society inflicts on non-Jews in general. For some non-Jews who land here by coincidence, this cultural character sometimes becomes an ordeal. At some stage my husband, having often enough been taken aback as a result of his dealings with my fellow Israelis, decided to start his own support group. It was specifically designated for frustrated English-speaking "goys" married to Israeli Jewish spouses. He started through the free small add section of *Ha'aretz* English edition's Anglo File on Friday, and soon about twenty men and women who shared his feelings presented themselves for the first meetings of GAGS (Grumpy Anglo-Saxon Goys). The group fell apart after a relatively short period, mainly because its members, who came from completely different backgrounds, locations, and age groups had little to offer each other except bitter criticism of Israel and the Israelis. As the free add kept appearing with our phone number, we continued to receive new calls from would-be members who were eager to join GAGS and relate the familiar tale of loneliness and alienation.

Mixed marriages are still considered a wild exception in the Israeli Jewish society, even among the most liberal. My own marriage seemed to me to be modelled strangely enough on a very traditional Jewish pattern. Jewish women always willingly supported and provided for their scholarly husbands, and this was the case in our family too. While my husband engaged in pure intellectual pursuits, my work earned us a living through many years. He was a late starter in academia but with hard work eventually made a modest name for himself in his particular field. Slowly but surely he was able to build up an impressive list of publications that included books and learned articles. His life in Israel was focused on independent research, supplemented by a single and untenured teaching course in the Overseas Student Unit of Tel Aviv University.

With the outbreak of the second Intifada in 2000, American Jewish students refrained from visiting Tel Aviv and even the part-time meagrely-paying job evaporated. Fortunately for him, at long last a British university was now ready to offer my husband a job. I was pleased for him and expected to join him soon in the pretty English country house that we had purchased together. I was all set on early retirement, hoping to move back into independent writing, and I actually started to work on my first book.

Two years later, I suddenly discovered that my marriage had broken up. While I was congratulating myself on the "Jewish Model" that allowed me to build a career next to a scholarly partner, the partner was actually living up to the family model favoured by Bedouin men. In our pretty country home near the university where he now had a good teaching job, he had been cohabiting with a good-looking divorcée, the same age as me. Frequent home visits to Tel Aviv and almost daily telephone calls were enough to sustain my illusion of a reasonably happy family.

My friends and family united in great condemnation of my renegade husband. His own family and friends in England were unsurprisingly more understanding of his sincere need to get away from what they saw as the "cultural gap" associated with the life of a foreigner in Israel. Remembering Hagit's hat I had to agree.

* * *

It was anyway time to admit that the marriage had failed long before I finally woke up to it. Had the union been truly solid, no "cultural differences" would have broken it – certainly no silly hats. Why did I fail to admit the obvious for so many years?

Some irony was there, entirely at my expense. After all, most of my time I was working on a book – the present one – critically agonizing over the irrationality of the society I grew up with. Why do Israeli secular Jews refuse to face reality? I was complaining while clearly turning a blind eye to my own comfortable home-made illusion. Suddenly I had a new perspective on the total devotion of my fellow Israeli Jews to a culture that renders them so miserable. The willingness of my friends and acquaintances to sacrifice their lives, the life of their children, a large chunk of their income, and their welfare – all this for the benefit of a national home that offers so little comfort and so much aggravation – no longer seemed incomprehensible.

* * *

The twist in my life turned out to be not so bad after all. New ideas, new pursuits, and new people soon presented themselves. Like most people in these circumstances, I discovered that families are not necessarily irreplaceable and that most homes are not eternal. One may always move out or renovate, or both.

The analogy is simplistic, but to me irresistible. With the disintegration of the Jewish-Israeli national home in full swing, an optimistic alternative is so much better than a defeatist depression. The break-up of old, unsuccessful unions is a prerequisite for the emergence of new, better solutions. With good will and sound management, this part of the world known historically as Palestine and presently ruled by Israel may and should be rebuilt over much sounder and more legitimate foundations. A serious discussion and consideration of a single democratic state of all its inhabitants, between the Jordan and the Mediterranean, is long overdue.

Part VII – Hopes (b)

And a sun as blue as the sea will rise upon us
A sun as warm as an eye
And it should await us so that we might ascend
For the time it would walk into the blue west

Dahlia Rabikovitz,
"The Blue West"[1]

[1] In "All your Waves and Breakers," 1972, author's translation.

25

A NIGHT AT THE OPERA, A MORNING IN RAMALLAH

"How do you feel about the idea of Two States for Two Nations?"

"Well if an idea is not becoming a reality after so many years, it probably should never **happen.**"

Israel Shamir,
member of an Israeli-Christian-Russian group aiming to join up with the Palestinians, in an interview to *Yediot Aharonot*, February 14, 2003

"I am glad I shall not live long enough to see this country fall apart altogether," my mother, the ex-fighter, ex-teacher, ex-staunch Young Socialist Guard, still a staunch Zionist, informed me gravely one evening. She was nowhere near dying, thank God. The same age as Ariel Sharon, who had just started office as Prime Minister at that time, and at the peak of his popularity, she was a very active, lively lady. I thought she looked great in a glamorous Turkish velvet jacket, tastefully embroidered. We were sipping free sparkling wine sponsored by a car manufacturer on the occasion of a gala performance at the New Israeli Opera, world famous for its quality grand productions.

Tonight's performance was Umberto Giordano's *Andrea Chénier,* featuring starving, furious peasants storming the ballroom of the Countess di Coigny with their spades and forks in Act I. The coquettish, preposterous dance of the gavotte came to a horribly bloody, messy end. The massacre of one group of decadent aristocrats on a country estate was only the beginning. The murder craze was soon to take over the capital of France. In the political opera, the Parisian mob joyfully cheers every day at the sight of hundreds of accused men and women paraded by cart through the streets on their way to *La Guillotine*. Many thousands of innocent people – including, unfortunately, the protagonist and his beloved – would pay with their lives for the wrongs of the greedy and the indifferent. Much blood, mud, and corruption would wash down the gutters before the French Revolution would go down in history as one of Europe's most heroic moments.

In the second act, a poor, blind old woman tearfully appeals to the sleazy Committee of the Revolution for special mercy: she needs an "exception" permit so that her last surviving grandson will be allowed to join the army and die massacring the Enemies of the Homeland as did all his brothers and uncles.

Am I the only one here moving uncomfortably in my seat? Or is there a message here for the Tel Aviv wine-sipping gala crowd? Thirty minutes' drive from the stylized postmodern architecture of the Performing Arts Centre, wretched women proudly posed for TV cameras, displaying photos of their sons and daughters who had turned themselves into live bombs in the streets of Israel, promising more of the same. This is the horrible March of the year 2002.

Perhaps the second Intifada will too, one day, become the subject of a musical performance with moving moments, carefully orchestrated melodies and a universally appealing moral. Perhaps the plot would concentrate on a fearless intellectual, modelled on Andrea Chénier, who would not give in to the murderous obsession. In the end, love in B minor would triumph over the mass-produced senseless death.

Peace Banner I:
Two States for Two Nations

Netanya's Park Hotel Passover night's massacre – thirty dead and almost a hundred wounded while sitting down to the Seder festive meal – happened just a few days after the gala opening night of *Andrea Chénier*. The Israeli government has decreed, "Something must be done" in the streets where mothers live with their would-be suicide bomber kids. "Something must be done" to appease shocked and furious public opinion. Israel's Defence Force, a colossal military machine made of tanks, D9 bulldozers, and thousands of highly motivated young men, has its marching orders to eradicate the "terror infrastructure."

Horrified at the prospect of the organized counter-carnage, several busloads of middle-aged women have set out for a peace rally near a rainy Palestinian town under Israeli military siege. We have come to chant for peace and call to end the occupation. A wall-to-wall coalition of peace organizations has declared a joint Israeli-Palestinian women's march to the barred gates of Ramallah. We have been asked to wear something white. The response is well beyond expectations, even though it is a stormy April day – hardly the weather for flimsy white shirts and scarves.

The buses drop about a thousand demonstrators – Israeli Jews and Arabs – in a large, empty plot at the outskirts of Kalandia, between Ramallah and Jerusalem. Large signs in Hebrew, English, and Arabic and banners for "Peace" and "End the Occupation" are available, as well as identifying marks for the many groups that answered the call: Gush Shalom, Bat Shalom, Doctors for Human Rights, Architects against Destruction, Zochrot – remembering the Nakba, Peace Now, Meretz, Hadash, and more. The rain is soaking us all as the march sets off toward Ramallah City.

"Israel and Palestine – Two States for Two Nations," the grandmothers in white rhythmically chant. I already have my doubts. Arabic speakers are better organized with "With soul and blood, we shall free you, Palestine." Some local young men and boys watch us with obvious disdain. "Israel – NO!" one of them throws emphatically to my face, and doubts or not, my heart sinks. Israel is, was, my homeland. The popular "Two States" slogan, dreamed up by the Israeli extreme Left many years earlier, is soon to be embraced and repeated by the Israeli mainstream, as well as some right-wingers, who consider it a clever trick that would halt any real progress.

Two States for Two Nations? Our one, well-confused national state had already managed to cause enough havoc and tragedy. There is nothing good to be expected of another such national organ. It has every chance to be loaded with its own threatening baggage of uncompromising hostilities and prejudice. Unarmed – as Israel insists – it will be a joke for the benefit of a gallery of helpless, probably corrupt leaders.

What is the point of working so hard for the establishment and preservation of two states with territories and borders intertwining like boiling spaghetti? If everybody in this march is so peace-seeking, why don't we call for a united effort toward rubbish disposal, sewage systems, water and transport maintenance, trade, medical services, welfare, and education? What else does one need a state for anyway?

More young Palestinians spot Israeli women and reward their effort with internationally accepted gestures of disgust. "Israel – No!" they chant. But too many Palestinians, I know for a fact, would be happy with merely a blue ID card and work permit. At the same time, too many Israeli members of the Peace movement consider the idea of more "Israeli Arabs" a nightmare. Hardly any understand or accept the need to bring back the population of refugees who still wait abroad for a return home.

A meticulously elegant Palestinian lady now scolds me furiously in very good English: "Sharon is Hitler! He is worse than Hitler!" I am made to feel responsible or at least a partner to the thuggish violence of my prime minister, a man I always loathed and feared, and his uniformed emissaries who are about to tear-gas me. Fifteen years earlier, in Washington, I was beside myself as Israel's then-ambassador to the United Nations, one Benjamin Netanyahu, declared on *The Week with David Brinkley*[2] that Yasser Arafat was "worse than Hitler." Four years as a correspondent in West Germany in the 1980s exhausted my patience with such cynical comparisons.

From a distance nasty yellow clouds of smoke go up gently. The large crowd starts a fearful retreat as tear gas is shot at it by the soldiers at the Ar-Ram barricaded entrance to Ramallah. Only a small dose of the gas hits us where we stand. It is my first ever encounter with this substance that burns the eyes and is painful to breathe. Palestinian women standing at the balconies of their nearby homes hurriedly throw onion slices at us, but I am a novice at this game and have no idea what to do with them. Why were we actually tear-gassed? We merely came to chant for peace. Tears run down my face and my eyes are sore.

---

[2] ABC network, April 10, 1988.

For media and PR purposes, our women's rally has a gimmick: the transfer of several trucks loaded with food and medical supplies for the Palestinians barred behind the Ar-Ram *Machsom* (checkpoint). One truck makes its way slowly through the long column of chanting demonstrators. The loudspeakers inform us that negotiations have started with the army to let it pass. The rain stops and then starts again. We have now been singing "We Shall Overcome" and "If I had a Hammer" for almost two hours, feeling young and pretending these are the sixties in Berkeley.

"Men step back! Only women forward," the organizers ineffectually plead over and over using loudspeakers. But this is the Middle East, and men are not going to concede their position at the top. I sense trouble as young men gather small rocks in their pockets. Are they about to induce an explosive end to the peaceful women's march?

We are really happy to notice the truck moving, at long last, toward the other side of the checkpoint. The army allowed it to pass, says the voice over the megaphone. Singing voices go up joyfully, and the sun shows up between the clouds, beaming some hope even at the outskirts of Ramallah. At this very moment, all hell breaks out. Had somebody chucked a stone or was it nothing more than some shoves, as somebody later insisted? Perhaps one or two of the demonstrators purposely pushed the limits of the nervous soldiers at the checkpoint, willingly provoking a violent reaction as per the teaching of comrade Leon Trotsky, alias Lev Davidovich? It is equally likely that none of these happened, and that it was actually somebody somewhere in the inflated hierarchy of Israel's Defence Army who had instructed the soldiers to inflict violence over the almost sleepy peace rally, to assert the true dimensions of the balance of power. The tear-gas salvos are no longer single shots but dozens of small flames, blowing up at eye level, forcing out the chemically-burning smoke into a thick, stinking bubble of pain.

Hundreds of panicking women, most of them venerable grandmothers, start another undignified, uncontrolled stampede in all directions. Screams of pain and fear fill the air; the smell of burning hair mixes with the terrible gas. I am terrified that within the yellow, stinking cloud, one of us will fall over and be left to be trampled on by the hysterical masses, unable to escape through the densely parked cars on both sides of the street. The pain in the lungs is now unbearable; my face is awash with streams of tears. It is the gas, of course; nobody would notice whether or not I am also sobbing, crushed with humiliation. Once out of the cloud, I notice the less fortunate women who were also burned and injured with the cartridges that hit their faces, shoulders, and arms.

The large white crocheted shawl I wrapped myself in this morning, a souvenir handmade by Savta Chaya at the old age pensioners' macramé group in the day centre at Ben Saruk Street, is now dragging behind me on the ground, soiled with the Middle Eastern mud.

We board the buses, sad and bruised. The organizers inform us that we might be on TV tonight, which means the demonstration was successful. "It ended relatively well; the truth is, we were afraid there might have been casualties," a satisfied young woman tells us before moving on to update the next bus, armed with notes and a megaphone. My panic level shoots up in retrospect. It is not at all certain that I would have willingly set out for action knowing there was a risk my family would see me next time in a box. Thank God we are already on our way home, heading for a warm shower, far away from the water shortage, the electricity breaks, and the lack of basic supplies in nearby Palestine.

Two States for Two People? Perhaps the priority should be to stop my one and only state scaring me to death, making me feel so guilty and so ashamed. Let's make this one state benevolent, responsible, and compassionate to all the citizens it controls. Let it stop trembling with well-orchestrated fear because some of them speak another language and (possibly) believe in a God that has a different name.

Are we really unable to join up with hundreds of thousands of human beings who more than anything else – just like us – would like nothing better than a nice home with a private car parked next to it, multichannel TV, and two trips to Europe every year? Is anybody really interested in "eradicating the infrastructure of terror" as the Israeli military mantra goes?

Peace Banner II: Dismantle Settlements. At Least Evacuate Unauthorized Strongholds

A year goes by. Suicide bombers occasionally manage sporadic killings. Retaliation and harsh measures are the answer, as well as more and more new settlers on occupied lands. It is Passover again, and a new, young, motivated Israeli group is determined – once again – to resuscitate the good old Peace Now brand. They have budgets and politicians standing by, hoping there is still a chance to create a mass movement that should bring them back to the coveted, elusive realms of democratic government. Disciplined veterans of the movement, which include my childhood friend Nira and me, willingly respond to the new summons.

The young people have come up with an idea that should produce a good media story. This time we shall travel to establish a so-called "Peaceful Stronghold" near the Arab town Hebron (al-Khalil). Unauthorized settlements are started almost daily by zealots with the not-so-clandestine support of most army officers. When complaints are raised, the army claims it is "unable" to dismantle them. It is our idea to find out whether or not the army will be unable to dismantle our own "illegal stronghold."

Nira and I experience our first-ever trip on "Jews-only" roads. The double tunnels highway, south of the capital, is an unparallelled ethnic-transport innovation. Over a hundred million shekels of the taxpayers' money was sunk in this infamously unique exclusive route, all in the futile hope that those Jews who willingly chose to reside in enclaves at the heart of "hostile population" would not have to fear frustrated stone throwing or violent ambushes on the roads of the occupied areas.

The bus goes past housing estates spread thinly on top of the hills. The very long banana-shaped suburban settlements, surrounded by barbed wire, are built as wedges that disconnect local habitats from one another as well as manufacture excuses for the removal of farmers and shepherds from their lands in the name of sacred security. The citizens of pre-1967 Israel, one of the most densely populated countries in the world, spend hours every day in traffic due to inadequate transport solutions, but few challenge the wisdom of pampering the commuters in the occupied lands.

We now witness these commuters at our leisure. Our bus has been stopped at a checkpoint, *machsom* in Hebrew. Local Jewish inhabitants of Judea and Samaria, easily identified by their uniform of yarmulkes and bearded faces and by their battered vehicles overloaded with children, sweep by with no hindrances; Arabs and obvious troublemakers like us have to get off the road and wait for higher authority to let us continue to our destination. As travellers on buses decorated with Peace Now banners, we are denied even access to the other side of the road, where a very large Jewish greengrocer's shop seems to do good business. Its construction of corrugated iron must have been erected by a settler with good contacts, which make building permits, business licenses, and probably trifles like VAT and other taxes superfluous. Israeli law enforcement had never seemed so selective to my inexperienced eyes. My kind of traveller is now forbidden even from moving inside the almost-empty parking lot to converse with a group of Palestinians whose bus, too, had been stopped and barred from entry into Hebron for seemingly no logical reason.

"What do you mean, we may not talk to them?!" I lash out haughtily at the uniformed soldiers, with the assertiveness imbued by fifty years of my Jewish-Israeli, much-privileged, democratic citizenship. "Is there a law now that forbids Jews from talking to Arabs in this country?"

"Giveret, please vacate the area," a sergeant in grey addresses and dismisses me with equally assertive authority. This is the Border Police, a cross between army and civil law enforcers. He has the authority to stop Israeli civilians. The army may only touch Palestinians, occupied with no civil status.

"I would like to take down your details, please," I insist. If this is the police, I may complain to the department for the investigation of corrupt cops. An obvious misuse of authority is being committed, driven by political considerations. Great scandal would erupt. This man is going to see sense now.

"My name is Machsomi," he tells me without a flinch. "Shachar Machsomi," he repeats, jeering. His subordinates are having a great laugh.

"Very funny," I sternly snap back. "No wonder you are afraid to even give your real name. This shows at least that you are well aware that you are acting illegally."

With deep contempt the border policeman points at the flap of his jacket pocket. The weird name Machsomi, "Mr. Checkpoint," is clearly embroidered there as a perfectly legal identification. There is an identification number as well, which I make a point of noting down, but my defeat is all too clear. The grey uniformed young men are savouring every minute.

"These are my orders," Machsomi thrusts at me, when I continue insisting on understanding what gives him the right to forbid my movement from the vicinity of one civilian bus to the next. His well-maintained calm is backed by an obvious physical advantage, which includes loaded weapons. Occupation is synonymous with violence. But in the Israeli media's thesaurus, only children throwing stones are violent rioters. The thugs who beat them up are our beloved children.

The Palestinians, well experienced in much worse molestations, wearily watch the internal Jewish strife. There is a much sharper confrontation on the other side of the parking lot, where a few young Peace Now girls break into the road, on the other side of the bar. Machsomi's soldiers, boys of the same age group as the girls, do not stop to ponder. Using the clubs they carry, they hit them with all their might. We are all stunned. Our impotence is total. Who should we call for help? The police?

The measure of the "Security Forces'" full identification with the settler movement and its senseless agenda finally sinks in. It is hardly a coincidence that this agenda is fully compatible with the vital interests of the officers' class: for more power, more influence, more taxpayers' allocations. Shachar Machsomi's brainwashed kids are cannon fodder to this unholy alliance. They will continue to do whatever it takes to provide the iron shield and the metal fists the settlers need to survive and the army professionals love to provide. The constantly dropping level of state education guarantees that only few would be capable of asking themselves – as some soldiers eventually do – what on earth they are doing in those checkpoints and in Palestinian villages and homes, and why they should club Peace Now girls rather than listen to what they have to say.

Still, we eventually get to stage our photo opportunity. Word comes from the higher echelons, and the soldiers now allow the demonstrators to erect a tower construction made of long metal pipes that came with us on the bus all the way from Tel Aviv. The idea was to raise it further up the road, but the checkpoint's parking lot will have to do. The construction represented an illegal settlement, the kind the soldiers never ever bring down when "real" settlers decide to populate yet another spot on the territory that belongs to others. As soon as the phantom new symbol is up, the cameras eternalize the gimmick, a speech is made, then another, and in return for this exceptional permission, the peace demonstrators dismantle their installation obediently as agreed. "We all realize now that when you put your mind to it, illegal settlements are being dismantled with no trouble at all," a voice over the megaphone says, addressing the uninterested soldiers. TV cameras capture the moment that would become a twenty-second item on the nation's screens. Nobody has the energy to spend any more time in this godforsaken area. It is time to go back home, weary but with a modest sense of achievement. In a few days the bruises caused by clubbing will be healed.

Bring down settlements? Dismantle illegal strongholds? The present Jewish state has no real will to disengage from the settlement movement. The 'Disengagement Process' that Prime Minister Sharon started in early 2005 marks no exception to this rule. Sharon and his subordinates openly declared that the very few settlements involved in the process had to be sacrificed in order to decrease pressure on the main bulk of the settlers' residential enclaves. The state continues to give maximum support to the residents of the Jewish enclaves within the Palestinian territories, and to make sure they should have no real reason to wish they were anywhere else.

The leaders of the fanatic nationalistic group in charge of the settler movement have a perfect understanding of the shaky all-Israeli self-confidence. They have smartly and efficiently built their own empire and illustrious careers all over its debris.

The interests of these apparatchiks are fully compatible with the needs of the giant professional army, gradually becoming dense with religious nationalists. Officers like Yitzhak Rabin used to speak about their longing for peace in a way that made one believe they meant what they said. These days, routine military rhetoric usually deals with the "eternity" of the Children of Israel, forecasting "another hundred years of war" as though there was nothing pathologically wrong with this promise. Fully paid military rabbis are dispatched to boost soldiers' morale with belligerent sacred verses. When the veteran, less fanatic, military officers started – too late - to wake up to the new reality and realized that their own positions and agendas were jeopardized by it, it was too late. In May 2016 Minister of Defence Moshe Yaalon (formerly the army's Chief of Staff, a prominent Likud politician) took a stand on minimum military ethics, and insisted on court martialling a renegade soldier who murdered a badly wounded Palestinian who earlier allegedly threatened soldiers with a knife. The killer soldier became a national hero. Prime Minister Netanyahu called his father to express sympathy with the religious settler family that produced the killer, then promptly fired the furious ex-general from his ministerial post.

"Regular" Israelis do not usually share the settler movement's blatant, self-serving and joyless nationalism. Yet the silent majority is oblivious even to the enormous public investment needed to maintain the "security" and the standard of living of the Jews in the occupied territories. While horribly crushing the lives of all the non-Jewish citizens in these regions, the state has no time and no money for the urgent need of its non-settler, non-military, regular taxpayers.

In September 2003 *Ha'aretz* courageously issued a special supplement discussing the cost of the settlement activity in the occupied territories. The issue carried a detailed disclosure of the billions of shekels poured out by the state every year for the benefit of the settlers. The carefully researched story made for interesting reading, as the country at the time suffered from high rates of unemployment and serious economic recession. Unusually, the supplement was almost free of advertising. In fact, the only ad it ran was by a distributor of an imported car brand, and this turned out to have been a mistake. The advertising agency that dared to have its client displayed next to such conspiratorial information nearly lost that client as a result of its bad judgment.

Many settlers have been lured by the enticing vision of the "quality living" the state openly promises to everybody who would move into these problematic areas. "Quality" in this case means "cheap": life on cheap land, sponsored water for agriculture, and free upgraded public services. Many "quality life" non-ideological settlers admit openly that they would be happy to live within the borders of older Israel, if only similarly spacious, gracious homes were given to them without any extra cost.

Peace Banner III: Save Israel, Get Out of the Occupied Territories!

It is September of 2003. Palestinians are not alone in their misery. The Jewish poor, spearheaded by single mothers, the handicapped, and the unemployed, are making themselves heard in public. Israel is a wealthy state, with an incredibly well-equipped army and a healthy economy. But for those not well-positioned in this economy, its policies in recent years offer a free drop into the abyss of despair. The Welfare State has been declared bankrupt, and at the same time, a much-discussed *Hudna* (provisional truce) initiative to temporarily halt the Palestinian-Israeli violence has been choked before it even got going. The young people of Peace Now again call activists to the flag. A mass peace protest rally is to be organized in the heart of swinging Tel Aviv. The email I received calls for volunteers to join a small convoy of cars that would sail through the streets of the city on a Friday afternoon, reminding the masses to present themselves in Rabin Square on Saturday night.

We meet by the railway station in Arlozorov Street. Our vehicles are covered with large orange posters calling "Save Israel, Get Out of the Occupied Territories."

"You are wasting your time," a young man tells me, looking at the posters on his way out of the station. "You do have a point, but what you do will move nothing at all."

"It moves some people at least," I say, trying to sound optimistic, knowing he is the one with the point. The real achievement of our demonstration will be a feeling of well-doing for its participants. It will make us feel that we are not responsible for all the bad things our state is doing in our names.

Save Israel? Get out of the Occupied Territories? This train has been missed long ago. The Occupied Territories are too deep inside our own state, just as our state is deep inside these territories.

Our small convoy goes up Arlozorov into the streets of my youth and my childhood: to Dizengoff up to the Dizengoff Centre, right into King George and into Sheinkin streets, past the usual Friday carnival of shopping and street shows. Down Hashmonaim and Carlibach Streets into Ibn Gabirol, past Rabin Square, we wave at the weekly memorial guard on the spot where Yitzhak Rabin was murdered eight years earlier. Five more minutes in dense traffic and we pass the yuppie-packed Basel Street then on Nordau Avenue to the sun-baked beach promenade. Driving next to the shiny sea, Tel Aviv's most brilliant decoration, we finally halt at the Hassan Beck Mosque parking area. Our mission is completed; we are thanked and get ready to take off the orange posters.

"But should we not drive further south, to the Tikva quarter, or to the centre of Bat Yam?" I find myself unable to hold back the question. Have the enthusiastic organizers of the convoy not considered that the peace rally message should be carried also to the less affluent regions of the Dan conurbation?

"This is something for future activities," one of the directors of Peace Now kindly informs me. "Our very first mission is to revive interest among our own public."

This for me summarizes the story of the Israeli Peace Movement. While working so hard to retrieve "our own" that had been lost to us, we have given up the ones who should have been "ours" long ago. As long as Peace Now and its offspring continue the ethnic, social exclusivity of its occasional ritual celebrations, the periphery would stick to the deep suspicion that when the Ashkenazi say "Save Israel," they actually mean save the good parts for their "own" only.

The Arab Jews' identity dilemma continues to produce powerful antidotes to suppress the pallid Peace Movement.

The Israeli malaise is everywhere in this land, not just in the occupied territories. Wherever we go, however well we retreat, the stress will stick and follow. It is the misery of our very self-determination: secular and religious Jews, Sephardic and Ashkenazi, rich and poor. We observe one another and find it hard to determine what it actually is that makes us one people.

"Getting out" of territories or being symbolically "disengaged" is relatively unimportant. Nobody can any longer define where the "territories" are these days. Which land is actually "ours"? Hard-core right-wingers often put forward an ill-meaning suggestion: why not redesign Israel's frontiers so as to include areas densely populated by Arabs in the "future Palestinian state"? In 1909 Tel Aviv, the pinnacle of Israeli liberalism, was established as a modern residential suburb of Jaffa on land purchased from local Arabs. All the property owners signed the regulations of the building society and committed themselves not to sell or rent out land or homes to Arabs. Until this day it is hard for a Palestinian to find dwelling in our city, outside the traditionally Arab Jaffa.

If you want to save Israel, you might as well just declare it a normal state and start to consider all people under its sovereignty as equal citizens living in one territory. This is not mission impossible. The world is full of such states and of such nations, which do not waste time and energy branding inhabitants according to what religion their mothers were born into.

26

THE BIRD MAN

I saw a perfectly beautiful bird
The bird saw me.
Such a bird, with so much beauty
I shall not see again before I die.
A vibration that came from the sun went through me
And I spoke words of peace.

Nathan Zach,
All that Milk and Honey[1]

It was common knowledge that a plush brothel was run on the ground floor of the house next door, just opposite the Shalva private secondary school. The couple who ran this institution had a son two years younger than I, who was known by the improbable name of Kacki. When a new baby was born to this family, it was named Bébé. As none of us knew that Bébé was French for baby, and in certain homes this word, just like Kacki, was used to describe the content of soiled nappies, the neighbourhood was quite mystified. At least one other young woman lived in this household. She was equally pretty and elegant, and her status in the family was quite vague – a sister, a sister-in-law, or a second wife? In any case she was part of the business.

Kacki once invited us to peek through the window into his parents' flat. Behind the lace curtains, I was mainly impressed with the floor rags that were woolly, colourful, and folded up at the margins, which indicated they were originally spread in much larger rooms. There were also crystal chandeliers, soft armchairs and sofas, woven wall tapestries featuring deer hunting, and other

1 Author's translation from Hebrew.

luxury items that I greatly admired. Nothing as lavish was ever going to decorate our own plain flat that was sternly ruled by the modern straight lines of fifties aesthetics and a tight budget. Nothing in the comfortable living room indicated sinful activity, but one could trust Kacki's indifferent reporting. The older boys in the street used to enjoy challenging him with the query, "What is your mother's job, Kacki?"

"Fucking," he would defiantly answer.

Kacki's father Marcel was a tall, bald man. One afternoon I came home complaining bitterly that Kacki had robbed me of all my *Goggos* collection, having lost in the game we ran in the empty plot on Weiss Street. My father, who was at the time at home with a leg in plaster following a work accident, and who could never see me cry without resorting to action, hurried down three flights of stairs to teach the boy a lesson. He grabbed Kacki's hand, shouted at him, and forced him to return every one of the apricot seeds that should have been legally mine. Now it was Kacki's turn to burst into a sobs and run home for paternal support. The muscular pimp immediately stormed out and without saying a single word charged straight into my father's head with his own bald skull. With one leg in white plaster my father chose to play the wise man rather than the hero. With everybody on the street holding their breath, he took the blow without the slightest attempt to hit back, spoke kindly and soothingly to the attacker, and somehow managed to calm him and make peace. For the rest of the evening, my furious mother could not get over the fact that due to my stupid *Goggos*, "I could have easily been left a widow today and you would have been orphaned."

We realized eventually that the next-door enterprise was quite famous in our city. Our subtenant Helen came back all excited one day, after a theft that had occurred in the office she worked for downtown. Like all the employees, Helen was questioned by a policeman who came to investigate the case.

When she gave her address the policeman raised his eyebrows. "5 Graetz Street, huh? Next door to number seven...?"

The news concerning the brothel came mainly from our next-door neighbour, a reputable seamstress, who worked at her flat and liked to pop in for her first cup of coffee every morning.

Marcel's escapades once or twice made the pages of the weekly *Haolam Hazeh* that my mother would not buy, read, or let into the house because it was so risqué and so negative about the government. At some stage Kacki's father got mixed up in a serious fight and was sent to prison for a while. Upon his release he had – so we heard – made a deal with the police. In return for clemency, the notorious pimp agreed to remove his profitable business from our quiet residential area in the Old North of Tel Aviv, five minutes' walk from the home of David Ben-Gurion and his wife Paula, and take his carpets, his chandeliers, and his pretty women as far away as was at all possible.

Until then, all I knew about Eilat was a line of a song by Meir Noy, which was a regular item on the weekly sing-along menu. It went: "*Somewhat south of Beersheva/ Desert wind is blowing/ the dirt road goes even further south...*"[2] The song further described Eilat, at the end of the long road down south, as "The Wondrous Pearl of the Desert." In reality Eilat was a punishment, a name by which one of the town's less attractive quarters (*Haonesh*) is known until this very day.

Like Australia for the English and the Western Indies for the French, Eilat at its beginning was a destination forced on "undesirable elements" of the young Israeli society. It had its advantages if you wished to avoid the law enforcers or any other of life's difficulties.

You could go there without worrying about accommodation, as sleeping on the beach and using the outdoor showers was pleasant in the warm nights through most of the year. Young people could always find day jobs. Long before the sands of Sinai had opened to Israelis seeking a simple, basic living close to nature, Eilat was the only shanty option, sixties style. Around a handful of hotels and the austere youth hostel, nightlife flourished – the infrastructure for latter-day Eilat's booming, never-legalized casino industry. Throughout the seventies shady figures associated with the underworld featured regularly in the Eilat "scene" that was documented weekly in *Haolam Hazeh*. It is possible that Kacki and Bébé grew up to become major Eilat personalities, or

---

[2] Lyrics by Haim Hefer.

maybe they did not. Our righteous next-door neighbour reported gleefully one day that their mother was spotted in Eilat by someone who reported back that "she looked a complete wreck."

Entrepreneurs, real estate sharks, and the tax-hungry state eventually spotted the potential of Eilat's scenic beauty, its dry climate, and the blue water of the bay, rich with tropical fish around the coral reefs. The cheap charter flight revolution that made international tourism so affordable pushed forward a construction frenzy. Tens of thousands of European and Israeli tourists stay during the year in enormous concrete blocks with fancy names that are piled up by the beaches and have irreversibly altered the landscape, the climate, and the human mix of the city.

Eilat's population is an interesting example of the Israeli melting pot. It is home to veteran Jewish Israelis of all ethnic origins and all political affiliations; Chabad Hassidic ultra-Orthodox and Shas supporters live next to professional divers, veteran navy commando machos, and nature lovers; the small but influential big-money elite keep expensive holiday flats and villas in gated estates; and masses of the underprivileged, multichild families, many of them single-parented cram into the ugly fifties-era estates. Thousands of ex-Bedouin, many of them with new names like Yossi and Amir, work for the tourism and commerce industries together with African and South Asian guest workers, many of them illegal. There is a massive presence of Russian-speaking immigrants from the states of the former Soviet Union as well as of immigrants from Ethiopia. A few Americans and Europeans who passed by, fell in love with the place, and stayed for good add some international flavour to the many pubs. Eilat thrives and also falls according to the seasonal demand for its sun, beaches, discos, music festivals, and natural beauties by tourists, who are the main pillar of the city's economy today.

It is a far less commonly known fact that the urbanization of the area had literally swept the ground from under the feet of about a billion tiny travellers who were accustomed to landing in the area of Eilat twice a year for the last hundred thousand years.

* * *

Earthwatch Magazine is an international publication well respected in matters of the environment and endangered species. Its May 1998 cover story was dedicated to what the editors considered "the most important habitat in the whole world." As far as *Earthwatch* was concerned, this habitat is located just north of Eilat. The story focused on Eilat's Bird Watching Park, which at the time was still a new project slowly emerging over a neglected garbage heap. With much effort, and against some resistance, a sanctuary for birds was being rehabilitated.

Until the 1950s, the north part of the Eilat Bay, an area today almost fully claimed by the hotel and recreation area, was one big salty marsh. It was a burning hot, unpleasant, mosquito-swarmed zone. Draining and drying it for the benefit of human habitation was therefore a classic Zionist achievement. But for no fewer than two hundred species of migrant birds that nest in Europe every summer and spend their winters in warm Africa, it was a vital resting area, indispensable for the success of their long journeys every spring and every autumn.

"Welcome back, my beloved bird," by Chaim Nachman Bialik[3] was canonized as the basic poetic text denoting the Jewish-Zionist longing for "the land of our ancestors." The poet, somewhere in half-frozen Eastern Europe, is asking a returning bird about the warm, old country. When the national poet wrote it in 1901, he could not have known that the migrant fowl would have dropped out of the sky and died of dehydration had it not been for the resting and feeding area of the Eilat marsh. It used to be the single green area between the Sinai Desert, the Sudan and the Arabian Peninsula in the south, and the Mediterranean coasts of Palestine and Lebanon in the north. Ornithologists estimate a billion birds patronize the Eilat stopping place in the amazing track of their biannual trip. This amounts to about one third of all the Northern European and Siberian bird population. For some species, it is almost 100 percent.

The salt marsh is long gone. Its remnants are some industrial drying pools of the local salt production industry. A shady deal with the Israel Land Administration turned the franchise owners into one

---

[3] 1873-1934.

of the richest families in the land, based on a controversial permit to turn the whole area into another residential quarter. The ancient natural bird habitat has disappeared altogether. Yet the birds are not drying out in the sky. About two miles north of Eilat, an artificial recreation area was created for them. It does not resemble the salt marsh at all, but is very successfully fulfilling its purpose.

The man who built and planned the Eilat Bird Sanctuary, and still runs it, Dr. Reuven Yosef, is an internationally renowned ornithologist but almost unknown in Israel. In the summer of 2000, his enterprise won a prestigious Rolex Award, and our firm was asked by the Swiss watchmaker to organize a proper venue in Tel Aviv to mark the occasion and honour the donors and the award winner. In October of that year, the breakout of the second Intifada scuppered this idea. As suicide bombers became an almost weekly horror, there was no room for celebrating a joyful public event on birds. We had a small event in Eilat instead.

The sanctuary survives through the support of several Israeli bodies, but the preservation of birds is still low on the scale of national priorities. Getting to know Dr. Yosef and his family easily brought me into the large circle of Yosef's admirers, most of whom are not Israeli.

Dr. Yosef is referred to with unusual superlatives in bird-expert circles. He spends much of his time at in international conventions, where his ecological achievements are the focus of much interest. During the migration period, volunteers and ornithologists from all over the world – including, whenever made possible by the Israeli authorities, Jordanian and Palestinian visitors – come to the sanctuary, and they are warmly received by Reuven and his wife Dalit. University of Arizona's Professor Michael Rosenzweig, author of *Win-Win Ecology*,[4] dedicated three chapters of his book to Yosef's stunning practical achievements in what he calls "reconciliation ecology" – the art of helping the earth's species survive in the midst of human enterprise.

It is from this book that I learned that Yosef became a bird lover's hero following some discoveries he made in Florida about the habits of a type of bird known as Loggerhead Shrike, also

---

[4] Oxford University Press, 2003.

known as the Butcherbird because it likes to nail its pray – big insects, lizards, even small mice – for display on to sharp thorns and spikes, to claim its territory. It was Yosef who discovered that male Butcherbirds attract the females with this display of hunting abilities. The Loggerhead Shrikes of Florida were an endangered species, as their numbers drastically diminished with the shrinking pasture areas, taken over by humans and buildings.

Yosef found out that each male shrike needed a private territory around a perch in the vicinity of his nest. Shrikes cannot fly as effectively as other birds of prey, and they prefer perching to hovering. Working in a large cattle ranch dedicated to ecological research, in an area that had already lost most of its shrike population, Yosef ordered wooden poles from a carpenter and stationed them close to the few remaining shrike nests. This cut down considerably the time parents needed to fly to find food for their chicks. It also enabled the shrikes to make do with much smaller private territories, which allowed more males to start families and build nests. The results of this experiment were dramatic: within one year the Loggerheaded Shrike population grew by 60 percent. Within three years of using this policy, this particular bird was no longer an endangered species.

The seemingly simple idea of artificially upgrading living conditions for birds as a compensation for human takeover of their territories was enthusiastically adopted by ornithologists in other parts of the world. Similar projects were started in Holland and in the Czech Republic. In the mid 1990s, when it was at last noticed in Israel that the Salt Marsh was almost gone, nature lovers managed to convince the authorities that if they did not care about birds, they should at least consider the potential for bird-watcher tourism. As a result Yosef received an offer to drop his nice job and secure scientific research future in Florida in favour of Eilat. He gladly came back and settled down south with his family.

The challenge he faced was formidable. The area designated as a bird sanctuary had been used until then as a dumping area, a real garbage heap. His first idea was to convince Eilat contractors to bring to this area all the soil from their excavations for building foundations. It made the base for the desert vegetation he was about to plant. Dozens of new species of plants, rich with proteins and resilient to Eilat's extreme heat were imported for the park. There is no lack of water in this bird diner: the city's sewage system has been channelled through the park, via an ecological filtering made of special plants.

The success story of the modest park did not go without some major problems. The development of the park required some building restrictions on the hotels around it, and several local tycoons were not too pleased with this idea. In his first years in Eilat, Yosef suffered some serious hostilities. The research hut in the sanctuary was twice burned down and three times broken into. The family's children one day came home to find their beloved German shepherd dog slaughtered and the carcass hanging from the door. The local police were not too enthusiastic about tracking down the obvious suspects. Then the thuggish intimidations quite suddenly stopped. Persistent rumours suggested that some old mates of Yosef, his pals from the time they all served as conscript members of an elite army commando unit, arrived in town one day for a private intimidation raid that sent a clear message to all the birds' enemies.

Watching his stout figure in a leather wide-brim cowboy hat, driving a powerfully-engined Land Rover over the barren plains around Eilat, one could easily cast Yosef as the typical Israeli ranger, army and kibbutz background and all. But his is a much more interesting species. A native of India, child of New Delhi's social elite, and a grandchild to a grandmother who started the first-ever nature reserve in the subcontinent, Yosef arrived in Israel as a single adventure-seeking teenager. Among other difficulties, he also had to cope with stereotypes and prejudices of his peers, the Israeli-born youth. You would not know about the cultural shock he went through if this information was not volunteered by his wife Dalit, herself kibbutz-born, smart as well as pretty, who was quick to figure out that the dark new Indian had great potential.

* * *

During the peak of the migrating season, one can find Dr. Yosef every dawn in his tiny hut in the Bird Park. Volunteers and interested tourists diligently run around the park, collecting fowl of a dozen species from the delicate nets that are spread there to catch them, into colourful cotton bags that Dalit Yosef made using an assortment of her children's clothing items. The loot is handed to the park's director and his assistants. With dexterity worthy of a Dr. Doolittle, Yosef pulls the fretting prisoners out of the bags one by one and puts them through a series of checks and measuring tests. Before being let free, every bird is marked with an identification ring that would make it possible to follow its trip if it were ever to be captured by a birdwatcher on the other side of the world. Sick or injured birds get to be hospitalized for a few days. Visiting children are often invited to gently hold the birds that are ready to resume their journey and personally set them free, sharing the magical moment of the resumed flight into liberty.

In Eilat's Bird Park, there is no room for nostalgia over the lost wilderness that not too long ago stretched over vast areas of quiet, salty desert. Every square inch of the former garbage dump is now used efficiently for the benefit of the tired guests. "This place is hardly five percent of the size of the ancient salt marsh, but since we now produce over twenty times the food quantity for each square unit, we supply the needs of the same number of birds as before," Yosef says, succinctly displaying his survival theory, so adequately adaptable for humans too, in this age of ever-increasing urban density.

* * *

There is nothing like the optimism of the Eilat bird man and his proven skills in saving endangered species in contended habitats to cheer up those of us who tend to sink into deep depression over the fate of our disintegrating homeland. Israel of the new millennium may uncomfortably be compared to a salt marsh on the verge of terminal dehydration; and Jews tend to consider themselves an endangered human species. Yet destroying the nests of other human species – conveniently calling them "terror nests" – and taking over other people's living spaces is not the way to cure one's own deep distress.

Religious and cultural communities, just like bird flocks, need no state laws to preserve their unique heritages. The preservation of

Jewish culture and faith over the last two thousand years is the best proof. Driving out three quarters of a million people who were not Jewish to make room for a Jews-only land was at best a mistake. The descendants of the expelled should be invited back. There is room enough for everybody. In his heyday, ex-General Sharon himself claimed the land can take 15 million residents. He was only wrong to insist on the right religion as an entry card – instantly welcoming Papa Marcel of my neighbourhood's bordello, and others like him, while barring the gates to the likes of Edward Said.

In this small area blessed by God and situated at a meeting point of three continents, some of our ancestors managed to launch useful social paradigms and produce truly sublime texts to support them. The whole of humanity took notice of these paradigms and these texts. They have little or nothing to do with the present weird, flawed, political-religious regime that tries to survive between Metula in the north and Eilat in the south, between the sea and the Jordan River, usurping human rights in the name of ancient, irrelevant decrees.

The establishment of the modern State of Israel was accompanied by several basic mistakes and evil acts, and for three generations we have been paying a high toll for these errors. We inflicted much higher tolls on others.

I know for a fact that my fellow Israelis – some of them my dearest friends and beloved family – honestly believe that we "happen" to live in a "complicated, unstable, explosive area." I try my best to make them see that there is nothing wrong with the area or with the neighbours, our "cousins" of other denominations. It is our own peculiar choice of differentiating people according to their mother's religious affiliation that created most of the present mess. How dare we criticize the Muslim Brothers for trying to change the Egyptian Constitution in favour of the *Sharia* – when our state never even ventured to produce a constitution, for fear it might not be compatible with the Halacha? Would our own "dear brothers" of the faith ever stand up for equal rights for their sisters? And as for my so-called secular Israeli Jewish fellow citizen: why are the only two Halacha laws they truly respect and follow the reshaping of baby boys' organs and the strict bans on fraternizing with non-Jews?

I set out to make some sense of the social puzzle I was born into, and my findings mainly indicate an ongoing inner crumbling process, due to the cracks in its original foundations. From around the debris, a new, solid, and more coherent base surely will be started. Since the publication of the first version of this book in 2004, I was fortunate to have met many people, young and old, who are dedicated, in different ways, to this necessary rehabilitation process. It will happen, sooner or later – let us hope without too much pain.

GLOSSARY

Glossary of frequently-used terms, Hebrew unless otherwise indicated

Abba – Father
Ashkenazim – Eastern European Jews and their descendants
Beit Midrash – Jewish study hall
Cheder – schoolroom for young Jewish children
Chevra Kadisha – burial society
Chuppa – canopy, under which Jewish wedding rituals is taking place
Eretz Israel – the land of Israel
Frenk – pejorative for Sephardi
Frum – devout (Yiddish)
Geveret - madam
Green Line – Armistice agreed of borders of Israel following the 1948 war
Gush Emunim – "the Block of the Faithful" national-religious settler movement
Habad –the largest Hassidic (see below) group also named Lubavitch after its rabbinical dynasty that originated in the Belorussian village Lyubavichi.
Haganah – Jewish paramilitary Organization during the British mandate in Palestine, affiliated with the Zionist socialist leadership
Halacha – the corpus of Jewish religious laws
HaNoar HaOved – The Working Youth, the Labour movement's youth movement
Haredi – ultra-orthodox Jew
Hassid/Hassidim – members of an ultra-orthodox Jewish movement. Emphasis is on emotion and faith and communities are led by spiritual leaders, usually of dynasties dating back to the 18th century.

Histadrut – Israel's organization of workers union, originally the "Hebrew Workers Union"
IDF – acronym for Israel Defence Army
Imma - Mother
Jabal – Mountain (Arabic)
Kibbutz – collective community, a Labor-Zionist form of (mostly) agricultural village
Kibbutznik – member of a kibbutz
Kippa – traditional Jewish male head gear, small round cap
Kollel – full-time religious study school for orthodox adult males.
Kosher - authorized by the Jewish Halacha (mostly food, but also dress material and other miscellaneous aspects of everyday society)
Maabara – temporary housing estate made of shacks or tents for new immigrants in the 1950's
Machsom –check point
Majnoon – crazy (Arabic)
masoreti – conservative (traditional)
Meshuge – crazy (Yiddish)
– ritual bath
Mizrahim – Literally Eastern, descendants of Jews from communities in Arab countries of the Middle East and North Africa. With the exception of the Yemenite community, they are also identified as Sephardi. The term "Arab Jews" is unanimously avoided (but has a comeback in politically conscious circles).
Mohel – performer of circumcision procedure in infants
Moshav – cooperative agricultural community of individual farms, established by Labor Zionism
Palmach – acronym for "Strike Companies", a paramilitary Jewish organization, the elite troops of the Haganah
Rabbi – spiritual leader also authorized legal authority on religious matters
Rebbetzin – wife of a rabbi
Sabba – Grandfather
Savta – grandmother
Seder – Festive supper ceremony starting the Passover holidays
Sephardi – Literally descendants of Jews from Spain and Portugal, however the term applies to all Jews from Middle Eastern and North African descent who have adopted the Sephardic style religious rituals.
Sharia – the corpus of Muslim religious laws
Shas – acronym for "Guardian of Sephardic Tradition", an ultra-orthodox party established 1984
shabbat haMalkah – The Glorious Sabbath

INDEX

C

D

E

F

G

H

I

J

K

L

M

T

U

W

Y

Z